ADVANCED
READING
SKILLS

Pauline Barr, John Clegg and Catherine Wallace

Longman

Longman Group Limited
Longman House, Burnt Mill, Harlow
Essex CM20 2JE, England
and Associated Companies throughout the world

First published 1981
Third impression 1983
ISBN 0 582 55904 9

Printed in Hong Kong by
Sing Cheong Printing Co Ltd

CONTENTS

CONTENTS

GENERAL INTRODUCTION

Advanced Reading Skills is for adults or young adults who have studied English to an advanced level. It can, for example, be used with English language students studying at university or preparing for the Cambridge Proficiency examination.

The book aims:
— to help you read effectively, not just to test your understanding
— to help you *think* about what you are reading
— to help you read different things in different ways
and above all to give you something interesting and provocative to read

The book consists of:
— ten Units; each Unit centres around a theme of general interest and has a focus, which is
    — either a skill, such as scanning
    — or a textual feature, such as formality
Each Unit consists of four Sections, each with one or more reading passages, which are authentic and drawn from a wide variety of sources
Section 1 introduces the theme of the unit
Section 2 introduces the focus of the unit
Section 3 gives practice in what you have learnt earlier
Section 4 explores the theme further

How to use the book
Start at the beginning and work through. There is a planned progression from one Unit to another. What you learn in one Unit is developed later. Similarly, within each Unit each Section leads on to the next.
Exercises are designed not only to check your understanding *after* reading, but to arouse your interest *before* reading, and to get you to think *while* reading. *The pre-reading exercises* are important. Reading starts before you even look at the page. When you pick up a newspaper or book you have a *reason* for reading, and you have ideas and expectations about what you will find.
The while-reading exercises are important because a good reader participates, that is he criticises, comments, queries,

agrees and disagrees and constantly anticipates what is coming next.

Many of the exercises help you to cope with unfamiliar words *without using a dictionary*. We do not need to understand everything we read. A good reader either ignores or guesses and reads on. The rule is, if you come across an unfamiliar word, decide first whether it is important. If the answer is NO, carry on reading. If the answer is YES, make a rough guess for the moment (often you will get extra help from the context later on) and carry on reading.

Reading means thinking about what you read. No-one else can think for you. There are many ways of understanding a passage and your interpretation may be different from other peoples'. Always be prepared to defend your opinion. Many of the exercises ask you to discuss. These are marked 🗨.

Answers for some of the exercises are provided in the key at the back of the book. These exercises are marked ⟨KEY⟩ Some of the answers in the key are only suggestions. You may have other ideas. These answers are marked ⟨___⟩ (in the key only).

To the student working on his own
The book has been designed not only for classroom use, but also for the student working entirely on his own. When you see the symbol 🗨 don't just ignore it. It is important that you *think* about the question, and then organise your thoughts on paper.

To the teacher
— All the passages are meant to be read silently. Do not read them aloud, or ask the students to do so.
— The material is designed to be student-centred, not teacher-centred. Try to reduce to a minimum the time you spend addressing the whole class.
— Many of the exercises are intended to be done in pairs or small groups. They are marked 🗨. During pair and group work, you should move from group to group 'eavesdropping', encouraging discussion, offering an idea when necessary, perhaps even playing 'devil's advocate'. Avoid the temptation to give the 'correct' answer.
— Students are often over-anxious about unfamiliar words. Encourage them to attach less importance to such words. Several of the exercises are designed to do exactly this. It follows that students should be discouraged from using dictionaries while reading. If they ask you the meaning of a word, do not give it immediately, but encourage guessing.

We are grateful to the following for permission to reproduce copyright material:

Associated Newspapers Group Ltd for an extract from the article 'The Not So Hidden Persuaders' by Yvonne Roberts from *London Evening News*, October 23rd, 1978; Beauty Without Cruelty for an extract from 'Beauty Without Cruelty Leaflet', 1978; the author's agent for an extract from *Room at the Top* by John Braine, published by Methuen; Jonathan Cape Ltd and Random House Inc for an extract from pp. 46–7 *The Body In Question* by Jonathan Miller; Central Office of Information for an extract from the advertisement 'Volunteers are Needed', reproduced with the permission of the Controller, Her Majesty's Stationery Office; the author, Professor P. R. Ehrlich for an extract from pp. 211–13 'Ecocatastrophe' in *The Environmental Handbook* edited by Barr and Allsop, copyright 1969 by P. R. Ehrlich; Faber and Faber Ltd and Harcourt Brace Jovanovich Inc for an extract from *Free Fall* by William Golding, © 1959 by William Golding, reprinted by permission of Faber and Faber Ltd and Harcourt Brace Jovanovich Inc; Friends of the Earth Ltd for an extract from 'Friends of the Earth Leaflet', 1978; Granada Publishing Ltd and McGraw-Hill Book Company for an extract from p. 232 *The Female Eunuch* by Germaine Greer; The Guardian for the article 'The Tent People' by Judith Cook in *The Guardian*, April 25th, 1978 and the article 'Denis Thatcher' by Simon Hoggart in *The Guardian*, October 1979; The Hogarth Press Ltd for an extract from *Cider With Rosie* by Laurie Lee; Michael Joseph Ltd and Tony Eady Associates for an extract from *My Brother and I* by Margaret Powell; Literary Magazine Society for an extract from the article 'A Place of Your Own' in *Prospect* Vol 3, Issue 5, August 1977; an extract from a Job Questionnaire in *Prospect*, 1977; and an extract from the article 'Professional Mechanical Engineers' by M. J. Harthill in *Prospect* 1977; the author's agent for an extract from *Of Human Bondage* by Somerset Maugham; the author, Susan Mayfield for an extract from her article 'One Room Living' appeared in *Singles*, 1978; Frederick Muller Ltd for an extract from pp. 122, 114 and 115 from *Small is Beautiful* by E. F. Schumacher; The National Trust for an extract from *Properties Open in 1980*; New Science Publications and the author, Michael Mann for an adapted version of the article 'The Working Class' in *New Society*, November 4th, 1976; New Science Publications and the author, Jackie West for the article 'The Factory Slaves' in *New Society*, February 24th, 1977; New Science Publications and the author, Jill Turner for the article 'Children Not Cattle' in *New Society*, August 24th, 1978; Open Books Publishing Ltd for the tables on pp. 74–76, reproduced from *Social Class Differences in Britain* by Ivan Reid; Private Eye for the 'Dear Bill' letter in *Private Eye*, August 31st, 1979; The Statesman and Nation Publishing Company Ltd for an extract from 'The Doll in the Golden Coach' by Mervyn Jones in *New Statesman*, July 3rd, 1977, reprinted from the New Statesman by permission; Syndication International Ltd for an extract from the article 'My Life on Sealand' by Princess Joan Bates in *Woman*, November 1978; an extract from the monarchy survey in *Woman*, October 28th, 1978; an extract from the article 'Ann and Brian Stainton' in *Woman's Own*, March 26th, 1977; Times Newspapers Ltd for an extract from the article 'Tessa, Ian and John' and 'Britain's Sorry Record Graph' in *The Sunday Times*, July 31st, 1977; an extract from the article 'Schools Out' in *Sunday Times Magazine*, January 15th, 1978; an extract from an article on middle class families in *Sunday Times Magazine*, January 25th, 1976; an extract from an article on working class families in *Sunday Times Magazine*, June 5th, 1977; an adapted extract from an article on windmills in *Sunday Times Magazine*, April 4th, 1976; an extract from the article 'Why the British Need to Have a Monarch' by Ronald Butt in *The Sunday Times*, June 1977; and an extract from an article on Ronald Biggs in *Sunday Times Magazine*, May 21st, 1978; the author's agent for an extract from *Hospital* by Polly Toynbee, published by Hutchinson Publishing Group Ltd, reprinted by permission of A. D. Peters & Co Ltd; The Tree Council for an extract from a 'Tree Council Information Note'.

Whilst every effort has been made, we are unable to trace the copyright holder of 'How Would You Like to Live in a Castle' by Belinda Black and would appreciate any information which would enable us to do so.

We are also grateful to the following for permission to reproduce copyright illustrative material:

Advertising Standards Authority for page 119; Alfred Dunhill Ltd., for page 55; Beecham Group Ltd., for pages 133 and 139 (left); BL Cars Ltd., for pages 136 and 137; Boots Company for page 139 (right); Butter Information Council for page 140; Central Office of Information for page 132; Central Press Photos Ltd., for pages 107 and 111; Cheese Information Service for page 134 (top); Chefaro Proprietaries Ltd., for page 120 (bottom); The Hon. Mrs Alan Clark for page 9; Dataslim Ltd., for page 121; Dateline International for page 122; De Beers Consolidated Mines Ltd., for page 120 (top); Elisabeth Photo Library for page 66 (bottom); Elisabeth Whiting Associates for page 15; Longman Photographic Unit for pages 65, 153, 154 and cover; Marks and Spencer Ltd., for page 168; Martak Ltd., for page 143; Maurice Nimmo for page 88; Peugeot Automobiles United Kingdom Ltd., for page 138; Rex Features Ltd., for page 95; Sandie Rolfe for page 60; Scotcade Ltd., for page 134 (bottom); The Sunday Times for pages 44, 47, 48 and 180; Syndication International Ltd., for pages 24 and 173; Volvo Concessionaires for page 135; Janine Wiedel for pages 31 and 42; Nick Yates for page 66 (top).

We have been unable to trace the copyright holder of the photograph on page 115 and would be grateful for any information that would enable us to do so.

A Place of Your Own

Section 1 Leaving Home

What do you think?

1 Young school leavers in Britain sometimes leave home to live elsewhere. Why do you think this happens? Do you think it is common? Note down your ideas briefly.

The extract below comes from an article in a magazine for young people in Britain about to leave school.

2 What are the advantages and disadvantages of living at home once you are grown up? Consider especially the following: – comfort
– expense
– independence
– friends

3 Next, make your own personal list of advantages and disadvantages.

4 Now read the first three paragraphs and note the advantages and disadvantages of living at home which are mentioned. Did you think of these?

A person's home is as much a reflection of his personality as the clothes he wears, the food he eats and the friends with whom he spends his time. Depending on personality, how people see themselves and how they allow others to see
5 them, most have in mind an 'ideal home'. But in general, and especially for the student or new wage earners, there are practical limitations of cash and location on achieving that idea.

Cash shortage, in fact, often means that the only way of
10 getting along when you leave school is to stay at home for a while until things improve financially. There are obvious advantages to living at home – personal laundry is usually still done along with the family wash, meals are provided and there will be a well-established circle of friends to call upon.
15 Parents are often quite generous in asking for a minimum rent, and there is rarely the responsibility for paying fuel bills, rates etc.

On the other hand, much depends on how a family gets on. Do your parents like your friends? You may love your family – but do you like them? Are you prepared to be tolerant when your parents ask where you are going in the evening and what time you expect to be back? Do they mind if you want to throw a party? If you find you can't manage a workable compromise, and that you finally have the money to leave, how do you go about finding somewhere else to live?

5 How *do* you find somewhere else?
Think of three possible ways of finding a place to live.

6 Now read on. . . .

If you plan to stay in your home area, the possibilities are probably well-known to you already. Friends and the local paper are always a good source of information. If you are going to work in a new area, again there are the papers – and the accommodation agencies, though these should be approached with caution. Agencies are allowed to charge a fee, usually the equivalent of the first week's rent, if you take accommodation they have found for you. But some less scrupulous operators may charge you a fee to look at accommodation which may be already occupied when you get there!

For students, many colleges, polytechnics and universities have accommodation officers who will do the necessary hunting. This is a difficult job in some areas where there is a large student population with scant residential provision and few locals who are keen to take students as tenants or boarders. But what sort of accommodation is available?

7 Before reading further, list the different kinds of accommodation you think might be available for young people in Britain.

8 Now read on, ticking off the items on your list as they are mentioned and adding any you had not thought of.

If you like the idea of living with a family (other than your own), or in a small house where there are a few other boarders, digs might be the answer. Good landladies – those who are superb cooks, launderers and surrogate mothers, are figures as popular in fiction as the bad ones who terrorise their guests and overcharge them at the slightest opportunity. The truth is probably somewhere between the two extremes. If you are lucky, the food will be adequate, some of your laundry may be done for you and you will have a reasonable amount of comfort and companionship. For the less fortunate, digs may be lonely, house rules may restrict the freedom to invite friends to visit, and shared cooking and bathroom facilities can be frustrating and row-provoking if tidy and untidy guests are living under the same roof.

60

The same disadvantages can apply to flatsharing, with the added difficulties which arise from deciding who pays for what, and in what proportion. One person may spend hours on the 'phone or wallowing in deep, hot baths, while another rarely makes calls and takes cold showers. If you want privacy with a guest, how do you persuade the others to go out; how do you persuade them to leave you in peace, especially if you are a student and want to study?

65

70

Conversely, flat sharing can be very cheap, there will always be someone to talk to and go out with, and the chores, in theory, can be shared. Even so, if you value privacy and a place of your own where you can put up your own posters, play your favourite music etc, perhaps it would be better to look for a bedsitter or a flat of your own.

75

The beauty of a bedsit is its simplicity. It is relatively cheap, easy to keep clean, economical to heat since it is usually a single room, and at its best a 'cosy' place to live. At its worst, the bedsit can be cramped and impregnated with cooking smells or cluttered with damp washing. It can also be very lonely if you are not naturally sociable and have moved to a new area.

80

A flat will usually give you more space, but you will have to pay for it, and, like the bedsitter, it can be a lonely start in a new area. In any dispute with a landlord over rent or responsibilities there is only you to negotiate, though of course you can take some problems to the local rent tribunal.

85

However, if you prefer entertaining at home and like having friends to visit, you will be spending less on going out, so the extra expense of a flat can be minimal. You will probably have your own washing and cooking facilities, and if the flat is not furnished, there is the fun of going to auctions and junk shops to choose your own furniture.

from *Prospect*, 1977

Check your understanding

KEY

9 Answer these questions. First locate the right part of the text, and then read that part carefully.
   a) What are the disadvantages of a bedsitter?
   b) Name two problems flatsharers might have.
   c) What do living in good digs and living at home have in common?
   d) For what kind of person might a bedsitter be a bad thing?
   e) What kind of person might prefer a bedsitter to a shared flat?

KEY

10 Which of the following six statements do you think best sums up the author's point of view?
   i) There are few advantages in living at home after leaving school.
   ii) Accommodation agencies are the best source of help when looking for somewhere to live.

iii) If one cannot live at home the best arrangement is to find a good landlady.

iv) One should carefully consider the advantages and disadvantages of all kinds of home before making a decision.

v) Living away from home is very lonely.

vi) Finding a flat of your own is the best solution of all.

 What do you think?

11 Is the situation described in the extract similar to that in your country? *Do young people move away from home, and if so, where do they move to?*

Section 2 A Roof Over Your Head

Once someone has decided what kind of accommodation he wants, the next step is to find something suitable. Small ads appearing in local papers and some magazines can be useful.

KEY **1** You are looking for somewhere to live. You've decided to look for shared accommodation. You want to live in a house, because you'd like a garden. You want to have your own room. You don't smoke. You eat meat.

Look *quickly* through the ads below and on the next page for something suitable. List the possibilities in order of preference. Give reasons for your first choice.

Rooms Offered

● **Mother and son** (5) want to share nice house north London (own kitchen, garden, share bath) with other single parent and child age 5–7—£18 a week—reduced rent for baby-sitting.

● **Quiet vegetarian couple** for spacious south London flat. Short let £10 p.w. each.

● **Couple or two share double room** luxury flat. £12.50 each per week.

● **THIRD PERSON WANTED** to share SC flat. Hornsey area, own room. Approx £33 per calendar month.

● **N.11** female 21 years+ wanted for congenial mixed house £35 month + elec. Foreigners especially welcome.

● **RESPONSIBLE PERSON** wanted to share house with two others in NW4.

● **BARNSBURY, N.1.** Responsible person (30's) for very attractive, peaceful loft room. Own cooking facilities, share luxury bath. £15.

● **COVENT GARDEN FLAT,** two adults and two year old. Room for four months (Nov–Feb). £13 p.w. Quiet. Amenable person possibly not spending whole week in London.

● **CENTRAL LONDON**—double bedsit or office combined overnight acc. Just vac similar Wembly opp. Stadium. Confidential. Please write fully.

● **SW10—OWN ROOM,** mixed house for non-smoker, vegetarian. No nuts. £60 pcm.

● **Large room mixed flat** for one or two prof. girls. Harrow.

● **SW3 person 23+**. Own room in shared flat. £10 p.w. inclusive.

● **Girl to share** flatlet. £4 p.w. Please write for details now.

● **MUSWELL HILL** girl (prefer vegetarian, non-smoking) to share house (two—own rooms, garden) £17.

● **WILLESDEN GREEN,** 5th person, own room in large mixed house with garden. Non-smoker. £31 pcm.

● **OWN LARGE ROOM** in shared house with lounge. colour tv, kitchen, gardens, etc. Near countryside, near Orpington. £39 pm.

● **OWN ROOM** in large Clapham flat for six months. £10 pw.

● **FEMALE** to share flat, o/r, SW11. £33.33 pcm plus deposit.

● **VEGETARIAN** for house in SW16. Own room, £9 pw plus expenses (deposit required).

● **TWO GIRLS** wanted to share large room in lovely modern flat. £9 p.w. inclusive.

● **MALE 24+** share house, E7. Own room. £8 p.w. Pref non-smoker.

● **SECOND PERSON** wanted (LADY)—three room flat, **BARNES.** Own room garden.

● **SECOND FRIENDLY,** relaxed person, late 20s/30s, non-smoker, vegetarian, preferably for o/room. Comfortable Harrow flat. Garden, car space. £65 pcm including C/H.

●**SMALL BASEMENT DUNGEON** offered exchange morning domestic work possibly pocket money. Dependent hours. Situated Mayfair.
●**HAMPSTEAD ROOM** for one in modern well furnished flat. C.H., TV, deepfreeze. £68 p.m.
●**Couple wanted** for large room in communal flat in N.W.3 to share with three others.
●**Own room (semi-furnished)** in mixed Earlsfield (S.W.18) house for male vegetarian non-smoker. £30 p.c.m.

●**Fourth person for** S / C flat, W.14. O/R. £40 p.c.m.
●**EALING**—own room. 3–4 nights baby sitting + £5.
●**E14**—single room for girl in large friendly, mixed house. Should like cats. £27 pcm. Deposit same.
●**LARGE ROOM** in cheap flat. Part furnished/Battersea. Share with touring clown—suit similar in theatre, music.
●**A pleasant room** in Bayswater flat for 1/2 persons. Sharing with student of painting and student of ballet: £16.50 p.w. All inclusive.

●**Share charming** Victorian house. Shepherds Bush. Lovely large room £15 p.w. plus bills. November-March possibly longer. Girl preferred or housework orientated guy.
●**N.20.** Large sunny room for one or two females. Central heating, own TV., shared kitchen and bathroom with one other dog and garden lover preferred. £60 per month.

> **When looking for a particular piece of information in a text, don't read the whole text from beginning to end. For example, with advertisements, read just enough of each to decide whether it is what you are looking for, or not. When dealing with other texts, glance through the whole text to find the relevant part and then read this more carefully. This is known as SCANNING.**

2   To help you understand the abbreviations used in ads, imagine you want to share a flat and make a list of things which would be important.

KEY **3**   Now try to work out what the following mean. If you are unable to guess what an abbreviation stands for, check in the key at the back of the book.

a)   M/F or 2F £28.50 p.w. ea. Sh Lge CH hse Phone 3364 aft. 6.30.
b)   1M to share comf. flat £27.50 p.c.m.
c)   f sh. rm. Lux. flt £51 pcm excl.

d)   Girl 20+ O/R in friendly mxd flat.
e)   3rd prof m to sh flat £65 pcm incl. all bills.
f)   Room in Mod hse to let. All cmfts, F pref. O/R £14 p.w.

KEY **4**   Two friends of yours, both girls, need somewhere to live, but they can't afford much. They don't mind sharing a room, and would like to share a large flat or a house with others. They don't know anyone else to share with, so they need to find a place for two. They want the cheapest accommodation possible. Suggest two or three ads they should follow up from those below and on the next page.

81●   FLAT SHARING

SHARERS
Now-September 1979. CHIS-WICK. W4. 2 twin bedrms., lnge., din. rm., k & b. 4 single sharers. £12.50 pw ea. Mrs Stutchburg. 994 2806. Streatham. SW16. Mod. block 2 twin bedrms., lnge., k & b. Ch. 4 single sharers. £12.50 p.w. ea. Mr. Charles, 6/7 3435.

F. 23 plus S/c flat SE24. £27 pm. 856 2877 days.
GIRL reqd for comfortable mixed flat. Willesden Green area. £63 per month inc ch & gas. Tel. 452 3891 after 5 pm.
GLDRS GRN M sh rm. £45 pm inc 455 7135.
GREENFORD. Sh lux hse soon. m/f £18. 557 3539.
HOLLAND PK. Dble £15.50 each. Dep. req. Evgs. 602 4663.

N8. Flat. girl to sh. room £46 pcm 348 4112.
N13 2 girls to share rm, mxd flat. £48.50 inc pcm. 882 2866 aft 10 am.
NW3. F. 20s o/r £46 pcm. 435 9244 eve.
NW4. M/f. Small rm mxd. hse. £48 pcm. 203 1711 eve.
PERIVALE. Room in house for mid 20s prof. person. Non-smoker. £60 pm. 997 9443.

FEMALE share flat. own rm. £65 pcm. Finchley. ‹‹6 16°7.
GL 20s o/r mxd flt SW4 cl Tube. £50 pcm. 673 2°77.
GIRL Sh rm in lov s/c flat. £41 pcm. £40 dep. ‹2° 8°72.
HIGHGATE. Girl share rm. mixed flat. £14 pw. 3‹° 53°° aft 6.
PROF m o/r SW4. £7.50 pw. ‹7‹ 7°°6 evn.
RESPONSIBLE young lady 18 is looking for room in nice flat. Central area. Ring Alison 7‹1 1°°8 after 5.30.
ST JOHN'S WOOD, female to share superb luxury one bedroom flat. 32° 6‹6° after 6.30 pm.
SE20, o/r £45 m. 7‹8 1398.
SHARE A FLAT for profs. No charge to landlords. 175 Piccadilly. 49° 12°° also b/b.
STH KEN 2 to sh rm. £20 pw ea. 589 2°°°.
SW15. 3rd person wanted for very comf. hse. O/r. C.h., c/Tv. £16 pw. incl. gas & elec. Ring 6°9 0°°i (after 6.30 pm).
W3, m/f. sh s/c. o/r £9 pw suit grad. 9°2 16i8 aft 6.

CHISWICK
W4 s/c flats. 2 twin bedrms lnge, dining rm. k & b, for 4 sharers. £12.50 pw each. Tel °°4 280°.

WEST KEN.
Large room with 2 beds available for 1/2 girls in lge flat with 1 guy. £15 single or £25 for 2. 6°° 243°.

STREATHAM
SW16 s/c flats. Mod block 2 twin bedrms. lnge. k & b. ch. For 4 sharers £12.50 pw ea Apply 46 Beechcroft Close. Hopton Rd. SW16. Tel °‹7 343°.

BRENT CROSS. Bed sit £18 per week. 4°8 477°.
BROMLEY, S/d bungalow Cnr psn. 2 beds, 2 rec., gge, gdn, £28.750. 6°1 95°°.
CROYDON. 3rd pers shr hse. £58 pm. C/h. 657 8119.
EASTBOURNE. Semi 3 beds, 2 rec., k & b. Open outlook. Large gdns, greenhse. Fitted carpets. £19,500. Tel. °°72°.

M/F to share rm in W1 flat. £70 pm. V comfortable. Contact °°5 195°.

M/F. 4 prof p sh mod spac flat. Greenford. 1 dble 2 sgls from £12 pw. 5°8 347°
N3. Prof m o/r mxd hse. £45 pm. 349 ‹°31.
N21. 2 sh hse. £14 pw. 6°4 7847. Fri 6-8.
NW9. 2 share rm mxd hse. £11 pw. Ring 2°° 677°.
PUTNEY. F. sh mxd hse o/r. £15 pw inc tel. 6°° 573° day: °°° 032° evng.
SE3. 2nd pers. pro. share flat. Own room. £57.50p mthly. Phone °‹8 3541 after 4 pm.

STUDENTS
NOW to JUNE '79
HAM'SMITH. 3 twin bedrm. lnge. k & b. 6 single sharers £13.95 pw ea.
W6. W12, SW5, 2/3 twin bedrms, lnge. k & b. 4/6 sngl shares. fr £13.95 pw each.
TOOTING, SW17. 2 twin bedrms. lnge. k & b. 4 sngl shares. £12.50 pw ea.
CRAWFORDS o°3 02°1

KEY **5** Some people prefer not to share with strangers, and so look for self-contained accommodation.

Work out what these ads for self-contained accommodation mean. Look up any you can't guess in the Key.

a) Furn. hse nr. stn and shops. 2 beds, 1 recep. Wd suit 3 shrng.

b) Central London flat for 4/5 shrs. 2 beds, lnge, k, b. £60 p.w.

c) Grnd flr. furn. flt. Parking. Sleeps 2/3. Refs essent.

d) S/C flt £45 p.w. incl. CH Suit overseas fam.

e) Large furn. bedsit newly dec. sh. kit and bath with 2 others.

f) Unfurn hse 2 beds 1 recep. all fac. incl CH. Min 1 yr. £100 p.m.

KEY **6** You have been posted to London for six months by your company. They are prepared to pay up to £85 p.w. rent on your behalf, but you have to find your own accommodation. You want a fully furnished 2 bedroom flat with a telephone. You won't have time for housework, so you're looking for a flat which is serviced (i.e. cleaned regularly). A colour TV would be nice. Find two ads which look promising from the selection on the next page.

79●FLATS & MAISONETTES TO LET

SUPER FLATS 1 to 5 bedrooms. Lux aparts from £50 to £1000. imm and advanced bookings. Call SUZYLET CO 262 ₃₋89

CORNWALL GDNS SW7 2 furnished flats to let. 1 dble 1 sgle bedrm. 1 rec. k&b. col TV, c/h. £100 and £80 pw. ₃37 002₀ aft 6 pm.

HOLIDAY FLATS in Bayswater 1-3 bedrooms. From £40-150 pw.w. Call LOMBARD HOMES 22₃ 005₃

ST JOHN'S WOOD Absolutely ideal fully furn. flat, beautifully situated. Mod with garage. Samuel & Co. ₃73 49₊₊.

SHORT LETS Luxury flats for visitors and companies LONDON APARTMENTS. 4₃7 9₃₃1 day: 4₃1 ₃6₁2 eves & weekends.

ON EALING COMMON. 3 bedroom quality 1st floor furnished flat in small block. Gas c.h. Yearly let. £70 pw. Brendons ₃28 2711.

RICHMOND. Superb gdn flat. Dble bedrm & dress rm, 20ft draw rm, k, b, shwr, bidet, chw, c/h, elec inc £60 pw. 4₃0 ₀583.

ST JOHN'S WOOD. Attractive 1 bed flat, adjoining Regents Park, Recep, k & b. balcony. Fully furn. 6 months-2 yrs. £70 pw. ₃22 212₃.

SELF-CONTAINED unfurnished entrance floor flat. Thicket-rd. SE20. Coming available end September. Accommodation: 2 large rooms, kitchen and bathrm with own garden. Good decorative condition. £900 p.a. exclusive (£75 monthly in advance). Minimum period 3 years. Good refs. essential. Give phone no. if available. Write to Box No. T224.

AT KNIGHTSBRIDGE. Dble £24 & sgle £16 S/c studio £40. ₃28 ₃302 FLAT-LAND

BED/SITTERS with kitchens. Dbles £17.95 pw. Hampstead nr. tube. Hol. let. 340 ₃414.

BEDSIT in Walthamstow. Large room, modern furniture & decorations. £15 pw. inc ch & electricity. 01-521 ₃84.

BELSIZE PARK holiday let. Luxury 2 rms, k & b. £65 pw. 734 7₃4₃ day: 722 7₃65 eves.

BOUNDS GREEN. 2 bedroom s/c flat, 6 months only. £45 pw. ₃69 7₃14.

BROMLEY, KENT. 24 mins. Victoria. Attractive mews. Newly decorated, central heating. Double garage. Four bedrooms, lounge, kitchen, bathroom. New fitted carpets throughout, part furnished. £60 pw. No sharing. 01-4₃₀ 04₀₀.

CHELSEA. Lux 2-rmd furn flat. K&b. £70 pw. Tel & view after 7 pm or w'ends. ₃89 477₃.

CHELSEA. Lux serviced holiday flats from £60 per week. Phone ₃₃2 641₃.

CHISWICK flat 3 rooms, k/b, wc. Phone. £60 pw. Short let 90₃ 1₃04.

EARLS COURT. Family flat 2 double bedrooms, suit company executive. £100 pw. Call ₃70 ₃670.

EALING. Beaut s/c flat. Lnge, 2 bedrms. £85 pw. ₀97 97₃4.

EALING. 3/4-bdrmd. £36-£60. Cosway. ₃98 995₀.

EARLS CT. Magnificent, s/c flat. 1 bedroom, 1 lounge, fit kit, bath, sun roof. ch. Near Tube. Suit 2. £60 pw. 7₃9 40₃5.

SHEP BUSH. Gd bachelor flat. 1 rm, k, b, £32 pw. 43₀ 05₃2.

SIDCUP, 4 r k & b. Suit couple or single professional £35 pw. 6 months only. Ring 30₀ 3₃44.

SOUTH KENSINGTON. Flats from £45pw: bedsits £15 to £30. Markham Bureau. ₃₃9 92₃3.

ENFIELD. One bedroomed flat £26 pw incl. Weybridge 4₃₃63.

FLAT. 3 rooms kitchen and bathroom. Newly furnished. Short term holiday let £120 pw. Apply 155 Queens Court, Queensway. W2. 9 am to 5.30 pm.

FURNISHED FLAT (small) offered rent free + salary for Nurse/Receptionist in doctor's surgery. Write Mrs J Dee, 2 Torver Road, Harrow.

GLOUCESTER ROAD SW7. Bargain flat for 2 months due to slight building work 2 bedrooms, reception, dining/kitchen, overlooking garden square. £70 per week. Phone Reigate 49₀₀6.

HAMPSTEAD. Luxury furnished flat. 2 dble bedrms. colour TV. Phone serviced etc, £85 pw. 43₃ 2₃/3.

HAMPSTEAD. Best part, 4 rms., 2nd flr. flat, k, b, CTV. CH. £95 pw. 4₃₃ 921₀.

HAMPSTEAD. Mod c/h furn flats. Tel col TV. 1-4rms. k & b. 32-89 gns. 7₃4 2₃89.

HAMPSTEAD. Ultra lux furn flat, 1bed, suit cple or exec. Refs essential. £100 pw. 01-435 8₃64 or 7₃2 3744.

HOLIDAY FLATS 7₃3 ₃₀1₃.

HOLIDAY flats 9₃₀ 798₀.

HOLIDAY LETS W9. Self-catering £10 per person per wk. 7₃7 51₀3.

HOLLAND PARK Pleasant, furnished flat overlooking garden. 2 r, k & b. £260 pm + electricity with £100 deposit. Maximum 4 months Phone 7₃7 98₀6.

KENS. Lux hol flat. CH. CTV fr. £60 pw. ₀37 30₃3.

KENS. SW10. Nicely furnished 2 dble bedrms., living/dining room, kitchen, bathroom. Colour TV Telephone, etc. £80 pw. Telephone ₃7₀ 1936.

KENSINGTON, W8. Pleasant modernised mews flat: fully furnished ch double bedroom, open plan reception, bath Cleaning included. £75 pw. 2₃9 2₃10.

KNIGHTSBRIDGE nr Harrods Lge furn flat £120 pw. Also smaller one £70 pw. 3₃2 9477 or 94₀ 1₃55.

LANCASTER GATE. Fully furnished, newly decorated, g/f flat. Lounge, bedroom, kitchen & bathroom/wc. £75 pw 48₀ 11₀2.

MAGNIFICENT maisonette to let W9 Suitable 5/6 sharing £120 pw for long let. Tel. 2₀₀ 667₃.

MAIDSTONE, Kent. Well furn s/c flat. Sleep 4. £40 pw. Ellis Estates, 8₀₀ 8033/₃970.

MARBLE ARCH, W1. Lux furn flat. 3 rms, k & b. £225 pw. 9₃9 27₀1.

MOVE IN now, buy later. Flats £15 pw. 474 1₀14.

N8. 2 bedrooms lounge kitchen, bath, toilet, 3/4 people. £45 p.w. Phone ₀1-348 5₃82.

NW10, s/c 2 bedroom flat, kitchen, lounge, bathroom. £35 pw. ₀65 3₃45.

POTTERS BAR 3/4 bedroom flat, 6 mths. let. Immediately all facilities, 2 baths, £65 pw Refs required, Fairgate College, Potters Bar (77) 42₃41.

PUTNEY. Sunny top flat for couple. £34 pw. 789 ₃0₃0.

QUEENS PARK. S/c lux furn apt. 1 dble bdrm. lnge, kit, bath/WC. 1-4 mths. £55 pw. VISITORS HOLIDAY FLATS 4₀2 8₃95.

QUEENS PARK. Flat. Sleep 5. £70 pw. 45₀ 85₃8.

SINGLE ROOM N2. 34₀ 5177, phone after 6.30.

SOUTH KENSINGTON. Flats from £45pw: bedsits £15 to £30. Markham Bureau. 5₃9 9₃43.

SURBITON near station. Superior self-contained flat in modern block, lounge, two beds k. & b. available six months. Suit visitors or company. £50 pw. ₃49 4₃64 after 2 pm.

SW7 Double room, private bath, lift. From £40 pw. ₃1-37₃ 4479.

SWISS COTTAGE Serv. dble bedsit, cook fac. 7₃2 834₃.

7 You and a friend need somewhere to live. Decide what kind of accommodation you prefer, and whether you want to share with each other, someone else, or not at all. Look back through all the ads for somewhere suitable.

Section 3 An Englishman's Home

Not all people live in houses or flats. The following passages are about what it is like to live in a castle and in a tent.

What do you think?

1 Before you read the text about living in a castle, make a list of the things you would like to know about the place and the people who live in it. An example is given; continue the list.

Wouldn't it be very cold?

The text comes from a weekly magazine

2 Scan it to see if your questions are answered. (Time limit: 3 minutes)

How Would You Like To Live In A Castle

Military historian and MP Alan Clark, tells Belinda Black about his Kent home

Unused to visiting castles and somewhat awed by the super-structure – the front 'door,' complete with . . .(a). . . is flanked by two lofty towers – I was immediately put at ease by its owner. Alan Clark, Tory MP for Plymouth Sutton and son of Lord Clark is witty, irreverent and immensely like-able, throwing open his home with gay abandon.

It took nearly an hour to do a tour of inspection, from the Great Library, to all around the grounds and the house. There is a secret garden and a ruined Knight's Hall, a torture chamber and a tiny museum, all quite separate from the castle proper. And lots of exits and entrances – it would be very easy to get lost.

'We've one hundred and twenty acres of land all told,' Alan explained, 'including six acres of lawn, four of which are enclosed by . . .(b). . . and . . .(c). . . Mowing the grass is enough exercise to give one a heart attack. My wife wears a pedometer, and reckons we average eight miles a day with-out leaving the castle walls. Not that there is the incentive to go out. It is so romantic and beauti-ful, with views for miles and a sense of total peace. I feel revitalised just being here, especially when we've been away. You feel very secure in a medieval . . .(d). . .

8

45 The castle is extraordinarily steeped in history, with a long and spectacular pedigree. Other than Warwick Castle, the Clarks reckon it is the best-kept privately-maintained medieval building in Britain, 50 though its origins go back much further.

A fortification was first known on the site in the year 488, when Romney Marsh was 55 covered by sea. The building, surrounded by forests, stood high on a ...(e)... between two streams. The lower trees dipped their branches in both 60 sea and stream, hence the name, Saltwood.

Prior to Lord Clark, Lady Conway owned Saltwood. She employed a team of ...(f)... 65 full-time for fifteen years, and restoration work is still going on. Alan Clark has since re-flooded the ...(g)... by the entrance gate, where we 70 photographed Jane, Andrew and a tame, hungry, and very mixed feathered assortment, from peacocks and chickens, to ducks and white doves.

75 'The outgoings here are unspeakable,' declares the debonair MP, not looking as though it gets him down. 'Even a boring bit of wall fall-80 ing out can cost £2,000 to resurrect, and it can happen while our backs are turned. 'We have central heating, but the windows don't fit, so the 85 heat loss is enormous. Double glazing, however, would look dreadful.

'The first time you came, we were without hot water for a 90 week. The downstairs boiler had to be replaced; it's like a furnace out of the *Mauritania*. As at Eton, one just gets used to physical hardship.'

95 The Clarks, you can see, have ...(h)... with their home like anyone else. It happens to be on a somewhat larger scale. Another thing I liked about 100 them – true aristocrats, they leave you to find out that they have three homes, a fleet of cars, vintage and otherwise, and a very comfortable private 105 income, preferring to amuse you at their own expense.

You enter the castle through the massive portals of the Keep, into a stone-walled en-110 trance hall, running the depth of the building. It is rather like a church. There are stained glass windows and ceilings with both ...(i)... and Gothic 115 drapery; the tapestries, paint-ings, pieces of sculpture look, and indeed, no doubt are, priceless.

Jane Clark, asked to count up 120 the number of rooms for which she's responsible, hazards a minimum of fifty; they include fourteen bedrooms and seven bathrooms. Married for nine-125 teen years, she can still be mis-taken for a teenager, except

when son James towers above her!

Out of a choice of reception 130 rooms, the family use the small library for formal gatherings and, a brisk up-and-down walk away, their delightful vaulted dining room. Here, at the back 135 of the house, is the kitchen, ripe for modernisation, and a modern family sitting room looking into the Inner Bailey. The Great Library is in the 140 grounds.

In summer the gardens are open to the public on Sunday afternoons, and to organised parties during the week. Says 145 Jane, 'We sometimes have three hundred people here on a weekend, and I both show them round and do the teas, which means baking mountains 150 of ...(j)... We all help to serve them on the lower lawn. When people say, "Do you know if anybody actually *lives* here?" I say, "Yes, the 155 Clarks." But my voice gives me away!'

3 Now read the above text more carefully. Ignore the lettered gaps.

KEY **4** Now look at the lettered gaps and try to guess the meaning of each of the original words. It will help you if you look at how and where the word is used. For instance:

visiting castles . . . the front door, complete with . . . a) . . .

. . .(a). . . must mean: a part of a castle.
           and: a part of the front door or entrance.

six acres of lawn, four of which are enclosed by . . . b) . . . and . . . c) . . .

. . .(b). . . and . . .(c). . . must mean: a part of a castle.
                and: something which encloses an open space.

You feel very secure in a medieval . . . d) . . .

. . .(d). . . must mean: something which you can be in, i.e. an enclosed space.
           and: something which makes you feel secure.
           and: something which existed in medieval days.

Now look at the other lettered gaps and guess the meaning of the original words in the same way. Write phrases about each word as in the examples above.

You can often guess the meaning of a word by looking at how and where it is used.
Consult a dictionary ONLY AS A LAST RESORT.

KEY **5** Now look at the original words in the key. Look each one up in a dictionary.
      Was your guess roughly correct?

The text below is from a daily newpaper.

KEY **6** As you read, answer the questions about the meanings of words by using the context to help you guess.

THE TENT PEOPLE

"WE ARE NOT," said Chris, the first comer in the tepee village, "playing Indians." The dwellers in the valley in West Wales have not chosen their way of life as an easy option.

5

a) *dwellers* is likely to mean:
    i) people
    ii) animals
    iii) ideas
    iv) trees

To get there at all you have a long drive over mountain roads, and after you leave your car at the "no vehicle traffic" sign you have a fairly long rough walk to find the hidden valley where the tepees cluster on each side of a stream.

The tribe, as they call themselves, are gradually buying up the land on which their tepees sit but the farmer – who bought his land at £10 an acre has upped his price recently to nearly £700 which makes it very difficult.

b) *tepee* is likely to mean:
  i) a kind of animal
  ii) a tree
  iii) a type of accommodation
  iv) a person

Each person coming in passes a kind of entrance test, building tepee. Carol, mother of four children, ranging from eight to fourteen, said: "I met a couple of people from the tepee village and they asked me to come. I said I would be there in a fortnight – but I uprooted and went straight away. My great grandparents were American Indians so I suppose I just felt at home. It took me a fortnight to make the tent. The village has a big old heavy duty treadle sewing machine you can use."

c) *tepee* is likely to mean:
  i) a camping tent
  ii) an American Indian tent
  iii) a commercially produced tent
  iv) a circus tent

Outside her tepee looks like a traditional Indian home. Inside it is immaculate and extremely comfortable. Its walls are lined with pockets, the bedding rolls into durry mats which double as seating, the floor is thick with woven blue and green mats. A fire burns on a bed of rushes and she cooks in old fashioned iron pots and griddles.

The women boil water over their fires for their washing, although sometimes they will go down to the launderette in Carmarthen.

They bake a kind of unleavened bread, rather like Indian chuppatis, in their griddle pans;

d) *chuppatis* are likely to be:
  i) made of meat
  ii) made of paper
  iii) made of metal
  iv) made of flour

one man produced a beautiful rich fruit cake he'd baked in a tin over his fire. None of the women I saw wore trousers, preferring long, thick skirts. They live together but independently. There is a tepee which is used for the occasional communal meal or meeting and there is a sauna, constructed by the stream, which all the village uses.

The women say they have discovered the need to get rid of possessions. There is room only for what is necessary, although there is no reason why that should not be decorative as well as functional. But anything irrelevant has to be shed.

The tepee dwellers took the recent arctic weather extremely well.

e) *dwellers* is likely to refer to people who:
  i) do a certain job
  ii) have a certain character
  iii) live in a certain place
  iv) have certain ideas

"We couldn't get out but then as we don't manage to get out often anyway, that hardly mattered. We had local milk and eggs and when you buy your flour, beans, lentils and so on in 70lb sacks as we do, then you're better off than most people in towns."

f) *lentils* is likely to mean:
  i) a kind of vegetable
  ii) spices
  iii) building materials
  iv) fuel for fires

Sid, in his third year in the village, says that there is no group way of life or communal philosophy. "We don't have special meetings or anything like that. Some people believe there is no place for technology at all and want to opt out completely. Others, of which I am one, think there is a limited place for some kinds of modern technology. There is also a place for crafts we don't have. To be truly self sufficient, we'd need our own smiths and potters.

g) *smiths* is likely to mean:
   i) activities
   ii) animals
   iii) machines
   iv) people

I think it doubtful we would ever achieve all that but I suppose it might be possible to help these crafts to continue. Our nearest smith, in Lampeter, will be retiring when he's sixty and there is nobody set to replace him.

h) *smith* is likely to mean:
   i) a skilled craftsman
   ii) someone who makes pottery
   iii) someone who makes tents
   iv) an intellectual

We do have old vehicles for getting into town but we'd like to be able to do without them eventually and just use horses and carts. You can't get the vehicles down here anyway."

The backgrounds of the tepee dwellers are mixed. Sid was brought up on a farm on Exmoor so the problems of boundary fences – much discussed after the ravages of the sheep – and subsistence farming are not new to him. Chris lived with what he describes as "the travelling people" in Ireland, much of the time being spent first in a tent and then in a tepee. Carol, too, had practical experience of hard living before she came. She was prepared to cook outside in the rain until she finished her tepee and runs her home with great efficiency.

Some of the others seem to have dropped out of middle class society and suburbia, retaining their accents and adopting their new way of life like fanatical converts to religion. Among this group were those who seemed to feel that any kind of technology was evil. One girl, with a gentle upper class voice, admitted to getting rather lonely and appeared to have drifted into the village through protest marches and ecological pressure groups.

Certainly when they all come into the local town on social security and shopping day they present a picturesque appearance, the women with waist length hair and flowing skirts – over wellington boots – and the men, also with long hair, flowing coats, beads, fringed bags and a weird assortment of headgear.

Children play around the tepees and many have small tepees of their own. The number fluctuates but there are usually about a dozen and as the villagers have convinced the local education authority that they can teach their children satisfactorily, they do not go to the local schools. Three babies are currently expected and the mothers will be going into the local maternity hospital although one would like to have her baby in her tepee. The district nurse and local social services people visit when necessary but it has been a joint decision that it would probably be safer for the mother to go away.

The village contains a high proportion of one-parent families – men as well as women. The women find the environment a supportive one after struggling along on their own. The men have mixed feelings. "The problem is," said one father who looks after his own son, "you have to do the traditionally masculine things, some of the really heavy work the women just can't do and also do all the mother's tasks. I think in this kind of society the one-parent father gets the worst of the deal."

They have had some criticism because some of them draw social security – others survive by doing odd jobs such as carpentry.

i) *carpentry* is likely to mean:
   i) a form of self-discipline
   ii) a learned profession
   iii) a way of earning a living
   iv) a technique for survival

155

160

165

"But local people," says Sid, "have been most tolerant and pleasant. Those of us who were travelling people were used to having a difficult time but we have run into very little prejudice in this little corner of Wales."

It is a hard life and not one that many would choose. Some villagers are now in their third winter and show no signs of wanting to give up. "When you've built your own tepee," says Carol, "it becomes yours in an almost magical way. It makes you feel truly independent, in charge of your own life, in a way you cannot possibly experience living in today's society. It's a very hard life and I wouldn't like people to think it's glamorous because it isn't. But in my case it fills a very deep-seated need."

from *The Guardian*, 1978

Check your understanding

KEY

7   The following table will help you to summarise the main information in both texts. Fill it in, referring back to the texts if necessary.

The Text	Living in a Castle	Living in a Tent
The people: Age		
Social background		
Job		
The facilities: Cooking		
Heating		
Sleeping		
Cost		
Advantages		
Disadvantages		
Other points of interest		

8 Now check the words in 6 a) – i) in a dictionary

9 Is there anything in the social or educational background of the people you have read about, which has led them to choose to live where they do?

10 Which of the two groups of people do you like best and why?

11 If you lived in any of these places, what would you find most attractive and least attractive about each?

Section 4 No Place Like Home

What do you think?

1 There are various decisions you need to make if you find yourself living in a single room, whether by necessity or by choice. How would you solve the following problems?

   a)   After moving into your room, you can only afford to buy 12 items of furniture or pieces of equipment over the first three months. What would you buy? Put the items in order (e.g. armchair, bed, curtains, record-player, second-hand washing-machine)

   b)   You want to make your room unusual and interesting. What would you do about: – the walls?
                                  – the floor?
                                  – the furniture?
                                  – the lighting?

2 Now read the article below and on the next page from a magazine for young people.

One Room Living

I've always believed that the challenge of decorating and furnishing one room to suit one person's individual needs, is one of the greatest life has to offer. If you are single
5 and have only yourself to please you have no limitations and you can do whatever you want in your own room. The freedom! (No-one standing there with arms aggressively folded, saying; 'Oh – I don't like
10 *that*!') You can be as nutty or as wild as you like, and your resulting room could be a creative masterpiece, designed exclusively by you and for you.

So I hope you don't mind if I offer you
15 ideas that I've seen and done myself to stir your imagination so that you can turn your bedsit, whether a flat or a bedroom in a shared house, into a personal haven, a

boudoir, a designer's dream, at a minimum of expense, to suit only you and whatever you desire.

Your room can easily change into a *sultan's den*. Buy as many second-hand velvet curtains and cotton bedspreads as possible and hang them on the walls. Paint what wall remains red or orange and pin up pictures of nudes or even odalisques. Now get hold of anything containing lots of fine material – a parachute, a net wedding dress – and drape it across the ceiling, from the centre of the room to the edge. If there's enough, drape it over the window and make a tent across the head of your bed.

If all this opulence strikes you as being a bit much, be really courageous and make yourself a *conceptual room*. Make every single thing in the room the same shade and make it a restful shade like cream, pale green, peach, beige or white. Hang your clothes and things on one wall and pull down in front of them same-coloured blinds fixed from the ceiling, so that the room looks completely bare. Put your bed on the floor and cover it with the same colour fabric. And that is all you have in your room.

This sounds horrifying at first, but after a while you find such a relief from the clutter of daily life everywhere else. You have a feeling of spaciousness and peace. You can meditate without distraction. When friends come to visit you, you will be able to psycho-analyse them by their reactions. The insecure people will be frightened; the conventional ones will be shocked and the egocentric ones will want to put pictures on the walls to add the impact of somebody's personality – theirs! Your conceptual room has a different meaning for everyone who sees it.

If you find this idea a bit dramatic but you still want a peaceful retreat from the horrors of city life, make yourself a *jungle room*. Paint a mural on one wall of either trees or plants. Add a sensuous effect by including sunshine and human figures enjoying themselves.

Get a piece of trellis to go over the window, especially if you've got an ugly city view, and hang trailing plants from it. Put five-foot high rubber plants or castor-oil plants in tubs in the corners of your room and cover one table with spider plants and african violets. Paint all the furniture in

your room white. If you want this atmosphere, but can't afford a lot of plants at first, a weekend by the sea can provide you with plenty of dried grasses, pebbles, driftwood, shells and other things of interest with which to decorate your room.

You may be into herbs and plants and herbal highs. Herbs in windowboxes do just as well on a table inside the window as long as you remember to water them. In the late spring, when the growth is at its strongest, clip them and dry them by spreading them on newspaper in a warm, dry place for about three days; or hang them in bunches near the fireplace. Put them in screw-top jars with labels and they make an attractive addition to any room.

If you like food and cooking, why not live in a *kitchen*? Use large bookshelves all over one wall (if you can't afford to buy them, make them from planks, supported at the ends by white-painted housebricks that you can get from a builder's yard) and display on them all your casseroles, crockery, food, cane baskets from Oxfam, stone mustard jars and cookbooks.

Get hold of a second-hand filing cabinet, which has no end of space in it, in which to hide all your clothes and non-kitchen possessions, and paint it the same colour as the walls so that it merges in. Cover cabinet and walls with spice charts, chopping boards, slimming plans, rush table mats, printed tea-towels, cooks' aprons, wine charts, pub mirrors – and plastic onions if you must! A plain table and rush mats on the floor finally complete the effect.

from Singles, 1978

UNIT ONE

Check your understanding

KEY **3** Answer the following questions. All these questions can be answered *from the text*, even if the words are new to you.

a) *Nutty* (line 10) is likely to describe someone who is
  i) unimaginative
  ii) conservative
  iii) intelligent
  iv) eccentric

b) *A boudoir* (line 19) is
  i) a room
  ii) a piece of furniture
  iii) a kind of house
  iv) an item of clothing

c) *Odalisques* (line 27) are likely to be
  i) exotic people
  ii) abstract shapes
  iii) plants
  iv) landscapes

d) *Opulence* (line 34) describes
  i) a colour
  ii) a piece of furniture
  iii) an atmosphere
  iv) a quantity of money

e) *Beige* (line 39) is
  i) a soft colour
  ii) a bright colour
  iii) a shape
  iv) a feeling

f) *Clutter* (line 48) suggests a feeling of
  i) darkness
  ii) spaciousness
  iii) crowdedness
  iv) silence

g) *A trellis* (line 68) is likely to be
  i) made of soft material
  ii) made of solid steel
  iii) made of wood
  iv) made of glass

h) *Planks* (line 95) are likely to be
  i) round and heavy
  ii) small pieces of stone
  iii) made of wood and rectangular
  iv) made of soft material

4 Now check the exact meanings of these words in a dictionary.

What do you think?

5 Imagine that you have decided on a 'jungle room'. List the items you will need.

6 Now imagine that you would like a 'kitchen room'. List the items you would choose under these headings:
- floor coverings
- furnishings
- wall-coverings
- kitchenware

16

People Who Matter

Section 1 Falling in Love

What do you think?

What is the best way to meet members of the opposite sex?

1 Look at these suggestions. Tick (√) those you think are good; put a cross (X) beside those you think are bad. Give reasons.

– at university or college
– at church
– at a political club
– through a shared interest, for example a sport
– through mutual friends
– at parties or dances
– through introduction by members of one's family
– at work
– on holiday

2 Imagine you have now met someone you like. What is the best way of getting to know him/her better? Should you:

– persuade a friend to help?
– ask your parents to arrange a meeting?
– just hope that you meet again by chance?
– write the other person a letter, asking if you can meet?
– find a way to meet the person again, making it look 'accidental'?

The following extract is from a novel written in 1959. In the extract, Sammy gets to see Beatrice, the girl he has fallen in love with.

3 Read the extract below and on the next page without pausing at unknown words.

> They were coming out of the training college already, I could see them, fair heads and mousy ones, giggling and laughing in flocks, tinkling their good-byes and waving, so girlish and free, the thin ones, tall ones, dumpy ones, humpy ones, inky ones, slinky ones, gamesy ones and stern ones with glasses on. I was in the gutter,

5

sitting on my bike, willing them to die, be raped, bombed or otherwise obliterated because this demanded split-second timing. And,
of course, she might not come out at all – might be – what the hell
did you do in the girls' training college at half-past four on an
10   autumn afternoon? The crowd was thinning out. If she saw me first
so obviously sitting my saddle in the gutter and waiting, the game
would be up. Had to be accident, I had to be riding when she saw
me; so I pushed off and balanced along with circus slowness,
half-hoping now that the crisis was at hand that she would not come
15   out and my misbehaving heart would be able to settle again,
wobble wobble heart and bike and she appeared with two others,
turned and walked away without seeing me. But I had rehearsed
this too often in my bed for my heart and swelling hands to let me
down. The whole thing was mechanical, fruit of terrible concen-
20   trated thought and repetition. I rode casually, one hand in my
pocket and the other on my hip. Look no hands, swaying this way
and that. She was past and behind me.
Startled I looked back, grabbed the handle-bars, braked and skid-
ded to a stop by the pavement, looked back brazenly as she
25   approached, grinned brazenly in immense surprise –

'Why, if it isn't Beatrice Ifor'! . . . .

4   What do you think happens next?
– Beatrice pretends not to know Sammy?
– It's not Beatrice after all?
– Beatrice talks briefly but then makes an excuse to leave?
– Beatrice is persuaded by Sammy to stay and talk with him
for a while?

5   Read on to find out . . . . .

. . . So they stopped all three while my rehearsed prattle left her no
chance of moving off without being rude; and those other two
moved on almost immediately, waving back and giggling.
30   ' – was just cycling past – never dreamed – so this is the training
college, is it? I come along this road a lot or shall do in the future.
Yes, a course. I prefer cycling between the other place and the
other place – no buses for me. Can't stand 'em. Course in litho-
graphy. Were you going back to your digs? No. I'll walk. Can I carry?
35   Are you enjoying it here? Is the work hard? You seem to be thriving
on – yes. Look. I was going to have a cup of tea before I ride the rest
– how – oh, but you must! One doesn't meet – and after all these
months, too!
There was a small round table of imitation marble on three iron legs.
40   She was sitting on the other side. I had her now for whole minutes,
islanded out of all the complexities of living. By sheer hard work and
calculation I had brought this about.

from *Free Fall* by William Golding, 1968

> It is often not necessary to work out the precise meaning of every word you don't understand; as in the text above, it is enough to grasp the general meaning the writer intends to convey.

What do you think?

6   Would you have chosen to do what Sammy did?
Would you have reacted as Beatrice did?

Section 2 Problem Page

Sometimes, people who are worried by a personal problem write to a 'Problem Page' of a newspaper or magazine for advice.

1   a)   What would you expect a letter headed 'Moody Gran' to be about?
   b)   To see if you were right, read the letter. As you read, try to underline the important words. Those in the first sentence have already been underlined.

MOODY GRAN

My <u>gran's moods</u> are very <u>changeable.</u> Sometimes she can be very domineering and difficult, at other times she'll be pleasant and quite happy. But whichever it is, the good is never quite as good as it might be and the bad is always worse – whenever my mother or I are involved. Frankly she seems happier to hear about our problems than our successes. I haven't seen very much of her since I married, although my mother still sees her about every three or four weeks. Occasionally she has outbursts about me and tells mum I'm no good. Other relatives have had this treatment and have moved away or lost contact. My mother tells me about her visits and I feel weighed down just by listening. But I feel guilty. She's my grandmother, not getting any younger and I'm taking the easy way out by not going to visit her.

2   Now compare your underlinings with the version in the key.

> Words which seem to give information which is essential are known as **KEY WORDS**. Picking out key words helps to summarise a passage. For instance, the problem in the above letter can be summarised:
>
> **The writer feels guilty because she doesn't visit her grandmother, who can be very unpleasant.**

3   a)   The letter on the next page is headed 'Boyfriend's Dreadful'. What do you think it might be about?

b) While reading the letter to check, underline no more than 14 key words in the letter, so that the underlined words explain the writer's problem.

BOYFRIEND'S DREADFUL

I expect you will think I am a silly, over-loving mother, but I am worried about my 16-year-old daughter. She is meeting a boy of 20 who is really dreadful. He has no education, is well-known for being a petty thief and is generally a loutish and unsavoury character.

She is our only child, and has been sensible until now. What can we do?

KEY **4** Which of these sentences best summarises her problem?
  i) She loves her daughter too much and is being over-protective.
  ii) She's afraid that her daughter is going to marry a thief.
  iii) She's worried about her daughter having an unsuitable boyfriend.
  iv) She is a silly woman, worried over something which is not important.

5 a) The next letter is headed 'I want to be me!' What could it be about?
  b) As you read it, underline not more than 15 key words which together summarise her problem.

I WANT TO BE ME!

I'm worried because at 23 I feel as if I'm just an extension of my mother. My personality is being suppressed inside, waiting to be developed. All my family are out-going, but I'm an introvert. When I do think of something to say, I usually miss the opportunity to say it. I've tried joining clubs but Mum just worried about me going alone. I don't want to live in her shadow, but I haven't the strength of character or confidence to help myself. I've no friends and I lean on my mother for everything, mentally and materially. I thought about getting a job abroad, anything that would take me away from her so I'd have to stand up for myself. Do you think that might work – that I'll be able to establish my own identity if my mother's not around?

KEY **6** Write a sentence summarising the problem. The key words will help.

7 a) The letter on the next page is headed 'Who has first call?'. Do you have any idea at all what the letter might be about?
  b) As you read the letter, underline not more than 30 key words which summarise the writer's problem.

WHO HAS FIRST CALL?

My husband and I are teachers—both in our early 20s. We have been offered, and have accepted, an exchange job in New Jersey. We would have all expenses paid and the two American teachers who are replacing us in London have offered us their flat in New Jersey, while they live in our house. We have been very excited, but now there has been a catastrophe. My widowed mother was in a car accident and is now in hospital. She is in a coma but could come out of it, and then she would depend on me taking complete care of her, although it's not thought that she would live long. When we telephoned New Jersey they were sympathetic but said we must either keep our date, or they must find two other teachers. This means we may never get another chance and it is so sad as it meant prestige and extra money for my husband. I am very torn. I want to stay with my poor mother, but the doctors warn me that she may linger on as she is, or be a permanent invalid. I am desperate. Who has first call? What I decide to do will affect my husband, and ought I not to consider him? They want us as a pair—we would have to work together.

8 Now compare your version with that of friends. Have you underlined different words? Which version is best?

9 Write two or three sentences summarising the problem. Do not write more than 45 words.

10 Look at the last letter again. Working with two or three others, list all the possible solutions you can think of. Decide which of these you favour. Then write an answer to the letter, in which you advise the woman what she should do.

Section 3 For Better, For Worse

Part A Marriage

1 Before reading the next texts, look at the words below.
How many of them do you know?
How many of them could you guess? (for example by splitting the words up: sub - servient; co - habitation)

subservient	strive
impediment	chore
cohabitation	gender
apt	prey
relapse	loot

2 Now look at these words in sentences. It should be easier to guess their meaning.

a) Women, long considered the inferior sex, are therefore expected to be subservient to men.

b) Intolerance can be a serious impediment to successful marriage.

c) Any relationship which involves cohabitation presents problems which are avoided if one lives alone.

d) Married couples behave in predictable ways. For example, they are apt to take on certain roles in the family.

e) In the early days of marriage husbands and wives strive to be on their best behaviour. Later, however, they may relapse into their bad old ways.

f) Gender roles tend to be allocated in marriage. For example, woman are expected to be responsible for cleaning, cooking and other household chores, while men are the breadwinners.

g) The hunter instinct survives in men. Women are still regarded as prey, to be caught and conquered.

h) Traditionally, men bring home the loot in the form of the weekly pay packet.

When you see these words in the text below it should be even easier to guess their meaning.

3 How many of the above statements on marriage do you agree with?

4 Think of ways in which you can describe the roles of husband and wife in marriage and the family.
For example,

Wife   *Husband*
cook   *breadwinner*
mother   *handyman*

List in order of importance

5 What factors do you think help to make a marriage survive happily? List them in order of importance.
For example,   *Friendship*
               Good financial position

The following texts are both about marriage. The first is from a magazine about human behaviour.

6 While you read the first text, decide if you agree or disagree with the writer's views, and note your reactions in the margin. If you agree, put √; if you agree strongly put √√; if you disagree, put X; and if you disagree strongly, put XX.

Traditionally, the woman has held a *subservient* position in marriage partnerships. While her husband went his way she had to wash, stitch and sew.
5 Today the move is to liberate the woman, which may in the end strengthen the marriage union.
    Perhaps the greatest *impediment* to friendship in marriage is the amount a
10 couple usually see of each other.

Friendship in its usual sense is not tested by the strain of daily, year-long *cohabitation*. Couples need to contrive separate interests (and friendships) as
15 well as mutually shared ones, if they are not to become inured to the more attractive elements of each other's personalities.
    Married couples are *apt* to exert
20 themselves for guests – being amusing,

discussing with passion and point – and then to *relapse* into dull exhausted silence when the guests have gone. They may compound the boredom by starting to accuse each other of points of inattention or illogicality or "disloyalty" that they noticed in the other.

As in all friendship, a husband and wife must *strive* to interest each other, and to spend sufficient time sharing absorbing activities to give them continuing common interests. But at the same time they must spend enough time on separate interests with separate people (without jealousy on the other's part) to preserve and develop their separate personalities and keep their relationship fresh.

For too many highly intelligent working women, home represents *chore* obligations, because the husband only tolerates her work and does not participate in household chores. For too many highly intelligent working men, home represents dullness and reproaches – from an overdependent wife who will not gather courage to make her own life.

In such an atmosphere, the partners grow further and further apart, both love and liking disappearing. For too many couples with children, the children are allowed to command all time and attention, allowing the couple no time to develop liking and friendship, as well as love, allotting them exclusive parental roles.

We live in an industrial society with universal education and universal suffrage and the ability to control the number of children we can cope with. Yet we nurture many *gender* prejudices suited only to slave or tribal societies.

However almost in spite of ourselves – in spite of our conditioning – we are seeing friendship between men and women. Most of the media deride the possibility – after all, if every man is not to regard every woman as dangerous *prey* and every woman is not to regard every man as a dangerous source of *loot* and flattery, a major part of sensationalist reporting and fiction is lost.

But it seems that friendship is possible between people of different gender. And it is also possible between people who are sexually involved with each other. It does not seem too soon for friendship to be recognized as a desirable component of the marital relationship. There can be few more rewarding activities than learning to make friends with your marriage partner.

from *The Family of Man*

7 Compare your reactions to the text with those of a friend. Decide on which points you agree, on which points you disagree, and why.

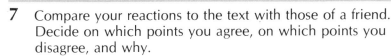

KEY **8** Look back at the text for factors which the author considers might be a danger in marriage. Group them under the headings: *Boredom   Gender Roles   Parenthood*

The second text is from a women's magazine. It is about a young couple with a small baby. The questions below are about the problems that can arise for such a couple.

9 First look at the questions; then, as you read, write down Ann and Brian's answers to them.
  a) At what point in their marriage should a couple have a baby?
  b) A wife with a good career may have to give it up when she has a baby; what dangers are inherent in this?
  c) How should a husband react to the boredom a wife may feel when she has to look after the baby all day?
  d) To what extent should the husband be involved in looking after the baby?
  e) Should husband and wife have separate evenings out?

Ann and Brian Stainton are a modern, intelligent couple who felt it was essential to establish their marriage and strengthen their relationship before having a baby. Ann also wanted to prove herself in her career, which she has done during the first five years of marriage, becoming personal assistant to two top executives in large London organisations.

We were sitting in the dining-area of their large L-shaped lounge. Ann, aged 25, made a graceful picture as she poured out coffee, her long hair framing her oval face. Her husband Brian is 30, enthusiastic, articulate and much more aware than most husbands of what it means for a career wife to find herself cut off from the challenge of mental stimulus of a responsible job.

"I worried about becoming a cabbage," she admitted. "I'm a person who needs people, who thrives on mental challenges. There are few neighbours with babies and anyway, I don't want to be eternally discussing child-care and recipes.

"The telephone is my life-line and I keep in touch with office friends. I also listen to the radio a lot – the talks, the discussions, the phone-ins. I became quite terrified that Brian would find me a dull companion." She turned to him and challenged: "Do you find there's not so much to talk about now I'm home all day?"

A one-sided conversation with a baby and a cat

There was silence while Brian considered. "I know you're concerned about this and there has been conflict I've had to overcome. I mean before, the two of us were at work, both earning and with jobs of equal importance and we talked mainly about them. I must admit I fought the temptation to say, 'Don't bother me – I've had a rotten day, I want to watch the telly and my job is all-important now and I want to relax.'

"A selfish attitude, I know, because I've only got to put myself in Ann's shoes, and I'd feel as frustrated as she if I had to face an evening of near silence after a day spent in a one-sided conversation with Joel and the cat! So we do range over a whole lot of topics, discussing what Ann's heard on the radio or what I've read in the papers. I'd say our horizons on the talk front are far wider. But it was another new pattern we had to learn."

I asked if they ever went visiting friends in the evening, taking Joel with them. "We tried it, but it didn't work very well," Ann confessed. "Joel is a happy, contented baby if kept to his routine. But if we were going out, he didn't sleep and then would cry from overtiredness. I think it will be easier when he's older. We're both determined to try and make him fit into our lives as far as possible."

Ann and Brian had agreed that he should be totally involved with the care of the baby. "Anyway, bathing and feeding Joel was a two-person job at first," Ann said. "He cried and his little arms and legs seemed to be moving in all directions and so Brian saw to the nappy end while I dealt with the upper half!"

Had they ever thought of separate evenings out? Lots of young parents had an evening each at leisure classes or spent a night visiting friends.

"Frankly, we prefer one another's company." Brian replied, "and if you're not careful, separate interests can lead to an even wider separation in your pattern of living".

from *Woman's Own*, 1977

KEY **10** Look back at the second text on marriage and choose one of the alternatives in the questions below;

    a) *A cabbage* (line 27) means
        i) a lazy person
        ii) a dull person
        iii) a happy person
        iv) a lonely person

    b) *Thrives* (line 29) means
        i) has no need of
        ii) feels physically healthy
        iii) feels cheerful
        iv) is stimulated by

    c) A *phone-in* (line 38) is
        i) a telephone conversation with a friend
        ii) a radio discussion conducted by telephone
        iii) a special kind of telephone
        iv) a radio programme about telephones

    d) *Challenge* (line 42) is to say something
        i) quietly
        ii) sadly
        iii) boldly
        iv) angrily

11 Do Ann and Brian seem to agree with the writer of the first text? Would they agree about:
– friendship?
– separate interests?
– the role of parents?

What do you think?

12 Now look back to your answers to 3 and 4 and consider whether the writer of the first text or Ann and Brian share your own views.

Part B Divorce

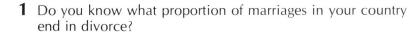

1 Do you know what proportion of marriages in your country end in divorce?

The text on the next page is from a government publication and gives figures for divorces in the UK from roughly 1970 to 1975. The graphs alongside the text illustrate possible trends in these figures, but only ONE of the graphs gives a correct picture of the figures given in the text.

KEY **2** While you read the text, decide which graphs are incorrect.

25

The fairly steady growth (averaging 9 per cent annually) in the number of divorces in the 1960s accelerated in the early 1970s following the 1971 Divorce Law Reform Act. (This applied only to England and Wales.) In 1972 the number of divorces in England and Wales was double that of 1970. The number fell back in 1973 but rose by about 7 per cent in each of the two succeeding years. It reached 120 thousand in 1975, slightly more than in 1972. This rapid increase led to a sharp rise in the number of divorced persons in the population and the number of young divorcees increased especially quickly.

a)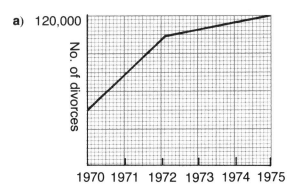

b)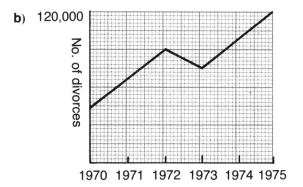

d)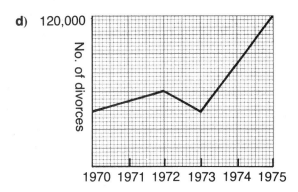

c)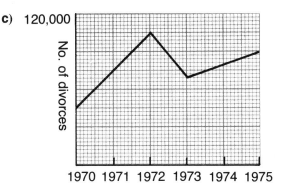

3 Does the text explain the steady growth in the divorce rate? Try to guess how the law must have been changed to cause this increase.

What do you think?

4 How easy should it be to get a divorce? If a married couple find that their marriage is so unsuccessful that they feel it necessary to get a divorce, what kind of reasons ought the law to recognise as sufficient?

This text comes from a magazine aimed at younger, educated, middle-class women.

5 As you read, underline the most important words showing the main grounds for divorce in the UK (in 1977).

Grounds For Divorce

As the law stands today, it has to be shown that a marriage has irretrievably broken down before a divorce can be granted, and, unless the circumstances are excep-
5 tional, you must have been married for three years before you can apply for a divorce.

If you genuinely feel that your marriage has broken down beyond repair, your
10 nearest divorce court can supply you with a booklet called *Undefended Divorce*, which outlines the necessary steps to take and five facts or grounds on which you can prove to a judge that your marriage has
15 truly broken down. Briefly, they are as follows:
1. Separation for a period of two years by mutual consent with both partners agreeing to divorce.
20 2. Separation for a period of five years. In this case, either partner can start divorce proceedings without the other's consent.
3. Desertion for a period of two years, but
25 you will have to supply evidence to show that you have been genuinely deserted.
4. Adultery, plus the fact that you cannot bear to continue living with your partner, although this does not have to particularly relate to the adultery. You will also have
30 to produce substantial evidence to prove that adultery really has taken place.
5. Unreasonable behaviour, to the extent that you cannot be expected to continue living with your partner. Again, you'll
35 have to provide evidence to support this claim and, in many cases, it's wise to consult a solicitor before starting any proceedings on such grounds. Your personal idea of unreasonable behaviour may be very
40 different from that held by the law. Boozy nights out with the boys might not make a man a roaring alcoholic, just as a possibly provoked slap might not brand him as a brute in the eyes of a judge. So make sure
45 you really know what's required to satisfy the court first.

Check your understanding

KEY **6** Could you get a divorce if you lived in the UK and . . . .
  a) your husband/wife is a very heavy smoker and is extremely untidy. You are very tidy and smoke makes you feel ill?
  b) you have lived apart from your husband/wife for three years but he/she will not agree to a divorce?
  c) your husband/wife has been living openly with someone else for some time?
  d) your husband/wife left you 18 months ago?

UNIT TWO

What do you think?

7 Look back to the list of reasons you wrote in 4. How do your reasons compare with those given in the text?
Do you consider that the laws on divorce in the UK are too lenient?

The following passage was written in the 1920s by a famous English philosopher who was well known for his outspoken beliefs on political and social questions. Here, he is writing for a general audience.

8 Read the text fairly quickly, underlining as you read the words which carry his main points on *grounds for divorce*.

The grounds which make divorce desirable are of two kinds. There are those due to the defects of one partner, such as insanity, dipsomania, and crime; and there are those based upon the relations of the husband and wife. It may happen that, without blame to either party, it is impossible for a married couple to live together amicably, or without some very grave sacrifice. It may happen that each has important work to do, and that the work requires that they should live in different places. It may happen that one of them, without disliking the other, becomes deeply attached to some other person, so deeply as to feel the marriage an intolerable tie. In that case, if there is no legal redress, hatred is sure to spring up. Indeed, such cases, as everyone knows, are quite capable of leading to murder. Where a marriage breaks down owing to incompatibility or to an overwhelming passion on the part of one partner for some other person, there should not be, as there is at present, a determination to attach blame. For this reason, much the best ground of divorce in all such cases is mutual consent. Grounds other than mutual consent ought only to be required where the marriage has failed through some definite defect in one partner.

from *Marriage and Morals* by
Bertrand Russell

KEY **9** Now fill in the following chart, using the information in the text. If you have to read parts of the text again, do so.

GROUNDS FOR DIVORCE

. . . .
. . . .
e.g. . . . .
. . . .
. . . .
Can you think of any other examples for this category?
. . . .
. . . .

. . . .
. . . .
e.g. . . . .
. . . .
. . . .
Best basis for divorce in this category: . . . .
. . . .

What do you think?

10 Do you think the grounds in either the first or the second category are sufficient for a divorce to be granted?

11 Do you agree that no blame should be attached to either partner when marriage breaks down due to 'overwhelming passion'?

12 How much, looking at your own list of grounds for divorce, do you find yourself in sympathy or agreement with Russell?

Section 4 A Death in the Family

The passage below is from a biography. In it, the writer recalls her parents in the last years of their lives. Her parents had moved into a flat for old people. Pat is the writer's sister.

1 Read the whole extract.

Dad had lost any purpose in life. We had to watch him getting frailer and frailer, while mum seemed even more energetic than before. She still had a job to do, shopping, cooking and running the flat. She was necessary. Dad felt superfluous. He died six years after they moved into the flat. I
5 think he died in self defence.
   He was the kindest and most generous man I have ever met. Yet I was never able to know him as well as I wished. He was reticent. I didn't get near enough to him. He never spoke of the things close to his heart. Perhaps he couldn't. I know that he loved all his children, but I think he
10 loved me in particular. Yet because in our family outward signs of affection were never shown, because mum and dad never kissed us goodnight, because neither of them said how much they loved us, some-how I have never at any time been able to express my love for them. I was with dad on the night he died and I longed to be able to kneel by his
15 bedside and say, 'Dad, thank you for being so good to us, I love you dad.' Every time I tried to I was overcome with embarrassment. I felt even at that time that he would think it wrong for me to try to clothe in words my private feelings.
   After dad died, all of us rallied round mum. We thought that to have
20 her children calling on her would be some sort of compensation. It was at first. I'd visit her twice a day and listen while she talked about her life with dad. Not for mum, a veil of silence over the dead. She would relate their lives and relationship together from the time she first met him. I think it was right that she did. The conspiracy of silence that so many relations
25 adopt about the dead doesn't help. It makes it appear as if those that are gone never lived. It was far better to talk about dad, to keep him alive in spirit. After all death is inevitable, it's only the way there that is different. The great thing about mum was that she had no regrets. She didn't keep

30   on about, 'If only I'd done this or done that.' All she wanted to do was relive their lives together. I remember once when Pat and I had been listening to her all afternoon, mum saying as we left, 'Now that I've talked to you both I feel ten years younger.' And as we went down the stairs I said to Pat, 'And we feel ten years older.' Yet we could both see the value it had had for her. It's all very well for me to say that dad died in self

35   defence, that mum dominated and overshadowed him. Perhaps this was what he wanted, someone to make all the decisions. Up to the very end he adored mum and she him. Perhaps towards the end he wanted more quiet, but who are we to say. It's only since he died that mum felt the need to talk about him; while he was there, her life was complete.

40   For the next fifteen years mum seemed to grow even more energetic. When she was well over eighty she thought nothing of walking from Hove to Brighton and back. Often she'd start by waiting for a bus but if one didn't come within a minute, she'd make an expression of disgust and decide to walk. She was always an impatient woman. The thing that

45   annoyed me, and I think my brothers and sisters, was that mum refused to allow us to compensate for dad. We tried so hard, visiting her, talking and listening to her, taking her flowers, chocolates and drink, but she'd always got her grumbles about how lonely she was. I used to say how fortunate she was to have five of us children and her grandchildren going so

50   regularly to see her. She'd just grunt. Then I'd compare her lot with that of so many of the other old people who lived around her, many of whom hadn't got anybody to care for them. 'What have they got to do with me?' she'd reply. What can you say to a woman like that? Only agree with her that contemplating other people's miseries doesn't help you to bear your

55   own. Mum resented that she was incidental in our lives; with dad she had been the only one.

from *My Mother and I* by Margaret Powell, 1972

Check your understanding

KEY **2**   Choose the best alternative.

a)   Why do you think the writer says *I think dad died in self-defence?* (lines 4–5)
  i)   He was unhappy with his wife
  ii)   He became weaker and weaker
  iii)   He was bullied by his wife
  iv)   He felt that, compared to his wife, his life was no longer useful

b)   What did Mum have no regrets about? (line 28)
  i)   Dad's death
  ii)   The way she treated dad
  iii)   The past events of their life together
  iv)   Talking about her life with dad

c)   What annoyed the writer about mum's attitude after dad's death?
  i)   She would not take comfort from her children's visits
  ii)   She was impatient
  iii)   She kept talking about dad
  iv)   She would not accept the family's gifts

d)   Mum felt resentful because
  i)   of the way her children treated her
  ii)   she was lonely
  iii)   no one could replace dad
  iv)   other people were better off than herself

Learning For Life

Section 1 The Happiest Days of Your Life?

What do you think?

1 Remember your own schooldays? How did you feel about:
   – the head teacher?
   – the other teachers?
   – the schoolwork?
   – the homework?
   – the other pupils?
   – sport and recreation?

The following extracts from modern novels describe unpleasant experiences in school.

The first extract is from an English novel written in 1968. Billy Casper has been called to the study of the Headmaster, Mr Gryce, with several other boys. They have been caught smoking in school.

2 Read the extract and find out what happens. The questions on the right will help you to work out the meaning of the words in italics.

	The boys lined up in front of the window and faced him across the carpet. Gryce surveyed them in turn, shaking his head at each face as though he was being forced to choose from a range of
5	*shoddy* goods.

'The same old faces. Why is it always the same old faces. I'm sick of you boys, you'll be the death of me. Not a day goes by without me having to deal with a line of boys. I can't remember a day,
10   not one day, in all the years I've been in this school, and how long's that? . . . . ten years, and the school's no better now than it was on the day that it opened. I can't understand it. I can't understand it at all.'
15   The boys couldn't understand it either, and they dropped their eyes as he searched for an answer

Why is he shaking his head? . . What must the 'goods' be like?

in their faces. Failing to find one there, he stared
past them out of the window.

'I've taught in this city for over thirty-five years
now; many of your parents were pupils under me
in the old city schools before this *estate* was built;
and I'm certain that in all those years I've never
encountered a generation as difficult to handle as
this one. I thought I understood young people, I
should be able to with all my experience, yet
there's something happening today that's
frightening, that makes me feel that it's all been a
waste of time. As far as I can see there's been no
advance at all in discipline, decency, manners or
morals. And do you know how I know this? Well,
I'll tell you. Because I still have to use this every
day.'

He picked his stick up from his desk and tested it
on the air. The first smoker stepped out and
raised his right hand. He proffered it slightly
cupped, thumb tucked into the side, the flesh of
the palm ruttled up into soft cushions.

Gryce measured the distance with the tip of his
stick, settled his feet, then slowly *flexed* his elbow.
When his fist was level with his ear, the hinge
flashed open swish down across the boy's palm.
The boy blinked and held up his left hand. The
stick touched it, curved up and away out of
Gryce's peripheral vision, then *blurred* back into it
and snapped down across the fingers.

'Right, now get out.'

White-faced, he turned away from Gryce, and
winked at the others as he passed in front of them
to the door.

'Next.'

They stepped forward in turn.

They all turned their heads when the door opened
and Billy walked into the room.

Mr Farthing, *perched* side-saddle on the edge of
the desk, stopped talking and waited for him to
approach.

'I've been to see Mr Gryce, Sir.'

'Yes, I know. How many this time?'

'Two.'

'Sting?'

'Not bad.'

'Right, sit down then.'

He watched Billy to his place and waited for the
class to settle before he continued.

'Right *4C*. To continue.'

from *Kes* by Barry Hine, 1968

The parents were his pupils in the old city . . . Where are they living now? . . So what was built?

What shape does this suggest?

What do you do with your elbow to bring your fist level with your ear?

How fast is the cane moving?

What kind of signal must a 'wink' be? Why does he do it?

Think about the teacher's likely position.

4C is obviously part of a numbering system, but what could it refer to here?

EY **3** Use a single word to describe:
   a) The boys' attitude to Mr Gryce
   b) Mr Gryce's attitude to the boys
   c) Mr Farthing's attitude to Billy

This extract is from a novel written in 1915
Philip, a crippled boy, has just started a new school.

4 Read the extract and find out what happens. The questions
   on the right will help you.

After breakfast the boys wandered out into the playground. Here the *day-boys* were gradually assembling. They were sons of the local clergy, of the officers at the depot, and of such	Are these the same boys who had just had breakfast?
5 manufacturers or men of business as the old town possessed. Presently a bell rang, and they all trooped into school. This consisted of a large, long room at opposite ends of which two undermasters conducted the second and third forms, and of a	
10 smaller one, leading out of it, used by Mr Watson, who taught the first form. To attach the *preparatory* to the senior school these three classes were known officially, on speech days and in reports, as upper, middle, and lower second. Philip	A kind of what?
15 was put in the last. The master, a red-faced man with a pleasant voice, was called Rice; he had a jolly manner with boys, and the time passed quickly. Philip was surprised when it was a quarter to eleven and they were let out for ten minutes'	
20 rest.	
The whole school rushed noisily into the playground. The new boys were told to go into the middle, while the others stationed themselves along opposite walls. They began to play *Pig in the*	
25 *Middle.* The old boys ran from wall to wall while the new boys tried to catch them: when one was seized and the mystic words said – one, two, three, and a pig for me – he became a prisoner and, turning sides, helped to catch those who were still	
30 free. Philip saw a boy running past and tried to catch him but his *limp* gave him no chance; and the runners taking their opportunity, made straight for the ground he covered. Then one of them had the brilliant idea of imitating Philip's clumsy run.	What was his limp stopping him from doing?
35 Other boys saw it and began to laugh; then they all copied the first; and they ran round Philip, limping grotesquely, screaming in their *treble*	What kind of voice do young boys have?

40

voices with shrill laughter. They lost their heads with the delight of their new amusement, and choked with helpless merriment. One of them *tripped Philip up* and he fell, heavily as he always fell, and cut his knee. They laughed all the louder when he got up. A boy pushed him from behind, and he would have fallen again if another had not

45

caught him. The game was forgotten in the entertainment of Philip's deformity. One of them invented an odd, rolling limp that struck the rest as supremely ridiculous, and several of the boys lay down on the ground and rolled about in

50

laughter: Philip was completely scared. He could not make out why they were laughing at him. His heart beat so that he could hardly breathe, and he was more frightened than he had ever been in his life. He stood still stupidly while the boys ran

55

round him, mimicking and laughing; they shouted to him to try and catch them; but he did not move. He did not want them to see him run any more. He was using all his strength to prevent himself from crying.

from *Of Human Bondage* by
Somerset Maugham, 1915

How can you make someone fall?

KEY **5** Describe:
a) The attitude of the boys to each other
b) The kind of boy Philip is

Section 2 Is There a Choice?

1 Find out what this text is about. Take no more than 10 seconds.

..ceable that, further education, once
ʌe left school is organised very flexibly. It
..vailable to young people of school-leaving
ge, and education is provided at all levels and

5

may be full-time, part-time, vocational or non-vocational.
   At the present time a third of young people receive some form of post-school education compared with a fifth in 1965. Many courses lead to

10 recognised qualifications, varying from degrees
and professional qualifications, through techni-
cian level to qualifications similar to those
obtained before leaving school. Further education is a broad term usually taken to refer to all
15 post-school education outside the universities.
Higher education (postgraduate, first-degree and
similar level work) is provided at universities and
on advanced courses at polytechnics and other
establishments of further education. Adults of
20 every age make extensive use of widespread and
varied facilities for the educational and cultural
leisure activities included under the term 'adult
education'.

The principal institutions of post-school educa-
25 tion are the 45 universities; the 30 polytechnics in
England and Wales and the 14 Scottish central
institutions, in which advanced (or higher)
courses outside the universities are increasingly
being concentrated; the Ulster College in North-
30 ern Ireland; and well over 600 other colleges
which are maintained or assisted from public
funds, some of which have a very wide range of
courses, while others concentrate on particular
subjects. These colleges include the 'liberal arts'
35 colleges and institutions of higher education in
England and Wales into which the former colleges of education (for teacher training) have
been assimilated. All these institutions offer
courses leading to recognised qualifications,
40 while their premises as well as school and other
premises are often also used for adult education

Apart from the universities, most est
ments of post-school education ar
and administered by
45 authorities. The

**To find out quickly what a text is about you can SKIM it.
This means running your eye quickly down the text and
picking out words which might indicate the content.**

You probably picked out words like –
*school-leaving age, courses, degrees, further education,
universities, colleges, qualifications, . . .*
– and can guess the extract is about post-school education.

2 Now skim this text to find out what it is about. (10 seconds) When time is up write down the words which stick in your mind.

e in different countries have hoped in different ways from different igins. But the educational systems of the urban, industrial economies are now on the move in response to increasingly similar pressures and in pursuit of increasingly similar goals. Before examining our own system we should look abroad, note this country's peculiar strengths and weaknesses, and see what can be learnt from the experience of other countries. It is to Europe, North America, Australia and Japan that we shall look. Such comparisons, if they are to be presented briefly, must be painted with a broad brush in generalizations which obliterate the finer points and omit the many reservations and qualifications which a longer account would include . . .

re age of eleven most of our children er a comprehensive school at which they will remain to the end of their school days. In most other countries the transfer to secondary education comes later; and in many there is a break at age 15 or 16 when children go to upper secondary schools of some kind. In this country the pupils who stay on to complete their course normally take public examinations at 16 and 18, and they specialize earlier and more severely than children in other countries. Elsewhere there is usually only one public examination, taken at the end of secondary education, and pupils over the age of 16 will usually be studying 5, 6 or more subjects. Here they are taking only 2, 3 or (more rarely) 4 subjects for examination purposes, althoug they do study other non-examinatic jects to aid their general educati

The eight extracts on the next page are taken from publications about education. Most are about different aspects of the British educational system.

3 Skim the extracts in order to answer the questions below within the specified time limit.

a) Which texts would you read to find out about universities, and which to find out about schools? (40 seconds)

b) Which would you read to find out about university opportunities for foreign students in Britain? (10 seconds)

c) Which would you read to find out about the problems faced by university students? (10 seconds)

d) Which would you read for an objective view of the English school system? (10 seconds)

e) Which would you read for a critical discussion of school? (10 seconds)

The deschooling of society implies a recog̶ faced nature of learning. An insistence on ski̶ be a disaster; equal emphasis must be placed̶ learning. But if schools are the wrong places̶ they are even worse places for getting an educ̶ both tasks badly, partly because it does not d̶ them. School is inefficient in skill instruction̶ it is curricular. In most schools a program̶ improve one skill is chained always to anoth̶ History is tied to advancement in math, and̶ the right to use the playground.

Schools are even less efficient in the̶ circumstances which encourage ̶ucation use of acquired skills, for which̶ education." The main reason for̶ ̶nd becomes schooling for schoo̶ company of teachers, whi̶ ̶e such company̶

ii)
̶e, lit & philology, ̶ ̶terature, BA, 3: yr 1: OE, Spenser & Donne & Milton. Shakespeare, Chaucer & 15th cent. & Malory & 2 of: tion. Shakespeare, A–S antiquities & either

DURHAM, English & Latin, BA, 3: English lit & practical criticism; yr̶ periods of English lit 1400–1837, epic poetry (the Aeneid & P̶

DURHAM, English & philosophy BA. 3: yr 1: English yr 1: as sin̶ peare, literary criticism, mod phil, metaphysics & aesthetics, mo̶ phil, hist & phil of science, phil of religion, & essay combining subjs̶

DURHAM, General studies BA, 3: ●English option yr 1: intro to poetry ̶ lang practical criticism lit 1600–1750 (excluding drama), selected 20th̶ wks, structure & hist of English with sp ref to 14th, selected 20th̶ Shakespeare, selected dramatists, optional subj (R: 73). 16th & 20th c̶

EALING CHE, Humanities, BA(CNAA)̶

iii)
̶or State system of education aims to give a̶ ̶ucation suited to their particular abilities. About 70 per cent of th̶ maintained secondary school population in England and Wales attend̶ 3,069 comprehensive schools which take pupils without reference to̶ ability or aptitude and provide a wide range of secondary education for all̶ or most of the children of a district. They can be organised in a number of̶ ways including schools that take the full secondary school age-range from̶ 11 to 18; the middle schools whose pupils move on to senior comprehen-̶ sive schools at 12 or 13, leaving at 16 or 18; and the comprehensive school̶ with an age-range of 11 or 12 to 16 combined with a sixth-form college for̶ ̶pils over 16. Most of the ̶emaining children receive their secondary̶ ̶ ̶s to which ̶ ̶ allocated after selection proced̶

iv)
How will you be Taught? Since all schools are multi-national̶ English is the language used inside and outside the classroom. Th̶ learning is learnt in small classes (seldom more than 12 or̶ students) led by skilled and enthusiastic teachers. Grammar̶ learnt as an intrinsic part of learning to speak and understa̶ (some may find that it is taught less formally than they have b̶ used to in their own countries). Audio-visual equipment is us̶ an aid to good personal tuition. ARELS schools co-operate̶ closely to ensure that the methods used are the best availa̶ prices within the reach of most students.

How Many Hours a Week do you wish to Study? N̶ ̶are 30 or 15 hours a week (6 or 3 hour̶ ̶eak periods. Schools entries s̶

v)
British graduate students are usually assisted by variou̶ grants, principally by research council awards. Local edu̶ also available, though, these grants are mainly in the field ̶ For the overseas student, there are many scholarships, fello̶ schemes, including those offered by their own governments̶ tions, and by international organisations such as the Unit̶ Kingdom's Ministry of Overseas Development makes awar̶ cooperation schemes, and the British Council also offers a n̶ fellowships each year. Details of all the British award schem̶ from the local Representative of the British Council, or fro̶ Embassy or the High Commission. Full-time graduate stud̶ ̶ve if the student does not have the benefit of an̶ ̶ven here relate to October 1976 and the eff̶ ̶nses fall into three main areas; t̶

vi)
The universities of England and Wales are a very mixed bunch. Like Topsy, they just growed. The only generalization one can make is that students go to them at 18 after gaining two or more subject passes at A level, follow on average a three-year course and emerge with a 'degree'. The degree is granted by the univer- sity itself and not by an outside body. For convenience the univer- sities can be grouped under six headings: Oxford and Cambridge, the Scottish universities, London, the federal universities, the civic universities, and the new universities.

vii)
̶ds are, earning their own living at seventeen̶ ̶ may occasionally remind him. He tends to think o̶ ̶e university as a means to a good job, and he looks forward to a̶ settled married life. While undergraduates appear more physically̶ ̶nature than their Victorian predecessors (and in consequence̶ more concerned with sexual security), the comparatively early age̶ ̶t which they enter the university, their lack of experience of life and̶ the inadequacy or total lack of guidance from their parents and̶ schools can cause acute unhappiness. There is much to be said for a̶ interval between school and university. Moreover many students̶ ̶re probably no more prepared morally for university and college̶ than the juvenile delinquent who may have attended the̶ They have not merely to work out for themselves̶

The country's children were sorted into carthorses̶ thoroughbred racers. The 1944 Education Act provi̶ modern schools, grammar schools and technical sch̶ meant to form the 'tripartite' system. As there we̶ technical school, it was in practice a bipartite syste̶ submerged three-quarters (as the report has called t̶ jumped-up elementary schools. The remainder we̶

37

The text below is from a guide to schools.

4 As you read the paragraph below, compare it with the notes on the right. Which sentences tell you what the whole paragraph is about?

Sending a child to school in England is a step which many parents do not find easy to take. In theory, at least, the problem is that there are very many choices to make. Let us try to enumerate some of the alternatives between which parents

5 are forced to decide. To begin with, they may ask themselves whether they would like their child to go to a single-sex school or a co-educational school. They may also consider whether he should go to a school which is connected to a particular church or religious group, or whether the school should have

10 no such connections. Another decision is whether the school should be one of the vast majority financed by the State or one of the very small but influential minority of private schools, though this choice is, of course, only available to the small number of those who can pay. Also connected with the ques-

15 tion of money is whether the child should go to a boarding school or live at home. Then there is the question of what the child should do at school. Should it be a school whose curriculum lays emphasis, for instance, on necessary skills, such as reading, writing and mathematics, or one which pays more

20 attention to developing the child's personality, morally, emotionally and socially. Finally, with disenchantment with conventional education as great as it is in some circles in England and certainly in the USA, the question might even arise in the parents' minds as to whether the child should be compelled to

25 go to school at all. Although in practice, some parents may not think twice about any of these choices and send their child to the only school available in the immediate neighbourhood, any parent who is interested enough can insist that as many choices as possible be made open to him, and the system is

30 theoretically supposed to provide them.

Sending child to school – not easy
Reason: many choices.
1) single-sex or co-ed ?
2) religious or non religious ?
3) state or private ?
4) boarding or day schools ?
5) curriculum : nec. skills
*   or develop personality ?*
6) compulsory or voluntary ?

In theory many choices possible

> **The sentence which sums up the content of a paragraph is known as the TOPIC SENTENCE. It is often found near the beginning of a paragraph. The topic sentence may be re-stated near the end of a paragraph.**

KEY **5** This exercise contains 4 jumbled paragraphs. The sentences on the left hand side of the page (labelled a, b, c and d) are topic sentences from 4 related paragraphs. The remaining sentences from the 4 paragraphs are in jumbled order on the right hand side of the page. Decide which paragraph each sentence belongs to and write a, b, c or d accordingly in the boxes provided.

a) Children thrive better in bad homes than in good institutions because a child's emotional lifeline is his relationship with his parents.

b) The closed world of boarding school is tribal and authoritarian. It trains children into accepting hierarchies.

c) Punishment in boarding schools tends to be regressive.

d) Not all teachers are good. A bad boarding-school teacher is more dangerous than a bad day-school teacher.

☐ The image of loving parents in the background is not enough especially for young children who are not capable of abstraction.

☐ Children are not free to see their parents when they wish.

☐ Progress through school is seen to bring increasing privileges including trivial ones like wearing clothes a certain way or walking on a particular piece of grass.

☐ Beating and drills are common in boys' schools.

☐ A boarding-school child does not know his parents.

☐ A child's dislike for a particular teacher affects both his achievements in school subjects and his emotional stability.

☐ When he comes home at the end of term, his parents are strangers.

☐ Physical exhaustion is frequently used as punishment.

☐ In any case, are teachers the best people to handle children?

☐ By the time he has got used to them again at the end of a holiday he has to return to school.

☐ These include undue submission to authority, unquestioning parochial loyalty, the subordination, often menial, of younger children to older ones, and various forms of snobbery.

☐ Punishment is often administered by the older pupils, which is bad for both punisher and punished.

☐ There is something odd about anyone who is prepared to spend his professional life in a single-sex institution.

☐ The more difficult a child is the more he needs individual care and the less likely he is to get it away from home.

☐ They produce on the one hand people who are oversubmissive to those above, dependent on hierarchy and arrogant to those below, and on the other hand people with a disregard for all rules and conventions.

☐ The regimentation of boarding school only makes children aware of their lack of freedom.

☐ The prefect system is at best silly: if the prefects beat, it is nasty as well.

☐ A glance at some boarding school rules suggests doubts about the wisdom of the people who enforce them.

☐ In fact, homes caring for children separated from their parents have realised the importance of boarding children in small informal family groups.

☐ It delays the time when they must learn to organise their own lives and it means that they can develop their private interests (if these conflict with group interests) only by rebellion.

from *A Guide to English Schools* by T. Burgess, 1964

KEY **6** The topic sentences are missing from the 2 paragraphs below. Read each one carefully, noting down the main ideas. Then provide a suitable topic sentence for each.

---

a) . . . .
. . . .
They differ in their biological make-up, their interests, their aspirations and their expectations. More important, they differ in their rates of development. At 13 girls are

5   gaining maturity, poise, and emotional attachments, while boys are still unruly, sissy-scorning toughs. Trying to teach them in the same class is like trying to teach two groups of different ages together. Left to themselves,

10   children naturally choose friends among contemporaries of the same sex.

b) . . . .
. . . .
Boys and girls exist. They live together in families, later they work together and get married to each other. The place for the sexes to begin learning to live and work together is at

5   school. Good emotional and social relationships depend to a large extent on the background built up from an early age, and segregated schooldays distort the background, making satisfactory relationships difficult later. Bringing

10   boys and girls together in their formative years creates a basis for understanding later; artificial barriers in childhood create problems, especially during adolescence, which are quite un-necessary. Education is not only a matter of

15   learning facts, it is a preparation for life. In co-educational schools the boys and girls learn how to get on with each other. Children from schools with only their own half of the human species are reserved and awkward with the

20   other half. After leaving school they go through a period of quite unnecessary misery and insecurity. Adolescence is bound to be made worse when schools pretend that sex is something that doesn't exist.

from *A Guide to English Schools* by
T. Burgess, 1964

What do you think?

7 What kind of school did you attend? What kind do you think is best?

Section 3 Alternatives   Part A What's Best?

Below is a letter to a magazine called WHERE which gives advice to parents on educational matters.

1 Read it very quickly, underlining the topic sentence in each paragraph. When you reach a reference to something unfamiliar to you, look quickly at the notes on the right to find the relevant information.

Choosing between the systems

We wonder whether you can give us some educational advice regarding our daughter, Penelope, aged nine. At present she is in the third year at the local county junior school. In her first year she was in the top five
5 per cent; in her second year she was in the top ten per cent. At present she seems to be doing well and enjoys school, although the staff do not appear to be stretching her and this year no homework is given out. However we are concerned about her prospects when she
10 moves in two years' time to the comprehensive secondary school in the neighbourhood. This school has only just become fully comprehensive, and we are disturbed by reports of poor standards of academic achievement (little importance seems to be given to
15 formal exams at CSE or O level) and poor discipline. One of Penelope's teachers has advised us that she should do better in a more academic setting.
We are therefore contemplating sending Penelope to a private prep school in the district. This school takes
20 children from seven to 13 years of age. Starting at the age of 10, Penelope would be just in time to start the school's science course, and also Latin. She would unfortunately have missed two years' French, and would find it hard work to catch up on this. The problem
25 really is that we shall find it hard to afford the cost of this schooling and we do not expect to be able to follow up three years' schooling at the prep school with continued higher costs at a private boarding school, unless Penelope is fortunate to win a scholarship to
30 one. There is no private day school in this area. It is therefore likely that Penelope will have to return to state comprehensive schooling at the age of 13.
Do you think that three years' private schooling is worth it, in view of the 'jolt' to the child on returning to a
35 state comprehensive. This raises the problems of mixing with a less disciplined group, finding that some of the interesting studies she was undertaking are either dropped completely or tackled at a much lower level and finding some subjects taught in a different way.
40 We recognise of course that she would be given a tremendous 'boost' by the period of private schooling, with a pupil/teacher ratio of up to 18 to one, and would have the opportunity of competing for a scholarship at 13.

Secondary Schools

The state system of education aims to give all children an education suited to their particular abilities. About 76 per cent of the secondary school population in England and Wales attend some 3,400 comprehensive schools which take pupils without reference to ability or aptitude and provide a wide range of secondary education for all or most of the children of a district.

No fees are charged to parents of children attending state schools (over 94 per cent of the school population) and books and equipment are free. Independent or private schools, however, receive no grants from public funds. These schools cater for pupils of all ages. The largest and most important of them are the public schools, which accept pupils at about 13 years of age usually on the basis of an examination.

Combined tuition and boarding fees in the public schools are usually about £1,800 a year, but some of this may be remitted for children winning competitive scholarships. A number of preparatory schools (or 'prep' schools) day and boarding coeducational and single sex, prepare children for entry to the public schools. Children at all secondary schools may be prepared for examinations at the age of 16 (called O level or CSE examinations) and at the age of 18, for A level examinations.

KEY **2** Below and on the next page are two possible replies to the letter. Parts of these are missing. Fill in what you think may have been left out.

a) We understand and to some extent share your anxieties over the secondary school in your area becoming comprehensive. Unfortunately the reputation for poor discipline and achievement is . . . .

As your daughter is academically able you obviously want her to . . . . and this might be achieved through the small classes and academically biased curriculum of a private school. There Penelope would almost certainly benefit from more individual attention.

However do not be too hasty to . . . .
Your local comprehensive may not, after all, be . . . .
You could go and have a talk with the . . . . to find out . . . .

Another point. What does Penelope herself think?
She might not want to leave her friends in the junior school,

where, as you point out, she seems happy. Equally, though, she might feel ready to . . . .

b) You say that you feel Penelope is not being sufficiently stimulated by her work in junior school. Certainly a private prep school would help Penelope to achieve more academically. Although some junior schools have high standards it is nevertheless true that on the whole private prep schools offer . . . .

For that reason we would agree that 3 years in a prep school would be to Penelope's advantage. The only problem, as you point out, is financial. With prep schools there is inevitably the problem . . . .

However, if Penelope went to the local prep school she would then have a chance of a scholarship to a boarding school. And even if she failed . . . . and was therefore obliged to return to state schooling at the age of 13, she would have benefited, in these three years . . . .

These advantages would remain with her in comprehensive school. She would have a stronger academic background than . . . . and we feel that she would be grateful for . . . .

Our advice is therefore . . . .

. . . .

Part B School's Out

What do you think?

1 Some parents decide not to send their children to school at all. Why do you think they might do this?
List any reasons you can think of.

The following text comes from a weekly news magazine.

KEY **2** Read the first part of the text quickly.
When you find a word in italics, decide which of the alternatives on the right give its meaning best. Use the context to help you guess.

SCHOOL'S OUT

The setting is every child's dream. A huge, rambling, 300-year-old house, warmed by log fires, overrun by pets, and set in acres of natural playground in the Norfolk Broads. And no school.

That is what makes the Kirkbride household so rare. James, 18, Tamara, 15, Tigger, 14, and Hoppy, 10, have spent the last four years doing what other children enjoy only at weekends and holidays.

They get up when they feel like it, breakfast at leisure, and spend the rest of the day doing what they want. They walk, swim, fish, paint, read, play musical instruments, perform their own plays, cook or just sit around and chat.

There has been no pretence at lessons since John and Melinda Kirkbride took their children out of the local school – James five years ago and the others a year later. Hoppy had been there only six days. "We did start with a sort of curriculum when we took James out," says John, 46, a large forceful man. "But we soon realised we were repeating the mistakes of the system."

"From the beginning, we both felt that packing them off to school was wrong," says Melinda, a German-born former actress. "Seeing their unhappiness and the *rigidity* of learning to the tune of a school bell made us re-examine our own school years, and remember how destructive they were." John, formerly a TV producer, began a teachers' training course at Norwich "to see if I could reform from within". He soon found he couldn't and, after completing the course and teaching for four months, he removed himself, and his children, from the system.

a)   i)   pleasure
      ii) inflexibility
     iii) failure
     iv) variety

3 What questions would you ask at this point?
List them.

4 Now read on to see if your questions are answered.

Persuading the local education authority to give its *blessing* was fairly easy, partly because John was now a trained teacher. The authority at first checked up frequently but now contents itself with calling every term and a half to see that the children are educated within the broad requirements of the law.

"Teach is a swear word in this house," says John. "It destroys the child's own natural talent and creativity. Now learning – that's a different matter. All our children learn when and if they want to learn something. They look it up in books or they go and ask someone who knows. They use their initiative – which is more than any school could teach them."

As proof of concentration, John points to Tammy, who has been playing the piano eloquently for the last two hours though she has never had a lesson in her life. Some friends did show her how to read music, however, much to John's disappointment. "She played with greater originality before," he insists.

b) i) approval
    ii) opinion
    iii) warning
    iv) disapproval

5 What questions still remain unanswered?

6 Now read on

If teaching is a swear word, examinations stun the talkative Kirkbrides into a *scandalised* silence. They are at the heart of what they find unacceptable in the education system, producing what John describes as school hurt – a fear of failure, a lack of confidence, conformity, rigidity. If one of his children wants to do something that requires qualifications, he agrees that sitting one may be necessary. "But at least it is being done for a specific purpose – it is not just years of wasted study, wasted pressures, wasted confidence just to produce a useless string of A or O levels."

If the personalities of the children were the only criteria, the experiment would be an undoubted success. They are articulate, confident, capable and considerate. All, including the two boys, cook and sew: Chores are shared without squabbles. Their courtesy to each other, and to the many guests who visit the household through the American University Without Walls scheme, is natural and unforced.

The household is a very open one. They all call one another by their Christian names. The stream of visitors, many from overseas, opens up endless discussions, ensuring, as James points out, that the family avoids *insularity*.

c) i) surprised
    ii) excited
    iii) disapproving
    iv) horrified

d) i) silence
    ii) contact with the outside world
    iii) a narrow point of view
    iv) openness

7 Can you think of any other questions one might ask this family?

8 Read on.

The practicalities of earning a living are seldom discussed. "Somehow, we've managed to keep going financially," says John. "There was a small inheritance and the rent at £2.50 a week is terribly cheap. Now, the inheritance has run out, I hope to make money from my paintings and from a book I have written about why I took the children out of school."

I asked the children what sort of work they would like to do when the time comes. James says he doesn't know yet but feels he will have a clearer idea in six months time. Tigger would like to do something in the theatre. Hoppy, at 10, hasn't thought about it yet. Only Tammy shows signs of being a rebel – and may yet do the unmentionable exams. "I want to be a professional pianist and if exams are the only way I can be accepted into a conservatory, then I will do them she says. "It would cause *havoc* in the family, with John particularly, because he dislikes them so much. But I think he would accept that it is my life and it's up to me."

Under the 1944 Education Act, the responsibility for education lies with parents – through regular attendance at school or otherwise.

The Norfolk Education Committee says four or five other families in its area are operating like the Kirkbrides. Each is monitored by an area educational officer whose job it is to ensure an acceptable overall standard of education.

from *The Sunday Times*, 1977

e)   i)   disappointment
     ii)) excitement
     iii) approval
     iv) great disturbance

9 Has anything been forgotten, do you think, in this discussion?

KEY **10** What reasons are given by the Kirkbrides for keeping their children away from school? (You should find four or five)

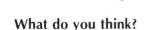 **What do you think?**

11 Think of the four children and what they want to do. Can you imagine what problems might arise?

12 Would you have liked not to go to school? Why?

Section 4 Never Too Late

What do you think?

1 Agree or disagree with these statements.

   a)   People should be educated while they are young and eager to learn

b) Education should be a life-long process
c) It's wasteful to spend money on educating the over-65s
d) Too much money is spent on educating people under 25 and not enough on older people
e) It's best to study for a degree straight from school when the brain is accustomed to studying

The following extracts are from a Sunday newspaper colour supplement.

2 Read them and answer the questions.

The Open University began to accept students in 1971. In 1976 there were 53,000 students on its degree courses, more than any other British university. Instruction is by post, radio and TV supplemented by a scheme of regional tutors, counsellors and summer schools.

In 1976, the Open University had 250 students over the age of 70. At an age when most people settle down to a quiet life, they are grappling with philosophy, literature, and so on.

Denis Riley

Denis Riley, at 76, already has one Open University degree, is currently studying for a second and looking
10 ahead to working for a Ph.D. When he received his first B.A. – in the arts and social sciences – in 1973 he was the star of the degree ceremony. "I staggered across and there was a lot of applause." Now he is working for a degree in philosophy. "University of second chance, they call it. For me it was the last chance."

He was never expected to live so long: the doctor told his mother he
15 was a weakling and she couldn't expect to rear him. He lived and prospered: left grammar school in Hanley, Staffordshire, at 15 and retired as the county's planning
20 officer. He spent his entire career in municipal engineering and planning, being twice president of the Royal Town Planning Institute.

Mr Riley planned his retirement,
25 too. At one time he said he'd spend it "preparing for death". Now he puts it differently. "People retire and die because there's nothing to do." Initially he applied for a B.Sc. econom-
30 ics course at London but found the mathematics so transformed since his day that he was advised against it.

So he was one of the Open Univer-
35 sity's first students, even though a car accident reduced his active retirement to a wheelchair existence. "It came at the wrong time, just as I was starting. But it never entered my
40 head to give it up." The accident has made him heavily dependent on his wife who ferries him to tutorials and summer school with the wheelchair in the back of the car. Her support
45 makes a big difference both physically and psychologically.

"Initially people couldn't understand me. They thought I was an odd fellow. But now the county treas-
80 urer, who's just retiring, says I'm an
50 encouragement to others. Anyway, my children think I'm marvellous."

Like other OAP students he has trouble with his memory. "I can remember what I learnt 20 years ago
55 but not what I read last night." And he struggles to hear the radio talks at dim hours: "I set an alarm to wake to hear *philosophy*." He thinks the Open University could do with more
60 tutors, fewer counsellors, but fundamentally he's a great enthusiast for his studies.

Certainly the life of study has brought Denis Riley great satisfac-
65 tion. "I was missing something at the office, absorbed in the day-to-day routine. Now I have a better sense of priorities. There's no need to bother about so many ordinary things."
70 He's a little disappointed, though, with the philosophy.

"Each philosopher says something, then the rest set to work to prove he's wrong – and they do. So in
75 the end there's really nothing in it. I suppose I was looking for an explanation, the answer to life, and philosophy doesn't give it. I can tell you that now. I don't know though
80 whether the tutors will agree."

Check your understanding

KEY **3** Choose the best alternative.

a) Denis was the star at the degree ceremony because:
  i) he was intelligent
  ii) he was unusually old to get a degree
  iii) he had to walk a long way to the platform
  iv) he got the best academic results

b) How long was Denis expected to live?
Choose the number you feel is closest to the meaning of the text.
  i) 10 years
  ii) 25 years
  iii) 40 years
  iv) 70 years

c) How do other people see Denis?
  i) People think he's marvellous
  ii) People are encouraged by him
  iii) He used to be considered strange
  iv) People don't understand him

d) Which of the following is true of Denis's memory?
  i) He cannot remember recent events
  ii) His long-term memory is poor
  iii) He can't remember what he hears on the radio
  iv) He has a good memory for very recent events

Florence Sephton

Florence Sephton is 77 and lives in a semi in Deganwy, North Wales. She is reading for an arts degree and has a firm idea of priorities. "I'm more of a 5 creature to polish my mind than polish my furniture. I don't let the house dictate to me. It takes second place while I put the studying first.

  "I was very happy at school and 10 had wonderful teaching. I matricu-lated and was ready to go to university but with World War One and the men away I went into banking. I was paid £1 a week. Manchester Univer-15 sity kept my place open for three years but I was enjoying the money and the freedom so I turned it down."

  She married, but like her mother, 20 was widowed young with two chil-dren then aged seven and four. Her motherliness belies a strong and individual nature. She was a pacifist, is still a cyclist ("I'm used to the 25 traffic but not so good at jumping on and off") and describes herself as a nonconformist. "I know I'm becom-ing an oddity around here."

  Mrs Sephton is now in the second 30 year of her Open University course and finding it hard work. She under-rates her ability. "I'm feeling fatigued more frequently. I can't do more than an hour's work at a time. 35 The memory's shocking. I'm sup-posed to be revising and I look up notes I did earlier this year and think, 'Have you read this before?' So I'm doing it very slowly – one credit a year, so it'll take six years. But if I'm not enjoying it, then I might pack it up.

"At the moment the greatest reward is simply the increase in knowledge – and the discipline. I had a salutory setback this week – an essay failed. It was on Blake and I know he's difficult. The tutor said I hadn't answered the question. I've been thinking about it all week. I know I haven't got the facility for essay construction. I just let myself go and get carried away. I feel more emotionally than I do intellectually. And I always feel sorry for the underdog . . . like Blake, who was considered a madman. I'm very ordinary really."

While protesting her ordinariness and laziness, Mrs Sephton is beavering away daily at her assignments. Last year she went almost weekly to Bangor University; this year she goes to Rhyl on Saturday afternoons. Her family are thrilled.

Mrs Sephton sees her studies as keeping her fit and independent. "Because of my life I've been horribly self-sufficient. It's not a very nice characteristic. It means I don't care enough about people. I can't say I find comfort in what I'm learning, so I'll be interested to see if there's a life ahead. But I am afraid of dying. I'd rather be knocked down and killed on my bicycle."

from *The Sunday Times*, 1976

Check your understanding

4 Choose the best alternative.

a) Florence never took up her place at Manchester University because:
   i) she was obliged to work
   ii) she was happy working
   iii) she no longer wanted to study
   iv) she didn't have the necessary self-discipline

b) How well does she work?
   i) Her mind is as good as it ever was
   ii) She devotes only half an hour a day to her studies
   iii) Age makes it more difficult for her to cope with the work
   iv) She has to read everything twice

c) Florence says she isn't a good essay-writer because:
   i) the essay-topics are too difficult
   ii) she responds to things emotionally rather than rationally
   iii) she's not clever enough
   iv) she thinks too long about the topic

d) Florence maintains that
   i) she's rather lazy, really
   ii) she's a hard worker
   iii) she has a strong character
   iv) she depends on other people

Earning a Living

Section 1 You and Your Job

Below is a light-hearted questionnaire which appeared in a magazine for young people in Britain.

 1 Read the questions, putting a tick by the answer you prefer. The questions in brackets may help you understand. Answer them as you read.

---

a) After a job interview the firm offers to pay your expenses. Do you

    i) Refuse to claim anything (*for what?*), thinking the firm will be impressed by your non-mercenary attitude (*to what?*)?

    ii) Make an honest claim?

    iii) Put in an exorbitant claim, amounting to a much greater sum than the expenses you have actually incurred?

b) At 5 o'clock the boss comes in and asks you to work late. You have arranged to go out with a friend. Do you

    i) Say yes to the boss immediately?

    ii) Flatly refuse (*to do what?*)?

    iii) Try to contact your friend to see if you can postpone the evening out (*why?*)?

c) In the middle of a busy period at work a rail strike is announced. Do you

    i) Stay at home in solidarity with your brothers on the railway (*why are they called 'brothers'?*)?

    ii) Do your best to get to work by some other means?

    iii) Take some blankets and sleep in the office (*why?*)?

---

d) The boss drives up in a new Rolls Royce. Do you

    i) Feel proud that the Company must be doing well?

    ii) Feel annoyed (*at what?*) because you can't afford even to run a bicycle?

    iii) Shrug your shoulders?

e) A woman in the office is driving you mad with her constant chatter. Do you

    i) Ram her typewriter down her throat?

    ii) Put cotton wool in your ears (*what for?*)?

    iii) Have a quiet word with the boss to see what can be done (*about what?*)?

f) A friend is sacked, unfairly in your opinion. Do you

    i) Immediately walk out in sympathy (*with whom?*)?

    ii) Improve your own performance to make sure you're not the next one to go (*where?*)?

    iii) Talk to your friend to see how he or she feels (*about what?*)?

g) Everyone expects you to make the tea all the time. Do you

    i) Suggest a rota for everyone to participate (*in what?*)?

    ii) 'Accidentally' drop a few cups and upset tea everywhere?

    iii) Learn all about different blends (*of what?*) so you can offer a range of choice teas to your thirsty mates?

h) Your favourite football team has a big mid-week match. Do you

    i) Provoke a strike so that you can get the day off work?

    ii) Take a day's holiday?

    iii) Go to work as usual and hope that they might show the highlights (*of what?*) on the telly?

2 Now check your score: count your points and read the comments.

HOW TO SCORE

a) i) **1.** They might give you a job on the grounds that they'll be able to take advantage of your naivety. Watch out!

   ii) **2.** Honesty is by far the safest policy in these circumstances.

   iii) **0.** You get no points. But you're the sort of person who'll cheat anyway and you'll no doubt award yourself 2 points for this answer!

b) i) **1:** Not a good idea. You'll get lumbered every time at this rate.

   ii) **0.** Perhaps you should have some sense of duty?

   iii) **2.** A spirit of compromise seems worthy of the highest points here.

c) i) **0.** Not that we're opposed to solidarity – see final score.

   ii) **2.** This is not always the right answer but is probably most appropriate in most cases.

   iii) **1.** You deserve a point for roughing it in such a way!

d) i) **1.** Perhaps he'll take you for a ride in it if you tell him how you feel?

   ii) **0.** Who wants to run a bicycle anyway?

   iii) **2.** You can't change the system. In many ways you must just grin and bear it.

e) i) **0.** We can't condone violence, no matter how provoked you are!

   ii) **2.** Perhaps if you ignore her she'll just go away.

   iii) **1.** It might work, but it might create lots of bad feeling and make everything much worse.

f) i) **0.** What will that achieve?

   ii) **1.** Won't the boss love you!

   iii) **2.** You never know – maybe your friend thinks the sack was justified.

g) i) **2.** Full points for a sensible approach.

   ii) **0.** They might deserve it, but this isn't the best way to win friends and influence people.

   iii) **1.** You can come and work for us if you like!

h) i) **0.** Strikes should really be taken a little more seriously.

   ii) **2.** Let's hope they win!

   iii) **1.** Not exactly positive, but not irresponsible either.

3

HOW MANY DID YOU GET?

10–16: You seem to be a sensible, well-balanced, thoughtful person.
6–10: You're far too humble. You should be a bit tougher, less self-effacing.

0–5: You certainly take a hard line. Try not to become too militant in your anti-work attitudes, however, or you might find you're totally unemployable!

from *Prospect*, 1977

Check your understanding

4 Choose the best answers from the alternatives below.

(from the Questionnaire)

a) *Exorbitant* (a) iii) means
   i)   too large
   ii) too small
   iii) just right
   iv) moderate

b) You *shrug your shoulders* (d) iii)
   when you feel
   i)   angry
   ii) indifferent
   iii) pleased
   iv) proud

c) *Ram* (e) i) means
   i)   push
   ii) pull
   iii) jump
   iv) hit

d) *Highlights* (h) iii) means
   i)   most important parts
   ii) bright objects
   iii) least important parts
   iv) players in a football team

(from How to Score)

e) *Lumbered* (b) i) means
   i)   rewarded
   ii) taken advantage of
   iii) criticised
   iv) promoted

f) *Roughing it* (c) iii) means
   i)   making yourself comfortable
   ii) being unkind
   iii) being untidy
   iv) tolerating discomfort

g) *To grin and bear it* (d) iii) is to
   i)   be pleased
   ii) be a revolutionary
   iii) put up with things
   iv) take action

(from How many did you get?)

h) *Self-effacing* means
   i)   humble
   ii) tough
   iii) arrogant
   iv) embarrassed

Section 2 All in a day's work

1 What do different jobs involve? Look at the text below about
a policeman's job and then answer the questions in the margin.

Any period of social change brings *its* conflicts as
well as *its* benefits and it is essential that solutions
can be worked out against a background of internal
peace. The deadly acts of the terrorist, serious
5 crimes that go undetected, violent protest, *each* in
their own way can threaten our democratic
institutions. The police try to ensure that these
dangers are averted. Less dramatically, it is *their* job
to see that ordinary life goes on with as little
10 disturbance as possible and that people can go
about their business safely and unhindered.

a) What does *its* refer to?
b) What does *its* refer to?

c) What does *each* refer to?

d) What does *dangers* refer
   to?
e) What does *their* refer to?
   police

KEY **2** a) Look at lines 4–5.
What are 'the deadly acts of the terrorist, serious crimes and violent protest' examples of?

b) Look at line 8 *less dramatically*.
What is considered dramatic?
What is considered less dramatic?

Words like this, its **or** each **make connections between parts of a text. It is important to realise what these words refer to. They may refer to a word, a phrase, a sentence, or several sentences in another part of the text.**

Sometimes connections between sentences are less direct. For instance, a word or phrase may be an illustration of, or a comparison with, something in a previous or following sentence.

The following text comes from a careers advice leaflet for young people.

KEY **3** Now read the text below and answer the questions in the margin, as you read.

Professional Mechanical Engineers

by M. J. Hartill, C.Eng, M.I. Mech.E, Schools Liaison Service, Institute of Mechanical Engineers

Do you realize that every time you take a step, the bones in your hip are subjected to forces between four and five times your body weight? When you are running, this *force* is increased further still. What happens if through disease a hip-joint ceases to be able to resist such *forces*? Like all fantasies the Bionic Man has an element of reality in *it*, and for many years hip-joints and other body joints have been replaceable either partially or completely. *It* is after all a simple ball and socket joint; *it* has certain loads imposed on *it*; *it* needs reliability over a defined life; *it* must contain materials compatible with the working environment. Any engineer will recognize *these* as characteristic of a typical engineering problem, which doctors and engineers have worked together

5

10

a) What *forces*?
b) *In* what? (you may have to guess)

c) What is *it*?

d) *These* what?

15 to solve, in order to bring a fresh lease of life to people who would otherwise be incapacitated.

This typifies the way in which engineers work to help people and create a better quality of life. The fact that this country has the most efficient agricultural industry in the world is 20 *another prime example.* Mechanical engineers have worked with farmers, horticulturalists and biologists to produce fertilizers, machinery and harvesting systems. The paintings of Breughel in the sixteenth century show farmers wading through shoulder high cereal crops. *This team effort* has now produced crops uniformly waist high or less so that they are 25 more amenable to mechanical harvesting. *Similar advances* with other crops have released people from arduous and boring jobs for more creative work, whilst machines harvest crops *more efficiently* with less waste. Providing more food for the rapidly increasing population is yet another role for the 30 mechanical engineer.

from *Prospect*, 1977

e) What does *this* refer to?

f) *Another prime example* of what?

g) Which *team effort?*

h) *Advances* similar to what?

i) *More efficiently* than what?

The following passage describes the jobs of women working in a tobacco factory.
There are three jobs which a woman can do here: weighing, labelling and boxing.

4 Read the text and find out which of these jobs you would find the most difficult.

Each week a woman spends a total of 26 hours in weighing, 13 in labelling and boxing. As a weigher, the woman takes a handful of "rag" – the loose, finely shred-5 ded tobacco – and places a small lump of it in the metal bowl of a scale. This about 500 times an hour. Above the scale there is a panel, rather like a temperature gauge, which registers the correct weight, indi-10 cated by a red light. A few drams out either way and the marker shoots up past the light or fails to reach it – whereupon she will deftly pull a few shreds of tobacco out of the bowl or throw in a few from her 15 left hand till the light comes on. The correct weight must be reached by the time at which the bowls are programmed to tip over, or the bowl will not empty its contents. A second out and it waits till the 20 next programmed second. She takes another handful of rag and throws it into the returned bowl. It empties, she takes another, and yet another ... If the machine stops or the woman is not work-25 ing her maximum, the group as a whole, or the women individually, may have to make up the amounts "lost" in the remaining minutes of that hour, or produce more than their minimum in the following hours of the day.

Plastic trucks of weighed tobacco pass in a constant stream, below and hidden by the scales, through an automatic process that wraps each in its individual "rice" paper and gold foil. Wrapped, they emerge in a virtually unceasing flow, like small packets of Kerrygold butter or ice-cream, down a conveyor belt into the hands of a woman sitting up at the labeller. She grasps them in rows of four, both hands in succession placing them onto another conveyor which passes them through a machine from which they emerge with green and yellow labels – the almost final product. Almost, because the eighth woman in the chain is there to grasp the labelled packets in fours. With each hand, in rapid succession, she slots them into boxes: 16 hand movements and she has filled a box, stacked on the side.

For a weigher, the red light can come to dominate the senses – a battle not of wits, but between the machine's autonomy and the woman's attempt to assert control. Not only must the correct amount be dropped in each time, but it must be done soon enough after the bowl returns to its upright position for the woman to gain the space of a few seconds in which to lift or turn her head and talk to her neighbour or opposite number. For labelling, a woman must learn to grasp several packets at once without more than a few slipping out, and to perform a number of different operations in rapid succession: place packets on the second conveyor; place lumps of unwrapped rag into a container for recycling; stack extras at the side or in trays. For boxing, she must learn to grasp wrapped and labelled packets in two hands at once; place one row after another in quick succession down into the boxes; once the box is full, fold over the two pieces of the top and slot them together; put it to one side; make the boxes as needed by taking the flattened card and pushing their sides in and upwards to form a carton. All this fast enough to keep pace with the speed of the conveyor, the stream of wrapped and labelled packets.

from *New Society*, 1976

Check your understanding

5 First locate the exact passages which tell you about:
   a) weighing
   b) labelling
   c) boxing

KEY **6** Now complete the following texts about each job:

a) A *weigher* ....
....about 500
times an hour. ....
...., a
red light goes on. If ....
....

she must add more tobacco or take some out. If the weight is correct, the bowl . . . . , returns and the weigher . . . .

b) The wrapped lumps of tobacco pass down a . . . .
. . . .
. . . . to the *labeller* sitting at the . . . . .
. . . . machine.
She has to do several things at once:
    —she takes . . . . packets in each
    hand, being careful to avoid . . . .
    . . . .
    . . . . and puts them onto another
    . . . .
    . . . . which leads to the labelling machine.
    —she puts . . . .
    . . . . tobacco into a
    container.
    —she . . . .
    . . . . in trays.

c) There are . . . . women in a team.
The last one does the *boxing*. Using one . . . .
. . . . after the other, she fills a box with . . . .
. . . .
She closes the box by . . . .
. . . . one piece of the top
inside the other and makes . . . .
. . . . out of a
. . . .
before the next . . . .
. . . .

What do you think?

 7 a) Which job do you think is the most difficult of the three?

b) In what sense is working in this factory more difficult than other jobs?

c) How do you think the job could be made less unpleasant?

d) The money the women earn is said to be good. Has the job any other advantages?

8 What kind of a job would you ideally like to do? List the characteristics of this ideal job, for example *good pay*

9 Now compare your list with the factory job in the text; how is it different?

Section 3 Situations Vacant

One place to look for a job is the 'situations vacant' column of a newspaper.

KEY **1** Decide what these ads mean:

> **a)** clk typist reqd for busy office. Exp. essl. £3000pa + LVs flexi-hrs 3wks hols.
>
> **b)** carpet salesperson reqd by lge co. basic wg + 10% comm. Dynamic pers. essl.
>
> **c)** imp/exp clk reqd in busy shipping off. Quick with figs, some typing. Willing worker.
>
> **d)** Friendly boss needs Person Friday, gd. tel. manner and sec. skills. Generous cndns.

 2 Solve the following job problems by looking through the ads below which come from a London evening paper.

a) You have a young English friend who is 16 and has just left school. She would like a secretarial job or one that involves some typing. She can type slowly. Select three ads she might follow up.

b) Peter is 20. He has had experience selling menswear, but is looking for a sales job which does not involve selling clothes. List 3 jobs he might consider applying for.

c) Imagine *you* have recently arrived in London. You have to find a job quickly. List any relevant skills you have and select three of these ads you might consider. Compare your choice with that of a friend.

CHEMIST Assistant reqd. for high class trade Hendon. Experienced in general sales and cosmetics essential. Salary to £50 p.w. 40-hr. wk. including Saturdays. Staff discount Phone ?02 89ս1.

COFFEE SHOP requires shop assistant. 5½-day week. Gd. wages. Preferably over 30 years. Tel. ?62 46ս0.

COSMETIC sales assistant required for City shop. No Sats. Phone ս53 914ս.

DESIGN JEWELLERY Golders Green, requires experienced Salesperson. Top salary to right applicant. Phone Mr Leslie Davis, 4ս5 30?7.

EXPERIENCED display assistant required for fashion interiors in new-look store. Good wages and prospects. Shopping discount. 4 weeks holiday, subsidised canteen, active sports and social club. Tel: Miss Hanton, 2?9 12ս4 Personnel Dept. Whiteleys, Queensway, W2.

EXPERIENCED Sales Staff for Notting Hill Gate. Separates and lingerie. 5-day week. 7?7 72?0.

EXPERIENCED retail carpet sales person wanted. SW11 area. Good basic wage plus comm. Phone Mr Mack. ?28 71ս7.

FRUIT and Veg. Manager/ess. Good working conditions. Experience essential. Salary negotiable. Apply Manager: Presto Supermarket 74ս ս/44.

GOODS INWARDS person required by The Scotch House, Knightsbridge SW1. Good salary + lvs. Equivalent 5-day week. Apply Mr G L Sellers. Tel. 01-5ս1 21ս1.

IF YOU have good stockbroking experience and you feel that salary and prospects are not what they could be why not give me a ring. I have a selection of positions available including valuations, rights, clients ledgers, contracts, transfers, etc. 1 also have vacancies for "O" level school leavers. Phone Cliff Bull on 2ս0 6ս32. Alfred Marks Staff Bureau, Stockbroking Division.

INTERVIEWER 21+ with City exp. (min. 1 year) for new Fleet Street Agy. to £60 + 10% comm. Tel. Kevin ս53 1?01.

INTERVIEWER/Management Exp. for busy City & West End branches. High basic + very good commission on all placings. Emp agency, 4ս9 937ս.

INVOICE CLERK for fancy goods wholesalers. 5 day week. W1 area. A. Henry ս36 94ս.

LEGAL Audio Secs. Choice of jobs at £3300. Jonathon Wren Consultants. Mrs Thomas. 6?3 12ս6.

LONDON metal exchange co. requires young person 18-20 to work on the exchange as junior market clerk. Good salary, L.vs. and annual bonus. Start immediately. Telephone ս26 438ս, ext 25.

LOVELY SPOT near the river in SW1 for an energetic young Clerk/Typist looking for more variety & interest. Pleasant working conditions; open plan office with two others. Plenty of perks, discounts, travel scheme, etc. Good salary too! Miss Baines CHALLONERS (Employment Agency) 8?8 3ս45.

MACHINE OP £3500!! printing co!! Help other depts!! Varied work!!! 4 wks hols!! Immediate start!! SOS Accountancy (Agy), 377 ս492.

MATURE CLERK for general office duties. £2500 + perks. 7ս4 782ս. DT Selection Agy.

MATURE Audio-Typist with general office experience required for small office, Knightsbridge. 10 to 5.30. Mon-Fri. From £2500 by negotiation. ?35 14ս4.

MEET THE STARS at big TV co. Some typing & phone work. £2600 m/f. ?5? 78?ս BROOK STREET BUREAU

MENSWEAR. Smart exp. salesman for West End shop. Tel. Waller, 4?7 42ս9.

MUSIC COMPANY in W.1. are offering £3000+ for a competent secretary to the music contracts manager. Lots of variety and scope, 4 weeks hols. Please ring Ronnette on 7?4 871ս Alfred Marks Staff Bureau, 34 Shaftesbury-ave., W.1.

MUSIC CO. req. bright young clerk typist £2400. Phone 7?4 78?? DT Selections Agy.

PERSON required to work in a busy hire division of a West End audio visual company. If you are interested in this responsible position which carries a good salary, then contact Stella Littlewood on ս52 2ս45.

PERSON FRIDAY to £3500. W1 for aviation co. Good all rounder with typing. Details 4ս2 054ս. Premier Personnel Agy.

PERSON FRIDAY. m/f. with typing for friendly publishers £2000 neg. 4ս0 04ս5.

PHOTOGRAPHIC sales staff required for our branch in Sloane Sq. experience essential. We will offer you an excellent starting salary + commission. Interested Then phone Margaret MacKenzie. 37ս 499ս.

RECEP/TYPIST. m/f. £2300 neg. Great new job at city co. Good prospects. 248 5923. BROOK STREET BUREAU Employment Service.

RECEPTIONIST. £3000 + Greeting clients & arranging appointments for this specialised co. Slow typing. 5 pm finish. Phone Chris Manley on 7?4 97ս.

SALES ASSISTANT required for exclusive children's shop in Kensington. Phone 9?7 8ս41.

SALES LADIES required for London's leading fashion house, full or part-time. Previous experience essential. Call in or write Mr Glazer Vogue, 1A gt. Cumberland-pl. W1.

SALESPERSONS required for modern jewellery in London stores. Good salary. Phone 74ս 027?.

SCHOOL/COLLEGE LEAVER with audio typing ability required for friendly West End solicitors office. Salary up to £2300 and subsidised lunch. Pleese phone Personnel ս80 9ս71.

SHORTHAND TYPIST required by NALGO. Salary up to £3440 p.a. according to age & experience. Office near Paddington Station & bus route. 35-hour week. LVs. Minimum 19 days annual leave & additional leave at Bank holidays. Partial mortgage interest rebate, opportunities for promotion. Tel.: Margaret O'Hanlon ս1-40? 52?7 or write to A. Jack, District Organisation Officer NALGO 34 Gloucester Gdns, Bishops Bridge Road, London, W2 6BF.

SHORTHAND SECRETARY £4000. Become the right hand of the finance director of this SW1 drinks company. ATLAS STAFF BUREAU, 183 Vauxhall Bridge-rd. 01-ս28 7ս81.

SW1. Garage requires bookkeeper, experienced preferred but not essential. Hours and salary by arrangement. Also required: Merchandiser, flexi-time available. Hours and salary negot. Phone 82ս 1?71 for more details.

TELEX/TYPIST £3000. International opportunity in this dynamic scene. Develop your talents by assisting the manager. Don't delay ring Terry on ս28 8ս55. Churchill Personnel Consultants.

THE DRAMA and music department of a SW1 college is seeking an audio secretary for the admin manager. Plenty of scope and interest involved. Must be a confident person with neat and accurate typing. 4 weeks hols. £1.75 LVs. flexi hours Salary £3000. Please ring Ronnette 7?4 871ս. Alfred Marks Staff Bureau, 34 Shaftesbury-ave., W.1.

THEATRICAL PRODUCERS W1 need young, bright Sec/Sh. Plenty of involvement. To £3000 aae. Phone 7ս4 8ս45. Hard Graftino Staff Agency.

Advertisements for vacancies in the professions are often larger and give more detail.

 3 Look carefully at this ad for a Warden and Deputy Warden for a hostel run by a charity. You (with two others) are on a selection panel. Make a rough list of the qualities and experience you would look for in applicants for these two posts. Base your list on the requirements of the ad.

CRYSTAL PALACE AREA—CROYDON, LONDON

WARDEN

Range 6 (Points 7–11)+ Supplement

DEPUTY WARDEN

Grade 5+ Supplement

ARE YOU LOOKING FOR A CHALLENGING POST WHERE YOU COULD REALLY BE COMMITTED TO THE TASK?

We are looking for a WARDEN and DEPUTY for an innovative Hostel project, due to open shortly.
We will offer temporary accommodation for twenty rootless young adults. Our aim is their rehabilitation.
Candidates for these posts should be qualified Social Workers, preferably with residential and/or community work experience.
Applicants should be in sympathy with the Christian principles on which Barnardo's work is based. Conditions of service broadly in line with Local Authorities. Transferable pension.
Applications to: Divisional Children's Officer, London Division, Гании s Lane, Barkingside, Essex. Tel: ^1-5ა1 ს011.
Enquiries to: Mr. P. Mann, Tel: Tunbridge Wells ა ა ٩٠4.

---

4 Now read each letter of application. As you read, decide whether the applicant has the qualities and experience you are looking for. Mark your list as you read.

5 Which applicant would you choose?

5 The Cottages
Earslmere Homes
Littleton
Derbyshire

25th February 1977

Dear Sir,

    I wish to apply for the post of Warden at your hostel in the Crystal Palace area.

    I have been in Social Work for over 25 years now. I began by organising voluntary helpers to visit and take an interest in poor, underprivileged families in my area. Later, I took up a full-time post organising a hot meals service for pensioners in our area. I was responsible for co-ordinating 50 lady volunteers, for running the kitchens and for keeping the accounts. For the last ten years I have been the Resident Warden of an Old People's Home. I am in charge of 16 domestic staff and 8 nursing staff and responsible for the welfare of 100 bed-ridden old people. The work requires much patience and understanding, qualities which are surely of use to all Social Workers.

    My Christian faith has been a great strength to me over the years, and I now feel that I am being called to take up work with young people who have had an unfortunate start in life and are at odds with society. I have always had great sympathy for young people from poor, deprived backgrounds and would be delighted to have the opportunity to help these youngsters.

    Sincerely,
    (Miss) M Saunders.

28 Greenford Rd
Bidwell Green
Hounslow
Middx

Divisional Children's Officer
London Division
T....ers Lane
Barling de
Essex   27th February 1977

Dear Sir

I wish to be considered for the post of Hostel Warden which was
advertised in New Society dated 24 February 1977.

After completing my degree in Social Science, I took up a post as a
Youth Worker with my local council for a year. At the end of this
year, reorganisation within the council meant that I became redundant.
I then took up my present post in an outer London Borough as a
Probation Officer. I have been in this post for nine years now, but
I am afraid I have not obtained a professional qualification as a Social
Worker.

Nine years in the Probation Service has made me consider very carefully
the procedures we follow in this country for dealing with young
offenders. I have concluded that the time a Probation Officer has
available for each of his clients is not sufficient to allow him to be
effective. Indeed, I feel that a more suitable approach would involve
the provision of non-compulsory residential care being made available
to homeless and unsettled young people, since this particular group
of people are likely to become habitual law-breakers. I am applying
for the position of Warden because I believe I can see the potential
of such a scheme as yours and am very keen to contribute as much as
I can.

I am not a Christian, but follow a broadly Christian code of ethics.
            Yours sincerely

            Paul Brown
            Paul Brown

Officers' Mess
Hayfield Barracks
Chichester
Essex

1 March 1977

Divisional Children's Officer
London Division
T....ers Lane
Barling de
Essex

Dear Sir,

ADVERTISEMENT IN NEW SOCIETY 24.2.1977

With reference to the above-mentioned advertisement, I wish to be considered
for the post of Warden in your new Hostel for 20 young adults.

I am 40 years old, unmarried with no family and will shortly leave the Army
after completing 20 years' service as an officer. When I return to civilian
life, I hope to obtain a job in which my Army training will prove useful. I
have earned quite a reputation in my unit for the speed with which I have
trained new recruits, even those from deprived backgrounds. Furthermore, as
you know, an officer is also responsible for the welfare of the men under him,
and I feel sure that 20 years of dealing with the problems of young and
inexperienced Army recruits who are away from home is most valuable experience
for a Hostel Warden in charge of young adults. I have always won the respect
of my subordinates and my commanding officers have praised my ability to
organise men and to obtain results.

I have served with the Armed Forces in many parts of the world, including
some of our ex-colonies, and I pride myself on having always established
cordial relations with the local inhabitants.

I am a practising Christian and attend church regularly.

I am most anxious to put the training and experience I have been privileged
to receive in the Army to good use, and I trust my long record of Army
service will compensate for my lack of a professional Social Work
qualification.

Yours faithfully,

W. Blake

W. Blake (Capt.)

Section 4 Unemployed or Unemployable?

What do you think?

1 Do you have unemployment in your country? How high is it?
Do you know any unemployed people yourself? How old
are they? Have they got skills or qualifications?
Have you ever been unemployed yourself? What was it like?
In your country, how can you help yourself when you are
unemployed and have no income?

The following text comes from a Sunday newspaper.

2 First read the introduction to the article.

● With the end of the school year, thousands of young people all over the country were last week entering their names for the first time on the unemployment registers.

5 Already *their* impact shows in the tragic unemployment figures announced last Tuesday – a rise of 163,901 in one month to a post-war record of over 1.6 million. More

10 than 100,000 of *that* rise is attributed to the new crop of school leavers, but even *that* massive figure underestimates the true position: in many parts of the country school term did not end until after this

15 month's count took place.

The young unemployment problem used to be seen as a seasonal *one* – recurring in summer, but correcting itself in the autumn. *That* is no longer so. For while some of the

20 new unemployed will find jobs within a few weeks, an increasing proportion stay idle for months or years. Even before the new crop of school leavers, there were already about 150,000 of *them* on the unem-

25 ployment registers from Easter, Christmas or last summer. A hundred thousand school leavers have now been idle for more than a year.

So chronic youth unemployment has

30 arrived. And the position could get even worse. We are now getting into the teenage "bulge" caused by the Sixties birthrate boom.

3 Now look at the italicised connecting words. For each
connector, draw a circle round the word or group of words
which it stands for and join the circle to the connector as in
the example.

4 Now read the rest of the introduction.

35 The youth unemployment tragedy extends beyond the immediate school leavers to cover a whole generation. The graph (right) is based on EEC figures for under 25-year-olds. Not only has

40 the total grown startlingly, but youth unemployment compared with total unemployment, has gone up in proportional terms too. Britain has the worst record in

45 Europe for allowing the burden of unemployment to fall on the young.

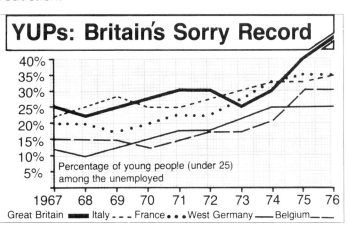

YUPs: Britain's Sorry Record

40%
35%
30%
25%
20%
15%
10%
5%

Percentage of young people (under 25) among the unemployed

1967 68 69 70 71 72 73 74 75 76

Great Britain ■■■ Italy - - - France • • • West Germany —— Belgium — —

KEY **5** Now use the information in both extracts and the table to fill in the gaps in the following passage:

The unemployment figures for the month of July 1977 show that in one month unemployment has risen by . . . . to . . . . which is higher than at any time since . . . . Of the total increase, school-leavers make up about . . . . %. Since many of these young people are likely to remain . . . . for months or years, unemployment among the young is now considered to be . . . . rather than . . . . Although this is the case in most European countries, it is most critical in . . . . In the European 'league' of countries with the worst youth unemployment figures, this country was in . . . . place in 1974, but has since then had the worst figures of all.

. . . . could be said to have the best record, though . . . . had the lowest figure in 1976.

6 Imagine you are the personnel manager of a large firm in an area of high unemployment. You have vacancies in your firm for a wide range of jobs requiring a variety of different skills. You are interviewing young people who have recently left school, in order to fill these vacancies. Make notes on them for your own personal record. On pages 65 and 66 you can see the cards which you have to fill in for each person.

First look at the following lists of opinions. Put a tick next to those you agree with and a cross next to those you disagree with.

a) A tidily-dressed person is always a better candidate for a job than someone who looks scruffy. ☐

b) You should never allow yourself to be influenced by such superficial matters as clothes. ☐

c) I would never give a job to someone who had been involved in crime. ☐

d) A person may have been driven to commit a crime by difficult social circumstances; one should give him a chance to mend his ways in a job before he ends up in prison. ☐

e) Good academic qualifications are usually the best sign of intelligence, responsibility, initiative etc. ☐

f) People in some of the most responsible jobs have started without any academic qualifications at all. ☐

g) If a person has been unable to get a job for some time, it must be ultimately his or her own fault – a sign of some personal failing. ☐

h) When there is high unemployment, even good workers cannot get jobs and should be helped to get one before their unemployment record gets so long that all employers will refuse them. ☐

i) A mature, experienced worker is always better than a young, inexperienced school-leaver. ☐

j) Young school-leavers must be given a chance to get a job as early in their career as possible. ☐

Now look at the following profiles of three school-leavers from Newcastle, an industrial city in the North-East of England with high unemployment figures.

KEY **7** As you read each text, fill in the record cards. Under 'name', 'age', 'qualifications' and 'job interests', write objective information, under 'general remarks' and 'suitable job', note your personal opinion.

a) TESSA

Tessa is 17, a tall striking girl with blue eyes, crinkly hair, five O-levels, two A-levels and not a clue what she wants to do.
5 What she needs is several temporary jobs to help her work it out. Eventually, she thinks she may settle down to nursing, but in the meantime she does not
10 dare wait around. So on leaving school she put in for "Assistant Scientific Officer" with the Civil Service – in real language a laboratory bottle washer. She
15 does not particularly want the job, but stands a good chance of getting it.

PERSONAL RECORD CARD
(confidential)

NAME:

AGE:

QUALIFICATIONS:

JOB INTERESTS:

GENERAL REMARKS:

SUITABLE JOB:

b) IAN

Ian, aged 16, is short, dark, anxious, keen. When he left school he had taken three CSEs but "knows" he failed two. Ian comes from Byker, a rough district of Newcastle where many children leave school without a qualification – in this respect they are typical of half the school-leavers on the national unemployment register. Ian could do with a job as a lab bottle washer but has little hope.

He left school before the end of term and has been without a job for nine weeks now and is sick and tired, he says, of acting as skivvy for the whole family (eight including himself) while his mother is out at work. The rest of the time he sits glued to the telly: "Wimbledon for two weeks . . . then a week of golf . . . then the Test."

What he would really like is one of those coveted craft apprenticeships at Parsons or Vickers. But failed CSE is not good enough. The lads starting at Vickers have O-levels, the *real* O-levels – maths, physics, chemistry – in many cases taken on the insistence of fathers who are themselves skilled engineers. Management calls it tradition. The union calls it nepotism.

In the meantime Ian knows as well as anyone that with every day that passes he gets less employable. He is just beginning to notice the difference in questions at interviews: "Have you done a job?" is becoming "Why have you not got a job?"

PERSONAL RECORD CARD
(confidential)

NAME:

AGE:

QUALIFICATIONS:

JOB INTERESTS:

GENERAL REMARKS:

SUITABLE JOB:

c) JOHN

John, meanwhile, is unlikely in the foreseeable future to get any job at all. He is just 16 and says he has more qualifications in theft than anything else.

John's appearance – single ear-ring, tee-shirt in tatters, jeans at half mast, dyed red hair – is not calculated to inspire confidence in the mind of an employer. He would have liked to be a garage mechanic (*would have,* he already uses the past tense about his aspirations). But, he says, a typical interview goes like this: "You go in. Say have you any jobs. No they say. Write your name down. Then you go out. It gets you down, man."

PERSONAL RECORD CARD
(confidential)

NAME:

AGE:

QUALIFICATIONS:

JOB INTERESTS:

GENERAL REMARKS:

SUITABLE JOB:

Youths like John are becoming the hard core of long-term unemployed. In Newcastle the number of young people who have remained on the unemployment, register for 12 months or more has increased fourfold in the past year. It is not only his attitude and manner that militate against his prospects. The type of unskilled work he might once have done is also fast disappearing.

In the past a strong uneducated lad might have found work doing the lifting, packing and moving now performed by the fork-lift truck; a friendly domesticated girl might have earned a living making the tea now supplied by machine. And the recession has destroyed the old lifeline of jobs on the building site.

But whether the loss of such jobs is permanent or cyclical, the effect on John and his like is the same. For his lot may not change even when the recession fades. There are plenty of older people now redundant and looking for work. They have employment records. And they wear their tee-shirts in one piece. By the time economic recovery comes, John will doubtless be rearing a family on the dole, if he is not in prison.

from the *Sunday Times*, 1977

What do you think?

8 If *you* were an employer, who would you employ? Who would you not employ?

9 Why do you think it is particularly difficult for school-leavers to find jobs?

10 What are the dangers of a situation in which there is always a fairly large number of people who are unemployed? What could happen to both Ian and John if they do not get jobs? Refer to the text, but also use your imagination.

UNIT FIVE

A Class-Ridden Society

Section 1 Going Up in the World

What do you think?

1 How do people judge social class in your country? Put the
   following factors in order of importance, adding any other
   factors you consider important.

   –how much you earn   –who your parents are
   –what job you do   –how you dress
   –how you speak   –where you live
   –how you think   –how well educated you are
   –how well mannered you are

The extract below is from a novel written in 1957.

*Joe Lampton is a clerk who has aspirations to marry a girl from a
higher social class. He has become involved with Susan Brown,
but has a rival for her affections. The rival, Jack Wales, is of the
same social class as Susan, who is what Joe calls a 'Grade 2'
woman whilst he himself is only 'Grade 8' (on Joe's own scale
of 1–10). In this extract, Joe is imagining the objections
(especially of Susan's father) to the liaison between Susan and
himself. He compares himself to his rival.*

2 Before you read, make a list of factors you think Joe might
   mention in comparing himself with Jack Wales (e.g.
   education).

3 Now read on . . .

   The impassable gulf between Grade Eight and Grade Two is
   sufficient reason in itself for the immediate termination of the
   relationship. But there is yet a stronger reason: the existence of John
   Alexander Wales. Born at about the same time as Lampton, he has all
5 the qualities which his rival so conspicuously lacks. He is at present
   studying for a science degree at Cambridge, acquiring not only the
   knowledge of technics which will qualify him ultimately for the position
   of Managing Director of Wales Enterprises Incorporated, but also the
   polish of manner, the habit of command, the calm superiority of
10 bearing which are the attributes of – let us not be afraid to use the
   word – a gentleman.

An illuminating insight into the characters of the two men may be obtained by examining the parts which they played in the Second European War. Mr Wales had a distinguished RAF career, which was doubly distinguished by his escape from Camp in 1942. Mr Wales is too modest to wish the exploit to be discussed, but it is sufficient to say that it reflects the greatest credit on his ingenuity, courage, and resourcefulness. It will be noted that Lampton, in the same position, made no attempt to escape, but devoted his attention to his studies, passing his main accountancy examination whilst actually a prisoner. This proves – we are anxious to be fair – that he possesses an admirable pertinacity of purpose, since it must have been extremely difficult to study under prison-camp conditions. It does not, however, say much for his manhood or patriotism.

Mr Wales was a Squadron-Leader at the end of hostilities and wore a DSO and bar, and also a DFC. Lampton has no decorations apart from those which all servicemen who served his length of time are given. And Lampton was, of course, merely a Sergeant from start to finish. He is not, it may be seen, officer material. We might feel differently about him if he were . . .

You fool, I said aloud to myself, you bloody fool. Why didn't you see it before? The whole of Warley's ganged up against you. I looked at myself in the mirror above the mantleshelf. Good-looking enough, but the suit was the one I'd had when I left the army. And I was wearing my shirt for the second day. I had the working class mentality; anything was good enough for work. I might as well face facts: Good-bye Susan, good-bye a big car, good-bye a big house, good-bye power, good-bye the silly handsome dreams.

KEY 4 a) What advantages does Jack Wales appear to have over Joe?

b) List the characteristics which Joe implies are typical of working class men like himself.

Later Joe gains entry to the world of upper-middle class people. He has been invited by Susan's father to a local Conservative Club, to Joe a symbol of prosperity.

5 Read how he describes his feelings:

I felt a cold excitement. This was the place where the money grew. A lot of rich people patronised expensive hotels and roadhouses and restaurants too; but you could never be really sure of their grade, because you only needed the price of a drink or a meal and a collar and tie to be admitted. The Keddersford Conservative Club with its ten-guinea annual subscription plus incidentals was for rich men only. Here was the place where decisions were taken, deals made between soup and sweet; here was the place where the right word or smile or gesture could transport one into a higher grade overnight. Here was the centre of the country I'd so long tried to conquer; here magic worked, here the smelly swineherd became the prince who wore a clean shirt every day. I gave my name to the commissionaire. 'Mr Lampton? Yes, sir, Mr Brown has a luncheon appointment with you. He's been unavoidably delayed, but he asked you to wait in the bar'.

55

60

He looked at me a trifle doubtfully; not having had time to change I was wearing my light grey suit and brown shoes, my former Sunday best. The shoes were still good but much too heavy for the suit and the suit was too tight and too short in the jacket. Third rate tailors always make clothes too small. I saw, or fancied that I saw a look of contempt in the commissionaire's eye, so I put back the shilling I was going to give him into my pocket. (It was fortunate that I did; afterwards I found out that you never tip club servants.)

from *Room at the Top* by John Braine, 1957

Check your understanding

KEY

6 In what ways does Joe remain self-conscious about his working-class origins?

KEY

7 What does Joe mean by
  a) *the centre of the country* (line 48)?
  b) *the smelly swineherd* (line 49)?
  c) *the prince who wore a clean shirt* (lines 49–50)?

What do you think?

8 Look back at your answer to 1. Are the characteristics of lower or working class people in your country the same as those implied by Joe Lampton?

9 Do you sympathise with Joe's reactions on this occasion? Give reasons why (or why not).

10 Could you imagine an occasion when you yourself might feel ill at ease because of mixing with a different social class group?

11 Would a marriage between two people from opposite ends of the social scale present problems in your country?

Section 2 Them and Us

Joe Lampton had very definite attitudes to social class. Would most English people share them?

KEY

1 On the following pages there is a passage from a weekly magazine. As you read, select the best connecting word.

Workers in Britain have a securer life than they did **a)** { and / but / as well as / including } no greater

b) equality. { Moreover / However / Similarly / Of course } they treat the class battle as a comic opera **c)** { rather than / as well as / in addition to / or }

a war. Britain is the only country in the world where comedy can consist quite simply

of the imitation of an upper class person. **d)** { However / In fact / On the other hand / Nevertheless } all over the country,

on T.V., in pubs and clubs people – especially working class people – are rolling about

with laughter because someone has made a simple statement in an upper class accent.

Comical provincial accents are recognised in most countries. **e)** { At the same time / Consequently / However / On the contrary } it

seems peculiarly perverse to laugh at a ruling class accent.

f) { Moreover / Consequently / In addition / For } are they not ruling you who are laughing? And what is funny about

that? Admittedly, laughter is often a way of handling vulnerability. **g)** { In fact / Thus / For / However } men

joke about mothers-in-law and homosexuality; **h)** { but / because / and / so } all working classes are vulnerable in roughly the same way to their rulers

i)
- so
- but
- of course
- as a result of which

why do

British workers alone joke about it? It seems that humour of this type involves three

factors.

j)
- So
- Firstly
- Therefore
- Moreover

there is a strong cultural sense of group identity, among the

'we' who laugh; secondly, there is a strong sense of threat from and hostility to the

'they' who are laughed at and

k)
- what's more
- on the other hand
- eventually
- lastly

there is an inability to change

the situation or remove the threat so that the only possible solution is to laugh. We

see

l)
- however
- for example
- therefore
- nevertheless

that jokes about mothers-in-law, homosexuality and the 'upper

classes' are a way of apparently overcoming

m)
- but
- and
- so
- since

in reality adapting to the threat

and the vulnerability.

from *New Society*, 1976

Words and phrases such as for example, however **or** consequently **show the logical relation between two sentences or two parts of a sentence. These connectors can help you to predict what follows.**

KEY   **2**   Read the following text. Wherever a gap occurs, underline the connector and continue the sentence in any way you think makes sense.

Among the many reasons which have been put forward to explain the economic decline of this country over the past decades, one of the most important is at the same time one of the least tangible: class. In an article in the German magazine 'Der Spiegel' in August 1977, several managers of German firms in England made quite clear that in their view the reasons for Britain's exports being less than half of West Germany's in 1976, apart from inadequate investment in the latest technology, were snobbery and bad treatment of the workforce on the part of the managers. British managers, they said, were 'educated in elite private schools and universities and their attitude to their workers was consequently ....
....

The German managers are not alone in their opinion. Whatever else foreigners tend to think of England and the English, one of the strongest impressions they take away with them is that English society is class-ridden. And it is the forms which this class-feeling takes which are significant. It is true that in all Western industrialised countries, there are classes with more money and power than others, but in England, although money is naturally important in distinguishing the social classes, ...
....

Englishmen, meeting someone for the first time, are never quite satisfied until they have been able to place their new acquaintance in a social class, and are immediately on the lookout for certain signals which will allow them to do so. One of the most important things to notice, for example, is ....
....

Most English people learn a lot about someone as soon as he opens his mouth. Much of this class-consciousness is strongly reinforced by the education system. In most other European countries, it is normally of no importance whatsoever to know where a person went to school. In England, however, ...
....

This is, of course, only of interest to middle-class people who have been fortunate enough to benefit from an extended education at school and university, but it is nevertheless vitally important. The Public Schools – exclusively middle-class institutions – educate about 5 per cent of the country's children, but at the universities of Oxford and Cambridge, they account for about 50 per cent of the undergraduate population, while the majority of the rest come from a small number of very middle-class state schools. And Oxbridge, of course is still a very good stepping-stone to responsibility, social status and political power. Most of the higher positions in government, the Services and the Church, for example, ...
....

The Civil Service, moreover, though its spokesmen are always anxious to prove that they will offer positions to anybody with the right qualifications, regardless of where they were educated, ...
....
....

Section 3 Class Classified

Whereas the fictional Joe Lampton divided social class into 10 grades, official censuses in Britain divide the population into 6 social classes based wholly on occupation. Children, housewives and others who are not normally 'economically active' are classified in the same group as the head of the family, the wage earner.

Table 1 shows the six social classes used for census purposes.

TABLE 1

Typical occupations by social class

Social class	Examples of occupations included
I Professional etc.	Accountant, architect, chemist, clergyman, doctor, lawyer, surveyor, university teacher
II Intermediate	Aircraft pilot or engineer, chiropodist, farmer, manager, Member of Parliament, nurse, police or fire-brigade officer, schoolteacher
III Skilled non-manual	Clerical worker, draughtsman, sales representative, secretary, shop assistant, telephone supervisor, waiter
III Skilled manual	Bus driver, butcher, bricklayer, carpenter, cook, electrician, miner (underground), railway guard, upholsterer
IV Partly skilled	Agricultural worker, barman, bus conductor, fisherman, machine sewer, packer, postman, telephone operator
V Unskilled	Kitchen hand, labourer, lorry driver's mate, messenger, office cleaner, railway porter, stevedore, window cleaner

1 Which do you think is the largest social class, and which the smallest?
Look at Table 2 to find out.

TABLE 2

Percentage of economically active and retired persons, males and females in each social class, Great Britain

	I	II	III (N.)	III (M.)	IV	V	All
Male	5	18	12	38	18	9	100
Female	1	17	38	10	26	8	100
Both	4	18	21	28	21	8	100

KEY **2** Looking at the first two lines of Table 2, answer these questions as quickly as you can:
  a) Which social class contains *most* 'economically active and retired' males?
  b) Which social class contains *fewest* 'economically active and retired' males?
  c) Which social class contains *most* 'economically active and retired' females?
  d) Which social class contains *fewest* 'economically active and retired' females?

KEY **3** The third line of the table gives figures for the whole 'economically active and retired' population. Do you think this consists of 50% men and 50% women? Look carefully at the table to see whether this could be so.

KEY **4** These six social classes can be crudely divided into just two classes. Manual and non-manual workers. Using only the information from Tables 1 and 2, fill in this table.

Percentage of economically active and retired persons, males and females, doing manual and non-manual work, GB.			
	Non-Manual	Manual	All
Male			
Female			
Both			

KEY **5** Now look at Table 3.

a) Do you know why it analyses voting *intentions* rather than *actual* voting?

TABLE 3

Voting intentions (Oct 74) (by social class)

	I	II	III N	III M	IV	V	All
Conservative	68	60	46	30	25	34	37
Labour	14	20	28	50	59	52	43
Liberal	19	19	23	18	14	12	18
Nationalist	–	2	2	2	2	2	2
Other	–	0.5	1	1	1	1	1

b) Which party was most popular with non-manual workers?

c) Which party was most popular with manual workers?

d) Did the Liberal Party rank higher than third with any of the social classes?

6 Now look at Table 4. Notice the column headings are slightly different.

TABLE 4

Religion by social class

	I & II	III N	III M	IV+ V	All
Church of England	67	64	67	63	65
Roman Catholic	9	7	10	12	10
Presbyterian Church of Scotland	9	9	6	10	8
Nonconformist	9	11	8	8	8
Atheist /agnostic	5	4	3	1	3
Other	4	4	5	6	5
Don't know/refused	–	1	1	–	1

Do these figures surprise you?

7 Look at Table 5, which shows average weekly working hours.

TABLE 5

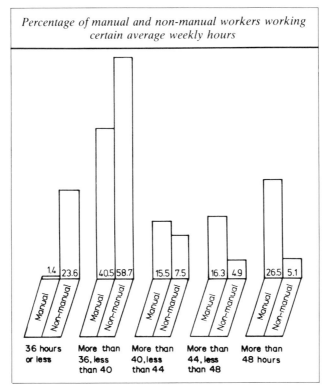

Percentage of manual and non-manual workers working certain average weekly hours

	36 hours or less	More than 36, less than 40	More than 40, less than 44	More than 44, less than 48	More than 48 hours
Manual	1.4	40.5	15.5	16.3	26.5
Non-manual	23.6	58.7	7.5	4.9	5.1

KEY **8** Choose the correct alternative according to Table 5.

a) About $\left\{\begin{array}{l}\text{half} \\ \text{two-thirds} \\ \text{three-quarters}\end{array}\right\}$ of manual workers work over 40 hours a week while 79.7% of non-manual workers work $\left\{\begin{array}{l}\text{less than} \\ \text{exactly} \\ \text{more than}\end{array}\right\}$ 40 hours a week.

b) 1 in 5 non-manual workers work 36 hours or less compared with only $\left\{\begin{array}{l}\text{1 in 3} \\ \text{1 in 80} \\ \text{1 in 500}\end{array}\right\}$ manual workers.

c) 1 in 3 manual workers had a working week in excess of 48 hours but this is true of only about $\left\{\begin{array}{l}\text{1 in 2} \\ \text{1 in 20} \\ \text{1 in 500}\end{array}\right\}$ non-manual workers

KEY **9** Although there's no such person as 'Mr Average', use the information in the above tables as a basis for a description of a typical British male worker and a typical British female worker.

	The typical British male worker	The typical British female worker
belongs to social class number:		
votes:		
is by religion:		
has an average working week of:		

from *Social Class Differences in Britain* by I. Reid, 1977

Section 4 Two British Families

You should now have a pretty good idea of the characteristics which British people see, officially or unofficially, as being typical of working-class and middle-class people.

The following two passages are taken from articles published in 1976 and 1977 in a weekly news magazine. They describe what the magazine considered to be typical examples of a working-class and a middle-class family.

1 Read both extracts; the questions in the margin may help you to guess the meaning of the words in italics.

The Cutters live a couple of miles from where they were both born and brought up in Wilmslow, a community which struggled hard to stay part of Cheshire in the *Redcliffe-Maud reshuffle*, and won. In reality, though, it is still regarded as part of Greater Manchester

5 conurbation and it functions mainly as a dormitory suburb, a preserve of the professional middle-classes.

Where they live is typical of the developments that have sprung up in the area since the war, a cul-de-sac of pale-brick and rather charmless detached houses, half-heartedly individualised with

10 coach lamps and timbered doors and small dimpled windows, and what the estate agents like to call 'rustic brick', haphazard slabs of purple and red. Being a cul-de-sac, it tends to attract young couples with small children, usually buying their first house. 'Susan lives in a wonderful avenue,' her mother says.

15 'Absolutely marvellous for people of her generation.' All the houses come with a garage, and to judge from the day-time parking, all the Triumph Heralds, Volkswagens, Fiats and Dafs, a second car is normal.

a) What do you think was intended to happen to Wilmslow in the process of the Redcliffe-Maud reshuffle?
So what do you think the Redcliffe-Maud reshuffle was?

Nicholas Cutter took over the family business, a small firm selling
imported woollen goods to domestic travellers, when his father
retired. He says that, relatively speaking, the business makes the
same amount of money for him now as it did for his father when he
was a young man, but he's *cagey* when it comes to estimating
exactly how much that works out at a week. 'My father used to say
"You won't make your fortune and you won't starve. It's the same
today".' The Cutters are not well-off, any more than their parents
were, but they're comfortable, and Nicholas thinks 'middle-
middle-class' is about the right description.

Susan Cutter, who is three years younger than him, at 33, has
been a housewife since they married 11 years ago. She says she
honestly doesn't have a clue how much her husband earns. They
have separate accounts and he deposits lump sums into hers
every so often.

Susan feels she's very inefficient as a housewife, certainly compared to her mother-in-law and her mother who are both *fastidi-
ously* tidy and who on the quiet, she thinks, probably consider her
a bit of a *slut*. 'I've never had more than a passing interest in
housework,' she says. 'I've got no routine; I never budget. I'm
terribly disorganised. For instance I spent half of yesterday morning helping to find somebody's cat, and then, of course, we had a
cup of tea afterwards. That's the sort of thing that happens. Oh,
yes, I've got lots of fruitless occupations. It's quite an idle life
really, but I'm happy being a housewife.'

In Summer, she plays golf as often as her mother ever used to,
maybe three afternoons a week, and she's a keen supporter of
the Wilmslow amateur dramatic and amateur operatic societies.
'Splendid productions,' she says 'Very adventurous. They did
Abelard and Heloise last year. The Rex also gets pre-London
runs of films you'd pay three or four times as much to see in the
West End.'

Mrs Cutter is doing an A-Level course in sociology that takes up
one morning a week, and now and again she drops references to
it in her conversations like 'total institution' and 'peer group' and
'nuclear family'. Her mother-in-law was horrified.

Susan did three years of a degree in town planning but gave that
up because the responsibility frightened her – 'You go around
and you see what these awful council estates look like, and you're
expected to dump something like that on lovely land' – and
anyway she wanted to get married. She's tried her hand at
various things since then, Spanish and shorthand typing among
them, and she goes to philosophy lectures, but Mrs Cutter says
she still doesn't know what she wants to do. 'I'm a bit of a
dilettante really, I never do anything thoroughly. I sort of *flit*
around like a butterfly. To get passionately involved in something
means much hard work, dedication, and such exclusion of other
interests.'

Nevertheless, she's the only one in the family to admit to *twinges*
of conscience. 'I do have a conscience about the fact that I have
more than other people. I feel sometimes life's a bit unfair. I feel a
bit uneasy about that. That sociology class I go to, the lecturer

b) Is Nicholas specific in his estimation of his income? Why?

c) How tidy do you think they are? and consequently . . .
d) What might they think about Susan?

e) How does a butterfly move?

f) How much does her conscience trouble her?

down there thinks there's nothing more *iniquitous* than inherited wealth, people don't learn to better themselves or anything then. It's stimulating, I think, to hear other points of view.'

75 (Susan and Nicholas have been sending their daughter to a private school, but recently they have had to think again about her education.)

The Cutters have already decided that the present boarding school rates are beyond them. But that's only one of the reasons why Joanna won't be continuing in private education. Nicholas

80 Cutter has got nothing against private education in principle, the opposite in fact, but he feels that, through the separation, both parents and children lose out.

'I wasn't miserable at school. I pride myself on being able to survive anywhere; it just to me seems such a pity that I had to be

85 away from home.'

The Cutters' problem is that by the time Joanna is 11, their local Grammar school will have gone comprehensive, and it's a system which Nick, anyway, is dead against. 'If she's clever enough we'll send her to a fee-paying day school. If not, we'll have to go to

90 the comprehensive and we'll get somebody in two nights a week as a tutor. I think that's probably the best way round a system which is designed to drag everybody down to the same level.'

Like his father and all his close relatives, Nick Cutter votes Conservative. 'It's the party of the middle-class,' he says, 'and I am

95 proud of being middle-class. I'm not one of those people who would try and insinuate that I'd got a working-class background, any more than that I was part of the aristocracy. Because if there wasn't a middle class, we'd be "Britain", full stop. There'd be very little of the "Great" left, would there?'

from *The Sunday Times*, 1976

g) Why does the sociology lecturer hold this opinion of inherited wealth? So what might this word mean?

2 Now read the second passage.

The Tranters haven't always lived in a Council house, but they do now. Thornhill Lees is an old estate outside Dewsbury, Yorkshire, that is dominated by the *slag* of a pit that Maureen's father used to work and, for one afternoon in 1947, was believed dead in.

5 As a child, Maureen used to *carom* down its slopes on pieces of cardboard. Neil Tranter was brought up in Batley, hardly two miles away, and his wife's parents still live near enough for their dog, a gnarled mongrel called Bobby, to be a daily visitor.

(Neil works mainly away from home. He installs freezer units.

10 Recently he was made foreman of his firm.)

Neil Tranter is known as a good worker. 'Good *grafter*, is Neil,' is the first thing anybody's likely to say about him. He's had one holiday, a week in Margate, in the twelve years he's been married, because he has always preferred to work his time off. And

15 just because he's home for the weekend doesn't necessarily mean his wife sees him; up to two months ago he ran a stall all day

h) How high is the 'slag'? What comes from a pit besides coal?
i) What word or phrase could meaningfully replace this?

j) What is Neil good at?

Saturday at Dewsbury market selling pouffes and cutlery and any other job-lots he'd been able to pick up; and on Saturdays now, and most Sundays as well, he works doing joinery, which is his
20   trade, eight till eight for a local contractor.

'I'm having to work away to *mek* a wage that allows me to live at the standard that I'm living at now, which I think is a nice standard. I think a family of our size should have every convenience there is possible, to make life easier, and none of us wants for anything.'

25   'Mind you, I never plan. I don't get that much money really, to save. The only cash I could really bank is what I make on the side; but what I get then, a tenner, say, for a day's work, nine times out of ten it goes on t'kids or *summat* like that. I work when I'm poorly, Maureen, don't I? I'm falling down an' I still get there. I never have
30   time off.'

'E don't bother much wi' banking,' Maureen said. 'He used to be wi' *Yorkshire Penny*, in Batley, but 'ed rather carry it about wi' 'im. I'n't that right?' Neil nodded that it was. 'I used to have a cheque book but it didn't interest me. Too much *faffin' about*. I like to know
35   money's in me back pocket. If I see anything then, I can turn round an' buy it. Because I make a lot more decisions than Maureen does. Not as regards kids, like, but as far as what we're having goes. As far as what we buy for t'house. I'll turn round and say, "I think you ought to have a mixer.".'

40   (Maureen Tranter works part-time in a local textile mill, where she used to work before she was married.)

Although the ten pounds a week that Maureen earns comes in useful, the main reason she went back to Ellis's mill with her mother was that when Barry started school at the beginning of
45   last year, she was bored. Apart from weekends, when Neil was at home, the only time she got out of the house was to go dancing at Thornhill Edge working men's club on Tuesday nights with her parents.

Maureen says she likes work, she doesn't know why, but Neil was
50   no happier to see her going back to the mill than her father had been to see her start there straight from school at 15. 'I'm not very confident. I'm not a confident person at all,' Maureen would say later at the pub where Neil's mother plays the piano and sings on Saturday nights. 'At work, though, I feel confident because I know
55   I can do it. I just like it. I feel safe there.'

Her new routine involves going out to work at midday and being delivered back home by her father in time to make the kids' teas.

As far as education is concerned, Neil and Maureen seem not to be particularly concerned about it. 'I've had the same education
60   as millions of people: standard secondary modern school. I did same as millions of other kids did,' Neil said, 'and I don't think I've *come off* too bad.'

Maureen's father, Terry Sutherland, is a £47-a-week lorry driver for the Co-op. Both he and his wife are life-long Labour voters.
65   Despite this, neither Neil nor Maureen are at all politically-minded: she has voted, she thinks, twice ('for Labour but don't ask me why. I have no idea about politics at all') and he has never

k)   What does *mek* mean? Why is it written in this way?

l)   What word could replace *summat*? What kind of word is this?

m)   What is the topic of conversation? So what is the 'Yorkshire Penny'?

n)   Why would a cheque book not interest him?

o)   What word or phrase could meaningfully replace this?

voted in his life 'I've never had time to sit down and think to meself: "Now what do I think of Labour or Conservatives or Liberals?"'

70 Mrs Sutherland summed up how they all felt. 'It allus turns out t'same,' she said, 'no matter what happens. They give you all the loud-mouth talk, then, when they get *there* you never see 'em. They get the *brass* an' that's it.'

Her husband said he would go on voting Labour regardless,
75 because he couldn't afford to vote anything else. 'We're working-class. We're not capitalists because we haven't any *brass*, have we really? They say, to be a Conservative today you haven't got to have the money, like, but I've still got the old theory that you have. Not,' he said, 'that I begrudge them as come into
80 money. I say good luck to them.'

from *The Sunday Times*, 1977

p) Where do 'they' go?

q) What does Mr Sutherland think you have to have to be a capitalist?

Check your understanding

 3 The following table will help you to summarise the basic information in the texts. Fill it in, referring back to the texts if necessary.

The family	The Cutters	The Tranters
Where they live: – the area		
– the house		
The husband: – job		
– spare-time occupation		
The wife: – job		
– spare-time occupation		
Earnings		
Political inclinations		
Other points of interest		

KEY **4** Choose the best alternative.

   a) From your impression of the general circumstances of the two families, would you say that:
-     i) the Cutters are rich and the Tranters are poor?
-     ii) the Cutters are considerably better off that the Tranters?
-     iii) neither the Cutters nor the Tranters are well off?
-     iv) the Cutters and the Tranters are both fairly well off?

   b) If you compare the wives, would you say that:
-     i) Susan has less opportunity to do things in her spare time than Maureen?
-     ii) Susan is less financially dependent on her husband than Maureen?
-     iii) Susan is less politically aware than Maureen?
-     iv) Susan is likely to have fewer money problems than Maureen?

   c) Maureen works mainly because:
-     i) she was bored when she wasn't working.
-     ii) she needs the money.
-     iii) she likes it.
-     iv) it gives her confidence.

   d) What is Nick Cutter's attitude to education?
-     i) He is against private education in principle.
-     ii) Whether he sends his daughter to a private school will depend on the expense involved.
-     iii) He is wholly against Comprehensive education.
-     iv) He objects to Comprehensive education on broadly political grounds.

   e) What is the attitude of the Sutherlands and the Tranters to politics?
-     i) They have always voted Labour.
-     ii) They are basically suspicious of politicians.
-     iii) They feel they are not wealthy enough to vote Conservative.
-     iv) They have firm views on politics.

The World About Us

Section 1 A Better World

What do you think?

1 Should we care about the effect man is having on the environment? Some people do worry about disturbing the balance of nature and about destroying our cultural heritage to make way for new things. Try to make a list of specific problems in this area. You could start with:

pollution from petrol engines

The following extracts are all taken from texts connected with the question of environment.

2 Skim them to find out as quickly as possible which specific problem they are connected with. (30 seconds)

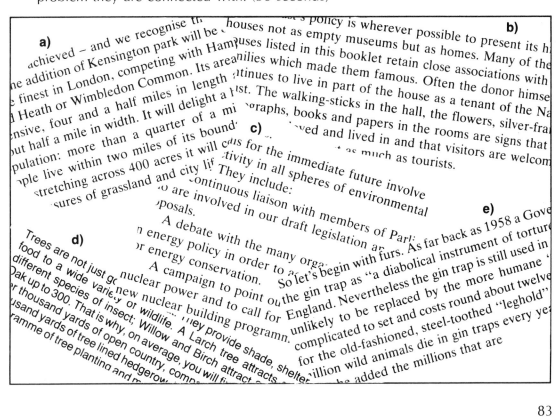

a) achieved – and we recognise th houses not as empty museums but as homes. Many of the he addition of Kensington park will be ⌐uses listed in this booklet retain close associations with finest in London, competing with Ham⌐ilies which made them famous. Often the donor himse Heath or Wimbledon Common. Its area⌐ ⌐tinues to live in part of the house as a tenant of the Na nsive, four and a half miles in length ⌐ıst. The walking-sticks in the hall, the flowers, silver-fra but half a mile in width. It will delight a l⌐ ⌐graphs, books and papers in the rooms are signs that pulation: more than a quarter of a mi ⌐ved and lived in and that visitors are welcom ple live within two miles of its bound⌐ ⌐t as much as tourists. stretching across 400 acres it will c⌐us for the immediate future involve sures of grassland and city lif ⌐tivity in all spheres of environmental ⌐posals. ⌐ontinuous liaison with members of Parl: o are involved in our draft legislation a A debate with the many orga. ⌐b)** ⌐policy is wherever possible to present its h**c)** They include: n energy policy in order to a So let's begin with furs. As far back as 1958 a Gove r energy conservation. the gin trap as "a diabolical instrument of tortur **d)** A campaign to point ou England. Nevertheless the gin trap is still used in Trees are not just go nuclear power and to call for unlikely to be replaced by the more humane ' food to a wide varie.y of new nuclear building programm. complicated to set and costs round about twelve different species of insect; wildlife. ⌐ıey provide shade, shelter for the old-fashioned, steel-toothed "leghold" ak up to 300. That is why; Willow and Birch tree attracts ⌐illion wild animals die in gin traps every ye r thousand yards of open country, you will f. e added the millions that are sand yards of tree lined hedgerow, comp ramme of tree planting and m **e)**

3 Were these issues on your list? Add them if they weren't.

4 Do you care about any of these things? Have you ever helped to protect or preserve something? Which item on your list do you see as potentially the most serious? What could you do about it? Compare your answers with a partner.

The following 4 texts describe the aims and activities of groups engaged in preserving or improving the environment.

KEY **5** As you read, note down the main aims and activities of each group.

THE
TREE COUNCIL

AIMS

The Tree Council was formed in recognition of the long-term crisis facing our trees and tree cover generally in both town and country. The Tree Council's aims are:

- to improve the environment in town and country by promoting the planting and good maintenance of suitable trees.
- to disseminate knowledge about trees and their care.
- to act as a forum for organisations concerned with trees, to identify the national problem and to provide initiatives for co-operation.

THE LONG-TERM NATIONAL TREE PROBLEM

For half a century or so tree population has been declining (apart from commercial woodland). Since the Second War the rate of decline in our landscape trees has become alarming. In some areas our tree population has been devastated by the rapid spread of Dutch Elm Disease.

THE TREE COUNCIL

WHAT DOES IT DO? The Tree Council uses every opportunity to alert the public to our long-term problem.

Each autumn the Tree Council initiates a campaign — National Tree Week — which by wide coverage on TV, Radio and in the press encourages tree planting plans for the future and in addition emphasizes the need for tree care. Throughout the country local authorities and voluntary groups join in the campaign in their own areas using supportive Tree Council literature.

A National Conference is organised annually.

A tree Fund was started in 1978 with the money raised through the BBC Nationwide "Crisis in the Countryside" series of programmes. This money is being used to support local community and voluntary schemes in both town and country for tree planting and care. Further contributions to the Fund will encourage even more local initiative.

a) Main aims: . . . .

. . . .

. . . .

. . . .

. . . .

. . . .

Main activities: . . . .

. . . .

. . . .

. . . .

. . . .

. . . .

The National Trust

For eighty-three years the National Trust has worked for the preservation of places of historic interest and natural beauty in England, Wales and Northern Ireland (there is a separate National Trust for Scotland). Under the National Trust Act of 1907 it is empowered to declare its properties inalienable, and these can never be sold, mortgaged or compulsorily acquired from the Trust without the express will of Parliament.

Today the Trust – which is not a government department but a charity depending on the voluntary support of the public and its members – is the largest private landowner and conservation society in Britain. Wherever you go, you are close to land that is protected and maintained by the National Trust. Over 400 miles of unspoilt coastline (more than a third of the finest that remains); 94,000 acres of fell, dale, lake and forest in the Lake District alone; prehistoric and Roman antiquities ranging from Hadrian's Wall to the Cerne Giant in Dorset; downs and moorlands, fens, farmland, woods and islands; lengths of inland waterways – even eighteen whole villages – are open to the public at all times subject only to the needs of farming, forestry and the protection of wildlife.

But the Trust's protection extends further than this: It has in its possession a hundred gardens and more than 200 historic buildings which it opens to visitors. Anyone can join the Trust for as little as £7 a year (£3.50 for each additional member of a family living at the same address), or there is a family group membership of £14 for parents and their children up to eighteen. Please note that membership cards are not transferable and that members will not be admitted free of charge unless they have brought a valid card. There is a membership application form at the back of this booklet. If you are not already a member of the Trust, and wish to support its work, we ask you to join the Trust today.

b) Main aims: . . . .
. . . .
. . . .
. . . .
. . . .
. . . .

Main activities: . . . .
. . . .
. . . .
. . . .
. . . .
. . . .

Friends of the Earth

What are our objectives?

We intend to generate among all people a sense of personal responsibility for the environment in which we live.

We intend to make the crucial environmental issues the subject of widespread and well informed public debate.

We intend to campaign against specific projects which damage the environment or squander our resources, and fight for their correction with every legal means at our disposal.

But above all we intend to campaign for the universal adoption of sustainable and equitable life styles.

How can we achieve them?

By helping to build up a powerful environment lobby that is not aligned to any existing political party.

By lobbying to change the law, and using existing laws to defend our environment and resources from abuse.

By making people aware of their rights and how they can use them to defend the environment.

By taking direct action to conserve and promote considerate use of the Earth's natural resources.

By creating channels through which the energies of committed people can be applied.

By raising money from organisations and individuals (such as yourself) to finance specific projects, central administrative costs and local group activities.

c) Main aims: . . . .

. . . .

. . . .

. . . .

. . . .

. . . .

Main activities: . . . .

. . . .

. . . .

. . . .

. . . .

. . . .

Why Beauty Without Cruelty?

People are now very aware of the fact that through the exploitation of soil, air and water and the misuse of animals, man is gradually poisoning and devitalising the world. And in line with a greater concept of the preservation of all life Beauty Without Cruelty suggests alternatives to cruelly obtained animal products that give everyone an opportunity to lessen the present vast-scale commercial exploitation of nature and alleviate animal suffering. To stress the need for non-animal alternatives, here are a few facts about the barbarous practices that flourish under the banner of commerce in the fashion and beauty businesses.

In the book, *Man's Dominion* by Monica Hutchings and Mavis Caver, it is stated that thirty million wild animals are killed each year for their skins alone. This figure does not include "farmed" furs, or "wastage", an untold number who suffered, died and then were discarded.

YOUR THOUGHT FOR THE FUTURE?
Beauty Without Cruelty provides alternatives to these products of inhumanity. Our own Beauty Without Cruelty range of natural toilet and cosmetic preparations are made from the finest flower, herb and plant extracts. When a chemical has to be used, as in the case of lipsticks and eye make-up, one is selected that has not caused suffering.

The replacement of animal products with natural substitutes not only makes life more pleasant for those who object to the abuse of animals, there is also a very practical need for such alternatives. The few figures given here relate only to the fashion and beauty businesses: when added to the numbers of animals used in other trades and in medical research annually the prospect of a world without animals looms grimly close. To help avert the tragic consequences of this there is a simple but effective preventative measure. As consistently as is possible, for ourselves and for the sake of future generations, buy only those products for which no creatures have suffered – buy your beauty without cruelty.

d) Main aims: . . . .
. . . .
. . . .
. . . .
. . . .
. . . .

Main activities: . . . .
. . . .
. . . .
. . . .
. . . .
. . . .

What do you think?

6 If similar groups were active in your country, what kind of support would you give them, if any?
1 None at all
2 Would contribute money if asked
3 Would support actively

Write the appropriate number in the box below.

A National Tree week	
An organisation like the National Trust	
A Group like 'Friends of the Earth'	
A Group like 'Beauty without Cruelty'	

UNIT SIX

Section 2 A Changing Landscape

The following extract is from a newspaper article about Elm Disease in Britain. This is a disease caused by the elm bark beetle.

1   As you read notice how the writer expresses certainty or doubt about what he says.

What is happening is nothing less than the extermination, by disease, of the most common tree in the hedges of England. Nearly all the old elms of the countryside will soon be dead, and a
5 lovely and familiar feature of the landscape will have disappeared, if not for ever, certainly until the middle of the next century.

As the landscape becomes poorer and barer, there is only one point of comfort. Over
10 the next few years, new elms will grow up from the roots left in the ground. It will be a long time before they grow large enough to have a significant effect on the landscape, and for at least 10 years they will be too small to provide homes for
15 the grubs of the elm bark beetles. So, with any luck, the disease which the beetles carry will largely die out, for lack of habitat. As the new generation of elms grows up we shall know a great deal more about them and their distribu-
20 tion; and, perhaps, we shall value the tree and its beautiful timber much more, now we have seen that they cannot be taken for granted.

The ability of the common elm to reproduce from 'root suckers' is not unique, but it is rare. A
25 tree left alone in ungrazed land will build a hedge around itself and this will eventually enlarge into a wood. Hedgerow elms expand sideways along the hedge. While the elm produces abundant flowers in February every year these rarely
30 ripen into viable seed. Even more rarely does the seed find the warm, moist bare soil it needs to germinate. It is thought that many individual elm clones have survived since the Stone Age by the purely vegetative process of suckering.
35 Such elms frequently haunt the sites of ancient settlements.

KEY **2**   Choose the best alternative.
- a)   Look at lines 1–3. Does the writer mean that the extermination (of the elm)
  - i)   has almost become a fact?
  - ii)   is definitely happening?
  - iii)   probably will not happen?
  - iv)   has already happened?

- b)   Look at lines 3–8. Which of the following statements is true?
  The elms will disappear
  - i)   for about 70 years
  - ii)   for ever
  - iii)   for half a century
  - iv)   for 100 years

c) Look at lines 15–17. Which one of the following
    statements is true?
    i)   it is possible but unlikely that the disease will die out.
    ii) it is certain that the disease will die out.
    iii) there is a reasonable possibility that the disease
         will die out.
    iv) there is a remote possibility that the disease will
         die out.

d) Look at lines 28–32. Make three sentences from the
    table below, which correspond to the writer's view

The elm	rarely	produces flowers
The flower	regularly very rarely	ripens into seed
The seed	never	germinates

e) Look at lines 32–34. Does the writer here
    i)   agree with this statement?
    ii) disagree with this statement?
    iii) give the opinion of other people?
    iv) say that few people hold this opinion?

Words like will, may, probably **and** certainly, **and phrases
like** nothing less than, with any luck **and** it is thought,
express a writer's certainty or doubt about what he says.

---

3 Now read the final part of the text.

The story of the elm in Britain is closely linked
with the evolution of the landscape and the history of man. Microscopic fossil records which
40 are our guides to early vegetation show a
dramatic reduction in elm pollen about 4500
years ago. Various theories have tried to explain
this elm decline, a prehistoric phenomenon
echoed by today's catastrophe. The climate
45 may have become cooler and therefore unsuitable for some species; or it may have been due
to Stone Age man clearing woodland for agricul-
ture; or to an outbreak of elm disease. Or, possibly, to all three.
50   Certainly the Elm Decline seems closely
linked with the settlement of modern man in this
country. Man's involvement with the tree and its
wood has continued ever since. A timber that

won't split and lasts indefinitely under water
55 obviously had a special value in an economy
which, from the Bronze Age to the Napoleonic
Wars, can fairly be described as timber-based.
Elms were planted and encouraged near
homesteads. They were coppiced and pol-
60 larded – both methods of using the wood while
preserving the bole, and they were allowed to
grow tall in the hedges. Only elms had the long
straight trunks necessary to make keels for
ships and barges.
65   Elm trunks were used for underground
water pipes, bored out by two men with a long
auger, at a speed of a few feet a day. Such pipes
are often dug up and found to be in good condition. There were elm wood parts in water mills,
70 and every wheel before the pneumatic tyre had

elm at its hub. Only elm would stand the shock of
the inset spokes as the iron tyre was shrunk on.
Almost every wooden chair had an elm seat.
The tradition survives.

75   Massive elm timbers are still used to repair
docks and locks, but the best wood goes to the
furniture trade. Wooden bowls are turned from
elm, but the wood is now not much in fashion for
tableware where it was once the only tableware

80   in the average cottage home. The grain pattern
or 'figure' of elm wood is warm, varied and rich.
We should harvest all our dead elms and make
use of the wood before it becomes a rarity.

from *Epitaph to the Elm* by
Gerald Wilkinson, 1978

Check your understanding

KEY   **4**   Choose the best alternative.

a)   Look at lines 37–44. Talking of the decline of the elm
4500 years ago, does the writer
i)   treat this as an established fact?
ii)   consider it likely, but not definite?
iii)   consider it unlikely?
iv)   treat this as the opinion of other people only?

b)   Look at lines 42–49; the writer describes three theories
which have tried to explain the prehistoric decline of the
elm. Which of the following statements best reflects the
writer's view?
i)   Each theory is equally likely.
ii)   One theory is more likely than others.
iii)   The theories appear in order of likelihood.
iv)   The most likely explanation incorporates all three
theories.

c)   Look at line 57. When the writer talks of an economy
which *can fairly be described as timber-based,*
i)   he disagrees with those who describe the economy
in this way?
ii)   he agrees with them?
iii)   he is not sure whether to agree with them?
iv)   he is not indicating his own opinion at all?

KEY **5** Group words from the text under the following headings even if you don't know their exact meaning.

a) (from both sections)
Words which describe parts of the elm or things that the elm produces e.g. flowers (line 29)

b) (from second section)
Words which describe ways of cutting the elm or parts of the elm e.g. harvest (line 82)

c) (from second section)
Words which describe objects that can be made from the elm or its parts e.g. pipes (line 66)

Section 3 The Energy Crisis

Part A Nuclear Power

What do you think?
One of the main questions facing all governments at the present time is where to get energy from, once present resources of coal and oil are used up. Many governments are putting vast amounts of money into nuclear energy, but projects like this are controversial and often violently opposed.

 1 What do you think are the reasons for this opposition?

The following text comes from a critical account of the economic structure of the Western world, written in 1973.

KEY **2** As you read the passage, answer the questions in the margin.

Of all the changes introduced by man into the household of nature, large-scale nuclear fission is undoubtedly the *most dangerous* and profound. As a result, ionising radiation has become the most serious agent of pollution of the environment and the *greatest* threat to man's survival on earth. The attention of the layman, not surprisingly, has been captured by the atom bomb, although there is at least a chance that it may never be used again. The danger to humanity created by the so-called peaceful uses of atomic energy may be much greater. There could indeed be

a) The *most dangerous* what?

b) *Greater* than what?

no clearer *example* of the prevailing dictatorship of economics. Whether to build conventional power stations, based on coal or oil, or nuclear stations, is being decided on economic grounds, with perhaps a small element of regard for the 'social consequences' that might arise from an over-speedy curtailment of the coal industry. But that nuclear fission represents an incredible, incomparable, and unique hazard for human life does not enter any calculation and is never mentioned. *People* whose business it is to judge hazards, the insurance companies, are reluctant to insure nuclear power stations anywhere in the world for third party risk, with the result that special legislation has had to be passed whereby the State accepts big liabilities. Yet, insured or not, the *hazard* remains, and such is the thraldom of the religion of economics that the only question that appears to interest either governments or the public is whether 'it pays'.

The most massive wastes are, of course, the *nuclear reactors* themselves after they have become unserviceable. There is a lot of discussion on the trivial economic question of whether they will last for twenty, twenty-five, or thirty years. No-one discusses the humanly vital point that they cannot be dismantled and cannot be shifted but have to be left standing where they are, probably for centuries, perhaps for thousands of years, an active menace to life, silently leaking radioactivity into air, water and soil. No-one has considered the number and location of these satanic mills which will relentlessly accumulate. Earthquakes, of course, are not supposed to happen, nor wars, nor civil disturbances, nor riots like those that infested American cities. Disused nuclear power stations will stand as unsightly monuments to unquiet man's assumption that nothing but tranquillity, from

c) What is the *example*?

d) Who are the *people*?

e) What is the *hazard*?

f) In this paragraph find 4 words or phrases which mean the same as *nuclear reactors*.

now on, stretches before him, or else — that the future counts as nothing compared with the slightest economic gain now.

We must be careful, however, not to get lost in the jungle of controversy that has grown up in this *field*. The point is that very serious hazards have already been created by the 'peaceful uses of atomic energy', affecting not merely the people alive today but all future generations, although so far nuclear energy is being used only on a statistically insignificant scale. The real development is yet to come, on a scale which few people are capable of imagining. If this is really *going to happen*, there will be a continuous traffic in radioactive substances from the 'hot' chemical plants to the nuclear stations and back again; from the stations to waste-processing plants; and from there to disposal sites. A serious accident, whether during transport or production, can cause a major catastrophe; and the radiation levels throughout the world will rise relentlessly from generation to generation. Unless all living geneticists are in error, there will be an *equally relentless*, though no doubt somewhat delayed, increase in the number of harmful mutations. K. Z. Morgan, of the Oak Ridge Laboratory, emphasises that the *damage* can be very subtle, a deterioration of all kinds of organic qualities, such as mobility, fertility, and the efficiency of sensory organs. 'If a small dose has any effect at all at any stage of the life cycle of an organism, then chronic radiation at this *level* can be more damaging than a single massive dose. . . Finally, stress and changes in mutation rates may be produced even when there is no immediately obvious effect on survival of irradiated individuals.'

from *Small is Beautiful* by E. F. Schumacher, 1974

g) What *field?*

h) What is *going to happen?*

i) What two things are *equally relentless?*

j) What *damage?*

k) What *level?*

Check your understanding

KEY   **3** The quotations on the following page contain the main ideas in the text.
Assess the degree of certainty or doubt which the writer expresses in each, by measuring each proposition on the following scale:

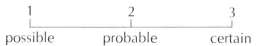

```
1              2              3
|_____|_____|
possible    probable      certain
```

Write an appropriate number by the side of each sentence.

a) Of all the changes introduced by man into the household of nature, large-scale nuclear fission is undoubtedly the most dangerous and profound. (line 1) □

b) Ionizing radiation has become . . . the greatest threat to man's survival on earth. (line 4) □

c) There is at least a chance that (the atom bomb) may never be used again. (line 9) □

d) The danger to humanity created by the so-called peaceful uses of atomic energy may be much greater. (line 9) □

e) . . . nuclear fission represents an incredible, incomparable and unique hazard for human life . . . (line 18) □

f) . . . the only question that appears to interest either governments or the public is whether 'it pays'. (line 28) □

g) The most massive wastes are, of course, the nuclear reactors themselves after they have become unserviceable. (line 31) □

h) (Nuclear reactors) have to be left standing where they are . . . perhaps for thousands of years. (lines 37, 38) □

i) If this is really going to happen, there will be a continuous traffic in radioactive substances from the 'hot' chemical plants to the nuclear stations and back again. (line 59) □

j) Unless all living geneticists are in error, there will be an equally relentless . . . increase in the number of harmful mutations. (line 68) □

What do you think?

4 On the basis of your results from the last exercise, say whether you find the writer dogmatic or reasonably objective?

5 What arguments can you think of in favour of the development of nuclear energy?

6 Do you agree or disagree with Schumacher?

Part B Windmills

Some people think we must find alternative forms of energy which are safer and not wasteful of resources – such as windmills.

The following text comes from a weekly news magazine.

1 Read the text and try to answer the questions.
Use a mask to cover the part of the text you have not read.

There is a burgeoning of windmills. They are springing up
in the fields and large gardens, some big enough to make
a useful contribution to the energy needs of the
household and others so small as to be only entertaining
experiments. Recently the world's governments have shown
an interest. The United States and Canada, West Germany
and Israel, Japan and the United Kingdom, all . . . . .

From the text above what features do these countries have in
common that is relevant here? Read on . . .

. . . . . have plans for wind-driven electricity generators.
There is even a project for a very large windmill on the
South Downs that will heat greenhouses. The attraction is
the energy that the wind will give us free. In reality, of
course, ...

What point is he going to make about the real situation?

. . . . you no more get free energy from the wind than you
get free steam power because someone happens to give
you a bucket of coal. You must harness the energy in
both cases. And although your windmill's raw energy,
unlike coal, is free, you still have to harness it in the most
economical way for your particular needs. Which is why
you may choose a . . . .

Can you say, in very general terms, what comes next?

20   .... bicycle-wheel windmill that will charge a car battery
   and thus keep your Sony TV going, or a home-built
   Cretan windmill that will warm your house.
    If windmills are to be more than emotionally attractive,
   the cost of the energy they produce, in terms of basic cost
25   plus maintenance, must compare with the cost ....

— of what?

   .... or at least, the only reasonably inflated cost, of energy
   from other sources. Even the bicycle wheel generator,
   unless you build it from scrap ....

What point will be made in the second half of this sentence?

   .... costs a lot more than the car battery it charges and
30   enormously more than the sum one would spend for the
   same amount of electricity from the local electricity
   board.
   However, we shall, probably within our lifetime, use
   up the coal reserves of Britain and the oil of the Middle
35   East: other reserves are certainly not infinite – we can
   make at least a near guess as to when they will run out.
   So ....

What conclusion does the writer draw here?

   .... we have to look to the renewable sources of energy
   if we have any thought at all for our successors, and for
40   many of us this means, quite precisely, ...

— who?

   .... our children. A child of five could live to see the
   end of coal and oil as common fuels, and increasing
   production of nuclear energy involves a correspondingly
   increasing gamble with safety. And while the pattern of
45   the way we use energy must alter, as it has altered since
   the oil-price increases of 1973, we must harness the
   renewable energy sources at reasonable cost if we are
   not to force our children to change their style of life
   very ....

—very what?

50 .... dramatically.
 The best way of using renewable energy, the main
 sources being sun, wind and water, is as a supplement
 both to fossil fuels – oil, coal and nuclear energy – and,
 where possible, to one another. In the temperate parts of
55 the world there is more sunshine in summer and more
 wind in winter, so a system that combines the two has a
 better chance of giving an even supply than ....

– than what alternative?

 .... one that relies on either. Whether, to get to the
 immediate point, you are choosing a windmill for a house
60 or a community, you will be choosing it as part, only, of
 an energy-supply system.
 When it comes to choosing or building your windmill
 you will find that the more energy you want from it, the
 more elaborate your windmill and its control system must
65 be and the higher it must be sited. But you cannot satisfy
 whatever demand you care to make, which is no bad lesson
 for those infatuated with the power of technology. First, ...

– Can you think of reasons why this is so?

 .... the windmill doesn't deliver constantly: with
 technology or patience you must adapt yourself to the
70 vagaries of the wind. And secondly, you cannot simply
 build bigger and bigger windmills to get more and more
 power. There always comes a point where scaling-up
 designs to larger versions doesn't work – there are
 engineering reasons, in other words, why an elephant is
75 not simply a large ....

– a large what? Think of something suitable.

 .... racehorse. As you increase the size of a windmill
 you reach a stage where you are trusting too much to
 present knowledge of design and materials: a windmill
 with 150ft sails would be a threatening object in a brisk
80 wind.
 A bit surprisingly perhaps, brisk winds are not usual in
 Britain. If you intend to produce energy from a windmill
 here you have to remember that, except in a few coastal
 zones, the average wind speed in Britain is 12.5 mph or
85 less. Although you must design your windmill to be safe

in more powerful winds you must predict your yield of power from this speed, with the mild consolation that the average is remarkably constant from year to year, so . . . .

– what implication do these facts have?

90 . . . . your energy production can be correspondingly predictable.

At this wind speed a windmill with a propeller diameter of 10ft produces a mere 300 watts or so, assuming it has an efficiency of about 70 per cent. This is enough for three brightish electric bulbs only – and you 95 have to remember that the wind speed is an average. A larger windmill is much better. You break into a kilowatt – an electric fire – of production at about 18ft diameter. These are the figures you must bear in mind if you are thinking of building or buying a windmill.

100 Once you have chosen the size of your windmill you have to get it into the wind. Because of the sheltering effect of buildings there is no great possibility of there being many useful windmills in towns, and even in the country you have to mount your windmill . . . .

– where?

105 . . . . high to get an undisturbed wind. Even on a relatively exposed site you can profitably use a 150ft tower, partly to reduce the effect of the drag that the ground exerts on the wind. There have been in the past much more dramatic plans than this. There was, for 110 example, a German project for a multiple windmill 1000ft high. In building high, you again have the energy production versus capital cost problem. The higher the tower the better, but . . . .

– what is the drawback of a high tower?

115 . . . . it costs more to build a high tower than a low one, and the gearing and drive from the high windmill can be much more complicated. You can solve the problem by going to the top of a hill – in fact the curve of a hill increases the wind speed, but you can't solve your tower problem by attaching a serious windmill to the building 120 you live in. The resulting vibrations tend to shake the stoppings from your teeth and the tiles from the roof.

from *The Sunday Times*, 1978

Check your understanding

2 Now decide whether each of the statements below is true or false according to the information given in the text. Write T (True), F (False) or D (Don't know) by the side of each statement. Refer back to the text carefully.
a) The energy that the wind gives costs nothing
b) If windmill X is twice the size of windmill Y, it will not necessarily produce twice the amount of power which windmill Y can produce.
c) A child born in 1973 will see the day when oil and coal are rare fuels.
d) A windmill with 150ft sails is a safety risk in high winds.
e) Wind speeds in Britain can reach 20 mph.
f) The power produced by one windmill will vary considerably from year to year.
g) On a relatively exposed site, it will pay to use a 150ft tower.
h) The Germans built a 1,000ft high multiple windmill.

Section 4 Has Man a Future?

What do you think?

1 What about the future? Are you basically pessimistic or optimistic? Do you feel that ultimately man will abuse his talents to destroy his environment, or exploit his skills to good effect?

Two opposing views follow. The first was written by an American ecologist in 1971.

2 Read the first passage to find out whether the writer is optimistic about the future.

Evidence that pesticides have long-term lethal effects on human beings has started to accumulate, and recently Robert Finch, Secretary of the US Department of Health, Education and Welfare, expressed his extreme apprehension about the pesticide situation. Simultaneously
5 the petrochemical industry continues its unconscionable poison-peddling. For instance, Shell Chemical has been carrying on a high-pressure campaign to sell the insecticide Azodrin to farmers as a killer of cotton pests. They continue their programme even though they know that Azodrin is not only ineffective, but often *increases* the pest density.
10 They've covered themselves nicely in an advertisement which states, 'Even if an overpowering migration [*sic*] develops, the flexibility of Azodrin lets you regain control fast. Just increase the dosage according to label recommendations.' It's a great game – get people to apply the

15 poison and kill the natural enemies of the pests. Then blame the increased pests on 'migration' and sell even more pesticide!

Right now fisheries are being wiped out by over-exploitation, made easy by modern electronic equipment. The companies producing the equipment know this. They even boast in advertising that only their equipment will keep fishermen in business until the final kill. Profits must

20 obviously be maximized in the short run. Indeed, Western society is in the process of completing the rape and murder of the planet for economic gain. And, sadly, most of the rest of the world is eager for the opportunity to emulate our behaviour. But the underdeveloped peoples will be denied that opportunity – the days of plunder are drawing

25 inexorably to a close.

Most of the people who are going to die in the greatest cataclysm in the history of man have already been born. Both worldwide plague and thermonuclear war are made more probable as population growth continues. These, along with famine, make up the trio of potential 'death

30 rate solutions' to the population problem – solutions in which the birth rate-death rate imbalance is redressed by a rise in the death rate rather than by a lowering of the birth rate. Make no mistake about it, *the imbalance will be redressed*. The shape of the population-growth curve is one familiar to the biologist. It is the outbreak part of an

35 outbreak-crash sequence. A population grows rapidly in the presence of abundant resources, finally runs out of food or some other necessity, and crashes to a low level or extinction. Man is not only running out of food, he is also destroying the life support systems of the Spaceship Earth.

from 'Eco-catastrophe' in the *Environmental Handbook* by
Paul Ehrlich, 1971

Check your understanding

KEY **3** Fill in the gaps in the following summary.

Ehrlich cites two examples of frightening trends visible at the time of writing: firstly, the . . . . effects of . . . .

. . . . on human beings, and secondly the use of . . . .

. . . . which gradually eliminates . . . .

. . . .

As evidence for the former, he claims that Shell is producing insecticides which are known to . . . . rather than . . . . the density of insects which attack . . . . crops. Shell, Ehrlich says, are well aware of this and refer to such a possibility as a '. . . . . ', which should be tackled by . . . .

. . . .; this in turn will of course benefit the company by
increasing the . . . . of the product.

The seas, he contends, are being . . . .
too severely.

Firms are making. . . . . to facilitate this,
although they know that in the end, fish stocks will . . . .

. . . .

In Ehrlich's view, the Western world is pursuing this blatant des-
truction because . . . . The
fact that it only has a limited time in which to do this, will also
prevent the . . . . from doing the same.
The pattern familiar to scientists, whereby a population . . . .
. . . . and then . . . . as a result
of . . . ., will assert itself. At present,
more people . . . . than . . . .
. . . ., but. . . . . , ...
. . . . and . . . . will soon bring
about the reverse.

The second text was written by Bertrand Russell in 1961; it
comes from a book in which he discusses the chance of
ultimate human survival. This is part of his conclusion:

4 Now read on.

> A pessimist might argue: why seek to preserve the
> human species? Should we not rather rejoice in the pros-
> pect of an end to the immense load of suffering and hate
> and fear which has hitherto darkened the life of Man?
> 5 Should we not contemplate with rejoicing a new future for
> our planet, peaceful at last, sleeping quietly at last after
> coming to the end of the long nightmare of pain and
> horror?
>   To any student of history contemplating the dreadful
> 10 record of folly and cruelty and misery that has constituted
> most of human life hitherto, such questions must come in
> moments of imaginative sympathy. Perhaps our survey

may tempt us to acquiesce in an end, however tragic and however final, to a species so incapable of joy.

15 But the pessimist has only half of the truth, and to my mind the less important half. Man has not only the correlative capacities for cruelty and suffering, but also potentialities of greatness and spendour, realized, as yet, very partially, but showing what life might be in a freer and 20 happier world. If Man will allow himself to grow to his full stature, what he may achieve is beyond our present capacity to imagine. Poverty, illness, and loneliness could become rare misfortunes. Reasonable expectation of happiness could dispel the night of fear in which too many now 25 wander lost. And with the progress of evolution, what is now the shining genius of an eminent few might become a common possession of the many. All this is possible, indeed, probable, in the thousands of centuries that lie before us, if we do not rashly and madly destroy ourselves 30 before we have reached the maturity that should be our goal. No, let us not listen to the pessimist, for, if we do, we are traitors to Man's future.

from *Has Man a Future* by Bertrand Russell, 1961

KEY **5** Now fill in the gaps in the following summary.

In Russell's view, a . . . . could well feel

that man's history has been so . . . .

that an end to it might . . . .

An optimist on the other hand might believe in the ability of man to

reach his goal of . . . . Russell himself

holds the . . . . view. Man, he believes, has the

potential for both . . . . and . . . .

. . . . and, although the latter has so far only been realised to a

very limited extent, he feels that this goal is well within his powers.

Today, ... , ... ,   .

. . . . and . . . . are all too

common, whereas . . . . and . . . . are all too rare.

In a possible future world, however, man might bring about the . . .

. . . . of the former and the . . . .

. . . . of the latter.

UNIT SEVEN

People and Power

Section 1 A Woman's Place

What do you think?

1 What power do members of a family have? In particular, what about the role of women in the family? How much power does a woman have as a wife or mother?
Say whether you agree or disagree with these statements.
Put a X in the margin if you disagree; a √ if you agree.
a) The role of wife and mother is the most rewarding one for a woman.
b) A woman is likely to be happier if she can work outside the home.
c) As wives and mothers women have a lot of power in the family.
d) A woman is inevitably subservient to a man in the family.
e) It is quite possible for men and women to be equal partners in marriage.
f) A mother is always the best person to look after her child.
g) We must look for alternatives to the traditional role of women in the family.

Below is an extract from a book by a writer, well-known for her feminist beliefs. In the book she challenges conventional views about women.

2 Read the extract below and as you read note whether you agree or disagree by putting √ or X in the margin (if you agree strongly put √√; if you disagree strongly put XX).

> The unfortunate wife-mother finds herself anti-social in many ways. The home is her province, and she is lonely there. She wants her family to spend time with her for her only significance is in relation to that almost fictitious group. She struggles to hold her children to
> 5 her, imposing restrictions, waiting up for them, prying into their affairs. They withdraw more and more into non-communication and thinly veiled contempt. She begs her husband not to go out with the

boys, marvels that he can stand in the pouring rain at the football and then be too tired to mend the roof or cut the grass on the finest day. She moans more and more that he doesn't care what the children are up to, that discipline is all left to her, that nobody talks to her, that she's ignorant, that she had given the best years of her life to a bunch of ungrateful hooligans. Politics is a mystery and a boring one; sport is evidence of the failure of men to grow up. The best thing that can happen is that she take up again where she left off and go back to work at a job which was only a stop gap when she began it, in which she can expect no promotion, no significant remuneration, and no widening of her horizons, for the demands of the household must still be met. Work of all kinds becomes a hypnotic. She cleans, she knits, she embroiders. And so forth. Every wife must live with the know-ledge that she has nothing else but home and family, while her house is ideally a base which her tired warrior-hunter can withdraw to and express his worst manners, his least amusing conversation while he licks his wounds and is prepared by laundry and toilet and lunch box for another sortie.

Obviously any woman who thinks in the simplest terms of liberating herself to enjoy life and create expression for her own potential cannot accept such a role. And yet marriage is based upon this filial relationship of a wife who takes her husband's name, has her tax declared on his return, lives in a house owned by him and goes about in public as his companion wearing his ring on her finger at all times. Alteration in detail is not alteration in anything else. A husband who agrees that he too will wear a ring, that they will have a joint bank account, that the house will be in both their names, is not making any serious concession to a wife's personal needs. The essential character of the institution asserts itself eventually. The very fact that such concessions are privileges which a wife cannot claim contains its own special consequence of gratitude and more willing servitude. And yet if a woman is to have children, if humanity is to survive, what alternative can there be?

3 What alternatives are there? List here as many as you can think of.

4 Continue to comment in the margin with X or √.

To begin with, the problem of the survival of humanity is not a matter of ensuring the birth of future generations but of limiting it. The immediate danger to humanity is that of total annihilation within a generation or two, not the failure of mankind to breed. A woman seeking alternative modes of life is no longer morally bound to pay her debt to nature. Those families in which the parents replace themselves in two children are not the most desirable ones for children to grow up in. There is no reason, except the moral prejudice that women who do not have children are shirking a responsibility, why all women should consider themselves bound to breed. A woman who has a child is not then automatically committed to bringing it up. A child must have care and attention, but that care and

55 attention need not emanate from a single, permanently present individual. A group of children can be more successfully civilised by one or two women who have voluntarily undertaken the work than they can be when divided and tyrannised over by a single who finds herself bored and imposed on. The alternative is not the institutionalisation of parental functions in some bureaucratic form,
60 nothing so cold and haphazard as a baby farm, but an organic family where the child society can merge with an adult society in conditions of love and personal interest.

from *The Female Eunuch* by Germaine Greer, 1971

What do you think?

5 Compare your √ and X with a neighbour. Say why you agree or disagree with the writer.

6 Look back to 1. Which of these statements sum up Germaine Greer's view about the position and power of women in marriage?

7 List the alternatives to traditional marriage mentioned by Germaine Greer. Now look back to your own list of alternatives. Did you think of the same ones?

Section 2 Above Politics

The family is an institution which we all know something about. What about powerful institutions beyond the family – national institutions? In Britain the monarchy is such an institution. The monarchy has no direct political power in Britain. But how powerful is it in other ways?

The two texts in this section were written by a pro-monarchist and an anti-monarchist on the occasion of the Queen's Silver Jubilee in 1977. The first passage is from a political weekly magazine with generally left-wing sympathies. The second piece is from a Sunday newspaper with no specific political sympathies.

1 Before you read the texts, look at the following sentences which are taken from them, and see if you can say whether they were written by the pro-monarchist or the anti-monarchist. In which cases is this clear and in which is it less clear?

a) For the Queen, if for nobody and nothing else, masses of ordinary people are anxious and willing to put out flags and throw a national party.

b) I believe that the English newspapers have largely failed to register the political significance of the greeting which the ordinary people of Scotland have just given to the Queen and the implications of this for the ultimate unity of the kingdoms.

c) In 1977 (the Jubilee has served the function of) covering every intractable problem with excuses for complacent resignation.

d) It's all for the tourists really.

e) We need a point of unity above and beyond the tensions of everyday public life and controversy . . .

f) Thus is the monarch valued, her heritage swallowed by commerce – an attraction worth more than Shakespeare's birthplace and the Soho porn shops rolled into one.

g) Today, I think we are in . . . need of our tribal loyalties . . .

h) Still, while the tourists take the front seat (to see the Queen), thousands upon thousands of British people are gawping from the galleries.

i) There is a natural longing in human beings for legitimacy in government, for an ultimate concept of authority which exists by some kind of legitimate right.

j) Such coaches were designed as moving containers of privacy, whose occupants could engage in absorbing discussion, doze or conduct seductions without being observed.

Some words always have positive or negative connotations,
e.g. *complacent* (negative)
    legitimate (positive)

Other words take on meanings in the text, by association with other words
e.g. *her heritage* swallowed *by* commerce (negative)
    we are in need of *our tribal* loyalties (positive)

Such words and phrases indicate the ATTITUDE of the writer.

---

2 Now read the texts. As you read, underline the words or phrases which you think show a fairly clear positive or negative attitude on the part of the author and write + or − in the margin. Three examples are underlined.

The state coach, <u>clumsily</u> shaped and about the size of an old-fashioned farm wagon, trundles slowly along. The windows are small and, from the pavement, it's difficult to see inside; such coaches were designed as moving containers of privacy, whose occupants could engage in absorbing discussion, doze or conduct seductions without being observed. A hand waves, a face appears. Leaning uncomfortably forward, the Queen is doing her best.

The wave is <u>mechanical</u>, the smile is a response to duty. When she walks, the Queen keeps to her ordained pace; she has never been seen to run or hurry. When she stops to speak to one of her subjects, she utters the correct number of words: no more, no fewer. All her public behaviour – and that means most of her conscious life – is programmed and regulated. One thinks, one can't help thinking, of those <u>dolls</u> which are wound up to produce a routine of actions and sounds.

It's all for the tourists, really. About that, the impresarios are brutally candid. Once, being summoned to take part in a television charade billed as a 'discussion on the monarch', I found myself seated close to the chairman of the British Tourist Board. What he had to say was simple: The Queen is his greatest come-on. A fanfare indeed for the descendant of Henry of Agincourt, of the scheming and commanding first Elizabeth, of the stubborn Charles who at least offered his head and not merely his smile. Thus is the monarch valued, her heritage swallowed by commerce – an attraction worth more than Shakespeare's birthplace and the Soho porn shops rolled into one. If Britain has become a quaint spectacle, a licensed and pensioned relief from the modern world, a Ruritania for condescending delectation, the monarchy is the special article for the customers with Diners cards.

Still, while the tourists take the front seats, thousands upon thousands of British people are gawping from the galleries. The monarchy mystifies, no doubt of that – in the full sense of the term 'mystification'. Its function is to spread a bemusing mist that conceals realities: to delude, to distort and to divert. Every Jubilee, to take the opposite case, has served a function. In 1887, to screen the poverty that had begun to worry the middle-class conscience and also to stifle a nascent republican movement. In 1897, to sanctify the trumperies of imperialism. In 1935, to conjure away the grimness of mass unemployment and the threat of Hitler. In 1977, to cover every intractable problem with excuses for complacent resignation.

Among socialists, whose presumed aim is to cleave through falsehoods and confront truths, this ought to be understood far better than it is. To put the monarchy on the immediate political agenda might well, for several good reasons, be foolish. But to assent to a consensus acclaiming its virtues is another matter. The monarchy is the apex of a structure of snobbery, unearned privilege, reverence for tradition unjustified by reason, and humiliating subservience – the complex of English vices that inhibit real social change. To make a simple point, it isn't conceivable that if we had no monarchy we should have an arbitrarily appointed House of Lords.

The monarchy is a dead hand, and that is bad enough; but it's a dead hand that could dangerously come alive. Dr Kenneth Morgan, in an erudite article details the steady decline in royal interference on the political scene. I'm not so sure that the monarchy hasn't gained a reserve power from its unquestioned impartiality between the established parties and its assumed devotion to a numinous patriotism. Parliamentary democracy is extensively discredited in the popular mind and not entirely secure; no one can be quite certain that the seams wouldn't have come apart if the second election of 1974 had produced no majority. The summons to an authoritarian saviour could, in distinctly possible circumstances, be put across if the move were made swiftly enough and respectably enough to disarm resistance. And who would provide the respectability? It was the King of Italy who delivered power into Mussolini's hands in 1922, and the King of Greece who absolved the colonels from illegality in 1967. Nothing in the record of the British monarchy, nor in the social sympathies and prejudices of Elizabeth II, guarantees a stand against the pressures that would be exerted in such conditions.

from *The New Statesman*, 1977

Here is the second passage.

Why does the idea of monarchy still draw so many people to it, even in an age as aggressively attached to equality as ours? Even Parliament is attacked as ineffective and out of date. Yet the monarchy remains, for the majority of people, sacrosanct. For the Queen, if for nobody and nothing else, masses of ordinary people are anxious and willing to put out flags and throw a national party.

Of course, the affection that the great majority of people have for the Queen personally has very much to do with it. So has an intuitive public understanding of the dedication which she and her family bring to an office which was once deemed almost priestly – and which still has something of that quality attached to it because of the total commitment in its wearer for which the Crown calls.

We need a point of unity above and beyond the tensions of everyday public life and controversy, and the monarchy to a great extent provides it – the more effectively because it requires loyalty to a person. The idea of Kingship evolved precisely from the leadership of a family or tribe – a kinship. Today, I think, we are in no less need of our special tribal loyalties, and the monarchy is an expression of them.

In the deepest and nonparty sense this is a political function. I believe, for example, that the English newspapers have largely failed to register the political significance of the greeting which the ordinary people of Scotland have just given to the Queen and the implications of this for the ultimate unity of the kingdoms. It may yet prove that the monarchy is the institution which will do most for national self-understanding of all parts of the Kingdom and for their unity.

Not least, there is the Queen's function as the arbiter of last resort in such matters of constitutional propriety as the dissolution of Parliament and invitations to form a government when a clear majority is lacking. It is a real responsibility, and it therefore encourages the politicians themselves to find answers to difficulties so as to do no violence to constitutional decency, and at the same time maintain the throne above politics.

Yet when all these practical functions of the Crown are acknowledged, they still do not altogether explain the most fundamental instinct of a nation towards monarchy – an urge which would exist even if Queen Elizabeth were not as successful and admired as she is. For people positively want to be respectful to this particular institution in a way that does not simply depend on the merits of particular incumbents, important and real as these have been since Queen Victoria.

What, then, is the nature of monarchy's magnetism? The answer is important less for what it tells us about the monarchy than for what it reveals about the instincts of the people.

There is a natural longing in human beings for legitimacy in government; for an ultimate concept of authority which exists by some kind of legitimate right, which stands for something deeper than the convenience of the moment, and did not invent itself. Our royal family, since 1689, has reigned by parliamentary title. The doctrine of the divine right of a dynasty died long ago. Yet what that curious doctrine stood for is a human way of thinking about government which will never, perhaps, entirely atrophy.

from *The Sunday Times*, 1977

KEY **3** a) Look at these words from the two texts. In the first column mark whether they are positive (+), negative (−) or neutral (N) as used in the texts.

The New Statesman	Text	Other	The Sunday Times	Text	Other
	−	*N*			
correct (line 14)			*equality* (line 3)		
regulated (line 16)			*commitment* (line 17)		
dolls (line 17)			*tribal* (line 26)		
stubborn (line 28)			*political* (line 29)		
mist (line 41)			*ordinary* (line 32)		
imperialism (line 47)			*unity* (line 34)		
socialists (line 51)			*magnetism* (line 58)		
snobbery (line 57)			*instincts* (line 61)		
subservience (line 59)			*longing* (line 62)		
authoritarian (line 76)			*convenience* (line 66)		

b) Look at the words again. Do they always have the same
connotations? Test this by first using 'horrible' or 'horribly'
with the word, then 'wonderful' or 'wonderfully'.
e.g. we can say both 'horribly regulated' and 'wonderfully
regulated'.
Therefore 'regulated' in other contexts may be *either*
positive *or* negative
So in the second column you should put N.
Now fill in the second column.

4 The following sentences are taken from the New Statesman
text. Each word in italics has a fairly fixed connotation. Say
what this connotation is. Then say what the connotation of
each of the alternatives is, and whether it would make sense
in the sentence. Discuss how the meaning of the sentence
might change.

a) The state coach, clumsily shaped and about the size of
an old-fashioned farm waggon *trundles* slowly along (line 2)
moves
glides

b) A fanfare indeed for the descendant of Henry of Agincourt,
of the *scheming* and commanding first Elizabeth (line 27)
clever
cunning
quick-witted

c) Still, while the tourists take the front seats, thousands upon
thousands of British people are *gawping* from the galleries (line 39)
gazing
staring
observing

d) In 1977 (the Jubilee has served the function of) covering every
intractable problem with excuses for *complacent* resignation (line 50)
happy
self-satisfied
satisfied

e) The monarchy is the apex of a structure of . . . . . humiliating *subservience* (line 59)
obedience
loyalty

What do you think?

5 Which of the two writers do you most agree with?

*What do the British think? The following article comes from a
popular weekly women's magazine.*

6   Read the first part.

The thrones of the world have top-pled one by one. But Britain's still stands regally, probably the richest and most influential of them all,
5 *decked out with pomp and pageantry. In this silicone-chip space-age, is Majesty out of touch, a waste of money, something which almost makes Britain a laughing stock amongst hard-headed industrial nations? The idea that*
10 *monarchy should be abolished seems to have gained support in recent years . . . But is it the belief of a noisy minority, or do the British really want their Royal Family to go? To dis-cover what the nation really thinks, we com-*
15 *missioned Opinion Research Centre, one of the country's foremost market research organisa-tions, to conduct this remarkable survey.* It is the first time such frank questions have been asked on a nationwide basis about a reigning*
20 *monarch and the members of her family.*

* The survey is based on a reliable and representative sample of 856 men and women over the age of 16, in 100 Parliamentary constituencies, who were interviewed in the privacy of their own homes.

KEY   **7**   Now complete the second part using information from the table.

Royals rule, O.K.?

The days when Europe glittered with Kings and Queens are long gone. Only half a dozen thrones are left now, with ours probably
5 the most regal. And if you believe critics of the Royal Family, you'd think most of us were just waiting to see the golden coach auctioned off and the royals retired!
10   But is this what the British people want? Asked if they thought monarchy was the best way of providing the country with a head of state or whether
15 they'd prefer to abolish it and elect a president instead, the vast majority _____ %–opted for the monarchy, almost half of these being "very strongly" in favour.
20 And enthusiasm was very evenly spread country-wide, and through the social classes, but women were more starry-eyed about royalty. Over _____ out of 10 men,

25 compared with_____
women, were pro-monarchy.
      Only ____ in 100 people wanted
to get rid of the monarchy. More
young people were ready for
30 change, but over_____
of the 16 to 24 year olds still
wanted to keep a monarch—
though well under a third of these
felt strongly about it. Royalist
35 feeling increased with age until,
among over 65s,_____
were promonarchy and nearly
threequarters of them strongly
so.

ARE YOU FOR OR AGAINST THE MONARCHY?

	All	Men	Women	16 to 24	25 to 44	45 to 64	65 plus
Monarchy provides the best head of state	86%	81%	91%	77%	86%	89%	92%
Abolish the monarchy and elect a president	8%	13%	4%	16%	9%	5%	4%
Neither	3%	3%	2%	5%	2%	2%	3%
Don't know	3%	3%	3%	2%	3%	4%	1%

from *Woman*, 1978

KEY **8** Is there any information in the text which is *not* given in the table?

UNIT SEVEN

Section 3 Power to the People

A referendum was used in 1975 to decide whether the UK should remain in the European Economic Community (the Common Market). The following extracts are all taken from propaganda published by various organisations before the referendum was held.

KEY **1** Scan each of the following extracts as quickly as you can to decide whether it comes from a pro-Market publication or an anti-Market one.

a) The EEC provides the most reliable and effective framework of international co-operation and solidarity for our future.

b) We would just be outsiders looking in.

c) Remember too that the Brussels machine, to which some of the sovereignty of Common Market countries is transferred, is nothing like as democratic as our own institutions.

d) The Campaign will voice the views and mobilise, the large and growing majority of our people, of all parties and in walks of life, who want to regain their self-government. They are insisting upon your right to decide your own affairs free of interference from Brussels.

e) The EEC has already emerged as an organisation of considerable weight and influence it can act vigorously in defence of its collective interests and help to shape global events. This is what sovereignty is really about.

f) MILLIONS of pounds are paid out under the E.E.C.'s crazy Common Agricultural Policy to destroy food to keep the price up.

g) So ask yourselves do you really want to become a citizen of an alien and artificial Continental state? Do you really want, finally and irrevocably, to throw away your heritage and your children's birthright?

h) The British people never wanted to be swallowed by the E.E.C. They do not want to be ruled from Brussels, with its bureaucracy, rigid regulations, constant wrangling, butter mountains, sugar and beef crises.

i) We can work together and still stay British. The Community does not mean dull uniformity. It hasn't made the French eat German food or the Dutch drink Italian beer. Nor will it damage our British traditions and way of life.

j) Remember Norway . . .
The same scare stories were spread in Norway during their referendum. Norwegians were told they would be ruined if they remained free. What happened? Exactly the reverse. Since Norway had the good sense to say "No" its economy has prospered as never before. In the past year currency has twice been valued upwards, whilst the £ has plummetted.

k) The real aim of the Market is, of course, to become one single country in which Britain would be reduced to a mere province.

l) The position of the Queen is not affected. She will remain Sovereign of the United Kingdom and Head of the Commonwealth. Four of the other Community countries have monarchies of their own.

112

KEY **2** Now look at each extract more carefully and note the words which enabled you to answer 1. For instance, in extract a),
(EEC) . . . . reliable and effective . . . international co-operation . . solidarity . . our future
indicate the extract comes from a pro-Market publication.

One of the issues during the campaign was whether Britain loses too much national sovereignty in the EEC.

KEY **3** Arrange the five sentences below in the correct order to make a paragraph claiming that Britain *does* lose too much sovereignty in the EEC. The first sentence is numbered for you.

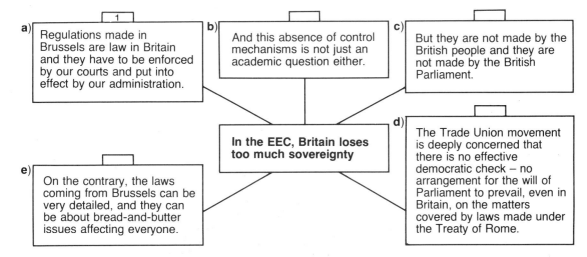

a) [1]
Regulations made in Brussels are law in Britain and they have to be enforced by our courts and put into effect by our administration.

b)
And this absence of control mechanisms is not just an academic question either.

c)
But they are not made by the British people and they are not made by the British Parliament.

In the EEC, Britain loses too much sovereignty

d)
The Trade Union movement is deeply concerned that there is no effective democratic check – no arrangement for the will of Parliament to prevail, even in Britain, on the matters covered by laws made under the Treaty of Rome.

e)
On the contrary, the laws coming from Brussels can be very detailed, and they can be about bread-and-butter issues affecting everyone.

KEY **4** Now do the same thing with these 5 sentences to form a paragraph to state the other side of the argument.

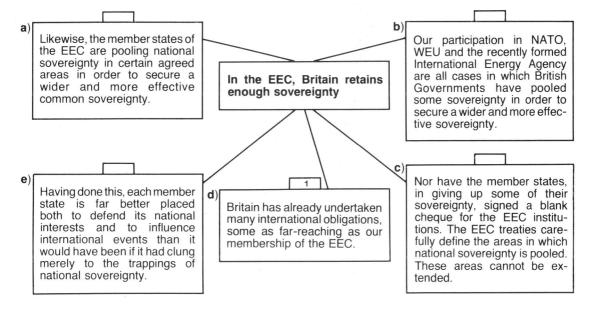

a)
Likewise, the member states of the EEC are pooling national sovereignty in certain agreed areas in order to secure a wider and more effective common sovereignty.

b)
Our participation in NATO, WEU and the recently formed International Energy Agency are all cases in which British Governments have pooled some sovereignty in order to secure a wider and more effective sovereignty.

In the EEC, Britain retains enough sovereignty

e)
Having done this, each member state is far better placed both to defend its national interests and to influence international events than it would have been if it had clung merely to the trappings of national sovereignty.

d) [1]
Britain has already undertaken many international obligations, some as far-reaching as our membership of the EEC.

c)
Nor have the member states, in giving up some of their sovereignty, signed a blank cheque for the EEC institutions. The EEC treaties carefully define the areas in which national sovereignty is pooled. These areas cannot be extended.

5 Decide whether each of the boxes below contains points in favour of Britain staying in the EEC (Pro) or against (Anti). All the sentences are about employment.

a) This means that after two and a half years' membership of the Common Market, our unemployment rate is now getting as bad as it is in France, Germany and Italy; and the longer we stay cramped inside the Market, the longer will the dole queues grow.

b) The bankers and financiers, of course, want us to stay inside so that they can shift their investment across the Channel, putting people out of work here.

c) And once outside this market, it is very doubtful if we could negotiate a free trade agreement with the Community.

d) Firstly, the flood of imported goods from the Market Six is throwing our people out of work. Secondly, investment means jobs, and each pound invested overseas means a pound less invested in Britain and so fewer jobs here.

e) Furthermore we could lose free access not only to the Community market itself, but to the 60 or more other countries with which the Community has trade agreements.

f) Even if we could, such an agreement would have damaging limitations and we would have to accept many Community rules without having the say we now have in their making.

g) Clearly, the prospects for the British worker for either employment or the creation of new jobs are not good whilst we remain in the Common Market, for the following reasons.

h) If we came out, our industry would be based on the smallest home market of any major exporting country in the world, instead of on the Community market of 250 million people.

KEY **6** The sentences above come from the main parts of two paragraphs. One argues in favour of Britain staying in the EEC and begins:

'Jobs depend on our industries investing more and being able to sell in the world.'

Its final sentence is

'The immediate effect of all this on trade, on industrial confidence, on investment prospects, and hence on jobs, could well be disastrous.'

The other paragraph argues that Britain should leave the EEC and begins:

'The dole queues are growing throughout the EEC: the number of jobless is soon expected to hit 5 million. And in this country there are now nearly a million unemployed.'

Its final sentence is

'After all, the Treaty of Rome is based on the "Free Movement of Capital". Money is to go where it will earn the highest return.'

Reconstruct both paragraphs.

Section 4 Children's Rights

Although most adults can exercise some power over their own lives, many still believe children should not have this privilege, and should be 'seen and not heard'.

The following extract is taken from an article published in a weekly magazine dealing with contemporary social issues. The article deals with the unusual case of a group of children who live not with their own families but under the care of a local authority, and who have decided to make their voices heard.

1 Read their story.

Society at work

Children, not cattle

Jill Turner

Eight young occupants of a salubrious residence overlooking Woodford Green are setting a national precedent in the treatment of children in care. They are demanding that their views should be heard and their feelings considered, and they will not be squashed. Tower Hamlets council planned that they should move out of their eight-bedroomed house with its ecclesiastical entrance, panelled hall and art nouveau leaded windows into a smaller more modern home and a nearby three-bedroomed council house some miles away. But since 31 July the date scheduled for the transplantation, the children have had a barricade of pickets at the front door and emergency stocks of food in case the councillors decide to take them by storm.

The children have lived at the home for seven years on average – "most of our lives" – and for the past six years the superintendent, Neil Weatherill, has looked after them. The result is a stable family home, more like the large family homes of North London professionals than a council children's home. The kids have their own friends nearby and go off shopping, swimming or playing football with them. Like all adolescents, they constantly test Weatherill's authority, but reckon he's a "good bloke." There is certainly no doubting his personal commitment to the children. Even the youngest needs the home to stay open only another 4½ years. By then they will all be grown up and out of care.

The children have a legal right not only to be considered but to be consulted on plans which affect them. It is spelt out in section 59 of the Children Act, 1975, which reads: "In reaching any decision relating to a child in their care, a local authority shall give first consideration to the need to safeguard and promote the welfare of the child throughout his childhood; and shall so far as practicable ascertain the wishes and feelings of the child regarding the decision and give due consideration to them, having regard to his age and understanding." Although the first part of this, the consideration, appeared in the Children Act, 1948, the second part, the consultation, was new in the 1975 act.

As yet, local authorities have taken little notice of it. Children are numbers in age batches and their objections, if voiced, have not been heard outside the walls of their homes. This time it is different: the Kingsthorpe children are making a public statement.

Tower Hamlets council, on the other hand, is doing its utmost to hush the matter up. The children's strong and well voiced feelings appear to have taken them by surprise. Meanwhile, Neil Weatherill is to be disciplined for talking to the press and for letting the children do so.

It is therefore difficult to ascertain, though all too easy to surmise, what consultation the children enjoyed under the 1975 act. A senior social worker who worked with most of the children apparently talked to them about it and drew the conclusion that while all of them would suffer from the move, three or four would be irreparably damaged. (One 14 year old boy, for example, had nine changes of home before he was seven; since then he has been at Kingsthorpe. "He's a nice well-adjusted kid." says one social worker. "But a lot of his stability is Kingsthorpe: the building, the people, his school and his friends.")

That report, however, was not what the council wanted. They sent somebody down from fieldwork management. The children were apparently asked whether they wanted to move to Harold Hill, the home now proposed, or to Dr Barnardo's. They didn't want either. This second report also came out against the closure of Kingsthorpe.

The children leave one in absolutely no doubt about what they want and there is clearly no need for the elaborate questionnaires some fear consultation would involve. Their friends and their relatives have warned them against the LCC overflow estate of Harold Hill. It's a rough area, "lots of punks," they believe. "My aunt Nelly says it's a disgrace there: there were all hooligans running about." They like their present school. "It's not a posh school and it's not Cockney either. There are some kids who swear there. It's just a normal school."

The council's one concession has been an offer to bus the children from Harold Hill back to their schools in Woodford Green. "We'd have to get up about half past five and we couldn't play after school."

It is clear that what the children would miss most would be friendships, built up over many years. "I've got more friends here than before." "We've got a lot of friends around." "I'd lose all me mates." As one social worker said: "It matters where your mates are when you're a kid – particularly when you're in care. It's hard to become one of the crowd." Those children who are in contact with their families also fear that they would see them much less if they were moved so much further out of the borough.

But the children also *like* the area. They are aware that they live in a nice house and are proud of it. They like the Green – for cricket, football and barbecues – and they know the shops. The neighbours are friendly: Weatherill has 700 numbers to ring if he needs help or support and there has even been a whip round for the siege fund in the local pub.

Meanwhile, Neil Weatherill has been accused of indoctrinating the kids and of setting them against the move. The charge does not stand up. "Neil said it was quite nice at Harold Hill, but we all wanted to stay in this area," says one of the older children. Weatherill says if the children changed their minds and wanted to move he'd happily go. He is not particularly partial to the area. He has asked the children several times whether they want to give up the struggle, but it was their decision not to be moved and it is their decision not to step down. "The councillors don't understand how we feel. They haven't come round. I've never met a councillor. I shouldn't think they're very nice."

from *New Society*, 1978

2   For each of the following questions, decide which is the best answer. There is not necessarily a 'right' answer. The point of the exercise is to discuss what you think is the *best* answer and *why*.

a) Tower Hamlets council want to move the children
 i) into 2 separate groups living near each other
 ii) into 2 groups living a few miles from each other
 iii) into a more modern home
 iv) away from the superintendent, who the council doesn't trust

b) According to section 59 of the Children Act 1975, a local authority making any decisions about children in its care
 i) is not allowed to take decisions about children which do not reflect the opinions of these children
 ii) should, as far as is reasonable, endeavour to find out how those children feel about any potential decision
 iii) need not take much notice of children who are too young to understand the details of the decision
 iv) must not do anything which is against those children's wishes

c) The main reason the children don't want to move is that
 i) they don't like Harold Hill
 ii) they want to stay at their own schools
 iii) they would lose touch with good friends
 iv) they like it where they are

d) The superintendent feels the most important thing is
 i) to defy the council
 ii) to unite the children in their fight
 iii) for him to support the children in their decision
 iv) to stay in a friendly neighbourhood

e) According to this extract, the council
 i) clearly did not consult the children as the 1975 act demands
 ii) did consult the children as the law demands but are now refusing to take the children's opinions into consideration
 iii) did consult the children but tried to get the children to say what the council wanted them to say
 iv) are angry that the children made the whole affair public and so are taking no notice of the children's wishes

3 Assuming that the facts, as presented in the New Society article are correct, look critically at the following three articles which report the same story. Two of the articles distort the facts. Identify the article which is factually correct and point out ways in which the other two articles are factually incorrect.

a) Tower Hamlets Council are expected to take strong action this week against a group of adolescents who are refusing to vacate council property. The super-intendent of these eight teenagers, who are in care, is urging them on in their defiance of the council. The children have taken the law into their own hands by barricading themselves into their house in Woodford Green – a house which is considered quite unsuitable for the children. The Council is insisting that they move to superior accommodation, but the youngsters are stubbornly refus-ing to budge. The reason they give is that the area the council wants them to move to is known to be rough. Mean-while, neighbours are complaining about the disturbance caused by pickets out-side their door and the Council is concerned lest matters get out of hand. They feel, understandably, that the children have at least been consulted. After all, legally, councils do not need to consult children in their care at all.

b) A group of teenagers have this week shown a determination to resist the decision of the local council to move them from their present home. The youngsters, all of whom are in care, have set up a picket against any attempt by the council to dislodge them from the house they have come to regard as home. They are adamant that they have decided on this course of action on their own, and their superintendent has indi-cated that he will go along with them, whatever they decide. The teenagers have the support of neighbours, who have even collected money to help them in their struggle. Meanwhile the council are planning to split the kids into two separate groups and move them away from their present neighbourhood. But perhaps the most important point is the legal one: the council are surely acting against the Children Act of 1975 in not properly consulting the teenagers. In a few years they will be grown up and so are already old enough to have their views taken into account.

c) A local council and a group of teenagers in their care are deadlocked this week over the council's decision to move the teenagers away from their home, run by Superintendent Neil Wetherill. The teenagers have refused to leave and have pickets at their front door and a well-stocked larder inside. They say that the council has not consulted them as the Children Act 1975 lays down it should. They feel that it is unreasonable to expect them to interrupt their education and start at different schools, and therefore they want to stay where they are. However, the council has offered to provide transport to their present schools from their new homes, which are in fact very close to their present home. Superintendent Weatherill thinks that this is reasonable and adds that, while he agrees with the children that Woodford Green is an attractive area, in the long term the children would benefit from the move to more modern accommodation.

In fairness to all concerned, it should be pointed out that the author did, in another part of her article, discuss the council's reasons for wanting to move the children. These include poor staff accommodation, high annual running costs and, possibly, the high market value of the house itself and 'constant damp'.

A Consumer Society

Section 1 The Professional Persuaders

If you find an ad unacceptable, don't turn the page: turn to us.

The Advertising Standards Authority. ✓

A.S.A.Ltd., Brook House, Torrington Place, London WC1E 7HN.

What do you think?

1 Do you think there should be more control over what advertisements say? For example, should an advertisement be allowed to say this kind of thing:

········washes your clothes CLEANER and WHITER than any other soap powder!

2 Look at this selection of ads and decide whether you find any of them objectionable in any way. If you yourself find nothing wrong, can you imagine anyone else objecting to them?

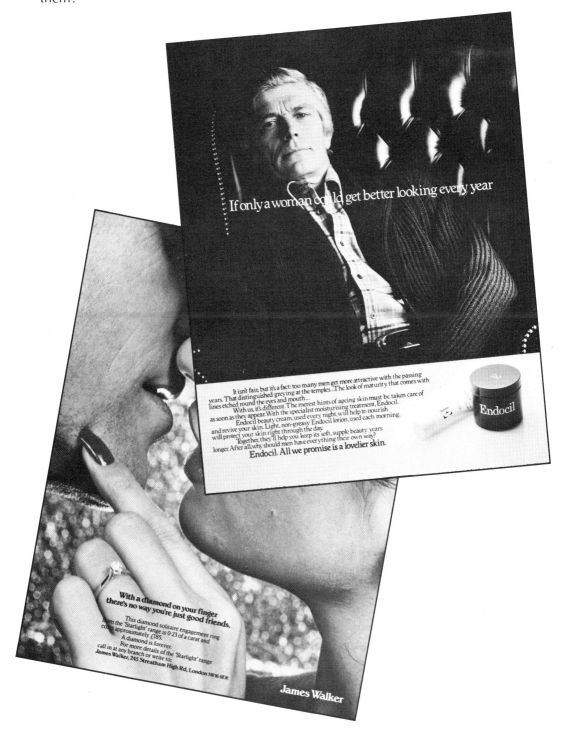

If only a woman could get better looking every year

It isn't fair, but it's a fact: too many men get more attractive with the passing years. That distinguished greying at the temples...The look of maturity that comes with lines etched round the eyes and mouth...

With us, it's different. The merest hints of ageing skin must be taken care of as soon as they appear. With the specialist moisturising treatment, Endocil.

Endocil beauty cream, used every night, will help to nourish and revive your skin. Light, non-greasy Endocil lotion, used each morning, will protect your skin right through the day.

Together, they'll help you keep its soft, supple beauty years longer. After all, why should men have everything their own way?

Endocil. All we promise is a lovelier skin.

With a diamond on your finger there's no way you're just good friends.

This diamond solitaire engagement ring from the 'Starlight' range is 0·23 of a carat and costs approximately £185.

A diamond is forever.

For more details of the 'Starlight' range call in at any branch or write to:
James Walker, 245 Streatham High Rd, London SW16 6ER.

James Walker

dataslim

eat your favourite foods
no additional exercise required
minimum change to your life style
and yet a guaranteed weight loss

A NEW DEVELOPMENT IN SLIMMING TECHNIQUE
For a total cost of £4.50 our computer will calculate how much you can eat — yet still lose weight.

Compare this method with other systems that drastically reduce your diet!

Let us provide you with a computerised DATA PRINT OUT which establishes a target weight for each day, personalised to your present weight, height, age, sex and general life-style.

Follow the computer's instructions and you CAN NOT FAIL TO LOSE WEIGHT as surely as you previously gained it, until you reach the satisfactory weight that the computer has calculated for you.

What's more, Dataslim's system is designed to help you

KEEP AT YOUR TARGET WEIGHT because it gives you bonuses when you reach it!

Dataslim is not yet another computer diet programme, as you may well be able to achieve your target weight BY ONLY A MINOR MODIFICATION OF YOUR PRESENT EATING HABITS (although helpful hints will be offered on this) and without the inclusion of additional exercise.

Just fill in the provided information section, enclose a cheque or Postal Order for £4.50 and you will receive your personal data print out and full information in a booklet.

IMPORTANT NOTE
Should you not be in 1st class health (apart from being over weight) it is important to gain clearance from your doctor.

Dataslim Limited, PO Box 10, 15–22 Fowlers Road, London SW10.

name _____

address _____

_____

	sitting	standing	walking	manual
work				
leisure				
	non active	active	v. active	vigorous

(tick appropriate box)

age [   ]   sex | M | F |

S1		

our guarantee

build — light | 0 | 1 | 2 | 3 | 4 | 5 | 6 | 7 | 8 | 9 | heavy — medium
(tick appropriate box)

If after completing the course you have not lost significant weight, return all the material we sent you and we will refund in full.

(This offer closes 10 days after the end of your course)

height [   ] feet [   ] ins

Please enclose cheque/PO for £4.50 payable to Dataslim Limited

weight [   ] stones [   ] lbs

Somewhere there is Someone who is Right for You.

DON'T GAMBLE ON FINDING YOUR IDEAL PARTNER

Dateline is trusted by **thousands to find that person.**

By yourself, you may not be able to find the perfect person for you – But we have locked away in our computer the information to match you to the partner who both interests and attracts you – the partner you are seeking, and who is looking for you.

When you complete the personality profile below, our computer will sort through tens of thousands of Dateline members to find the one who best matches your requirements. You will receive FREE and entirely without obligation, a computer print-out giving your partners details, a

Free – computer test to **introduce your perfect partner**

list of their interests and their Dateline membership number. Should you agree with us that this match is right for you then they will be included among the other partners selected for you when you join Dateline. If not, don't worry. We will try even harder to satisfy your needs.

REMEMBER this is a test. If you decide to join Dateline you will complete a longer and much more detailed questionnaire that will allow us to select you partners with even greater accuracy.

Start here 1

BY TICKING THE PHOTO THAT APPEALS MOST TO YOU

2 Do you consider yourself:

Shy: ☐	Generous: ☐
Extrovert: ☐	Outdoor type: ☐
Adventurous: ☐	Creative: ☐
Family type: ☐	Practical: ☐
Clothes-conscious: ☐	Intellectual: ☐

3 Indicate which activities and interests you enjoy by placing a '1' (one) in the appropriate box. If you dislike a particular activity, write a '0' (nought) in the box. If you have no preference, leave the column blank.

Pop music: ☐	Cinema: ☐	Creative writing/painting: ☐
Fashion: ☐	Good food: ☐	Poetry: ☐
Pubs and clubs: ☐	Politics: ☐	Philosophy/Psychology/Sociology: ☐
Sport: ☐	Classical music: ☐	
Pets: ☐	Art/Literature: ☐	
Folk music: ☐	Live theatre: ☐	History/Archeology: ☐
Jazz: ☐	Science or technology: ☐	Conversation: ☐
Travelling: ☐		

4 Other services from Singles House.
(Tick the box for further details.)

☐ **Singles Society**
Countrywide meetings and parties.

☐ **Singles Magazine**
On sale bookstalls. The only U.K. magazine for single living. 40p

☐ **Singles Holidays**
Unique holidays for the unattached.

☐ **Breakaway Weekends**
Ease the stress of a working week.

5

BLOCK CAPITALS ONLY – ONE LETTER PER SPACE – LEAVE BLANKS WHEN REQUIRED

Your Sex ____ M or F

Your Age ____ yrs

Your Height ____ ft ____ ins

Age I would like to meet ____ MIN ____ MAX

Christian Name (one only) _____

Surname _____

Address _____

_____

_____

_____

Nationality _____ Religion _____

Occupation _____

6 I enclose 2 first class stamps for postage of my free computer test and brochure. I am genuinely interested in finding my ideal partner.

SIGNED _____

Send today to: Dateline, Dept. (NAT). Singles House, 23 25 Abingdon Rd., London, W.8. (01-937 6503)

Dateline leaves nothing to chance

3 Make a list of the grounds people might have for objecting to ads, for example:

making unprovable claims

The following extracts are taken from an article published in a popular national daily. The article is about a group of TV and radio advertising executives who are holding a conference on 'The Role of Broadcasting in Marketing'.

4 As you read the extracts, find out what standards the 'admen' seem to set for themselves, according to the writer. Clues in the margin will help you work out the meaning of the words in italics.

The not-so-hidden persuaders . . . . .

The occasion, on the whole, seemed to be used less as an exchange for new ideas, more as an opportunity to add polish to the profession's collective ego.

Even if we, the public, regard advertising men as a
5 crowd of smooth young tricksters in three-piece suits out to cheat us into buying packets of Instant Happiness, the advertisers themselves, naturally enough, think differently.

'Responsible persuasion', they agreed, over Wembley
10 Conference Red Table Wine, is a wholly admirable activity, a wholly *innocuous* business.

Admen were most definitely dedicated to the service of 'truth, decency and fairness'. At least, so thought chairman John Freeman of London Weekend Tele-
15 vision, speaking in a hall reminiscent of the setting for the Hollywood Oscar presentations.

PUNCHY
slogan

Commercials must not, said the admen, offend taste or a sense of fairness, or mislead.

They must make no emotional appeals to children
20 (buy Daddy a Ferrari for Father's Day); they can no longer make claims on *phony* scientific tests (nine out of ten babies prefer bottled milk to breast-feeding) and

Does this word have positive or negative connotations? Which word in the context tells you?

Is the example scientific? How would *you* describe this test?

they cannot encourage individuals to 'acquire' prestige by advocating drinking, smoking or enjoyment, for that matter, of any of the other Deadly Sins.

'We do have *integrity*, you see,' announced a man in a grey flannel suit and glasses sitting in the body of the hall. He made integrity sound like a commodity as attractive to the market as a Barbara Streisand movie.

'All we do is direct the consumer to an educated choice. And business in the last couple of years,' he adds, unable to restrain himself, 'hasn't been bad at all'.

Independent television was born in 1955 and christened with its first commercial, an advertisement for SR toothpaste.

Now one in eight homes have two TV sets or more, and six minutes in every commercial TV hour, for 15 hours a day, is devoted to delivering a message to the consumer.

What began as a novelty has developed into a science. Products are researched, test-marketed and *launched* (and relaunched) with a vocabulary full of terms like 'bursts', 'drips' and 'O.T.See' (Opportunity To See a Commercial.)

Television provides half the outlets for all advertising and the major advertising agencies can make £1 million to £1.5 million pre-tax profits a year.

In short, advertising in broadcasting has grown into a £400 million a year industry (*boosted* five years ago by the arrival of independent radio).

And today, if you launch, for example, Carrot Spread, a Revolutionary New Concept in tea-time eating, it's almost certainly not going to succeed on its merits alone.

Instead, it needs the power of a punchy slogan (Go to Work on an Egg . . . Guinness is good for you) and the magnet of television advertising.

PLAN OF
campaign

First you must begin with a commercial. Perhaps it shows four successful young people taking tea, absolutely at the Centre of Life, relaxing in Monte Carlo. And all because of Carrot Spread. For 30 seconds worth, that may *set you back* £70,000 or more.

Look at the preceding list of things admen must not do. What, in this man's view, does the list prove?

When a product has been researched and tested on the market, what is the next step for the admen to take?

What effect would the arrival of independent radio have on the revenue of the advertising industry?

What other word could you meaningfully use here?

Then comes the campaign itself, designed by an advertising agency's media planner and negotiated into *slots* with the TV companies by a time-buyer.

Who negotiates with the TV companies?
What does his name suggest he does?
What is meant by 'time' here?

SAFE
attractions

65 If a campaign for Carrot Spread or whatever, is to make any impact at all, a client has to expect a bill for about £300,000.

Advertising revenue this year produced almost £33 million for the independent television companies. They
70 used it to make more programmes, many of which are the safe predictable audience attractions which the advertisers like. And so the cycle goes on.

'We've gone past the era of the Hidden Persuaders' explained one adman. 'The public have graduated into
75 consumers. They are more *wary*; we have to be more careful. But when it comes down to it, there'll always be some kind of market for wrapping products in a promise or two.'

Have the public changed for the better or for the worse?
What would make admen more careful?

adapted from *The Evening News*, 1978

5 What are the admen's standards?
Do the ads you looked at in 2 contravene their standards in any way?

What do you think?

6 Do you agree with the standards the advertising men have set themselves? Or would you make the standards even stricter?

7 Draw up your own code of practice for advertisers. An example of an item in your code might be:

advertisers should not make unverifiable claims

Section 2 Your Country Needs You

The Army is a major advertiser in the United Kingdom. Since compulsory military service (known as National Service) was abolished in 1960, the army has been purely professional and has advertised to attract new recruits.

What do you think?

1 Do you have compulsory military service in your country?
If so, at what age can you be called up?
Are both women and men eligible?
How long is the period of service?
Can you opt out? If so, what procedures must you adopt?

2 What type of people do you think the British Army
authorities want to attract as officers?
Try to specify:
  – sex
  – age
  – education
  – interests
  – other qualities

3 What would make this kind of person want to join the
Army?
List the appeals you think an advertisement like this would
make, for example

  sense of adventure

*The text on pages 127 and 128 is an advertisement for the
British Army which appeared in a daily newspaper in 1976 and
whose aim was to attract new officer recruits.*

KEY **4** The sentences below are extracts from the ad. Read each
sentence and say whether the writer is:
  i)   giving information
  ii) expressing an opinion or a feeling
  iii) addressing the reader directly
Notice that in a single sentence he may be doing more than
one of these things.

  a) In our opinion (compulsory National Service) gave the
     Army a bad name.
  b) We're a member of NATO.
  c) Is the job worth doing?
  d) We want you to volunteer out of a mature realisation of
     what the Army can be like.
  e) You'll be fit, alert and active.
  f) You'll also get a tax-free bonus of £1,395 when you
     leave.

**Language is used for different purposes. The aim may be,
for example**
a) **to give information, as in statements which are a matter
   of fact. For example,** 'We're a member of NATO'.
b) **to express opinions or feelings as with statements which
   contain adjectives such as** fit, alert, active.

---

c) **to make contact with the reader, for example with
direct questions or the use of words like** we **and** you.
For example, We *want you to volunteer.*
**The writers of advertisements make use of a), b) and
particularly c) in order to persuade the reader to act or
think in certain ways.**

5 Now read the advertisement and note the places where the
writer
  i) gives information
  ii) expresses an opinion or a feeling
  iii) addresses the reader directly

Volunteers are needed for three years national service

There are still people who regret the end of compulsory National Service.

In their opinion, it was the solution to everything from vandalism to the divorce rate. It taught boys to be men and it gave the Army a cheap work force.

In our opinion, it gave the Army a bad name.

It's true that we got some good men. But we also got a lot of boys who begrudged lifting a finger and lived only for demob.

Who could blame them? They didn't volunteer. They were forced labour.

We were glad to see the end of that kind of National Service, and even more pleased to start building an army of professionals.

Now we have what is considered to be one of the most efficient fighting units in the world.

We don't need conscripts because we have enough people who think the job is worth doing.

Our hope is that the day will come when every young man at the end of his education will at least ask himself whether *he* thinks the job is worth doing.

And whether he's prepared to spend three years as an Army Officer helping to do it.

So it might help if we tell you exactly what the job is.

DEFENDING A MAN'S RIGHT TO BE A COMMUNIST

We may as well start right at the top, however high-falutin' it sounds; your job will be to defend democracy.

Because, make no mistake, it is threatened.

There are nations and there are terrorist organisations who have pledged themselves to its destruction.

We can't go into the whys and wherefores of their beliefs now, but already over half the peoples of the world live under one form of dictatorship or another.

These people do not have the rights you take for granted.

The right to vote, the right to worship as you choose, to speak your mind, to strike if you feel you're being exploited.

In short, the right to live your life as

you want subject only to the wishes of the majority and the laws of the land.

55 This is what you might be asked to fight for; to defend even your neighbour's right to be a pacifist or a communist.

And don't forget, because we're a member of NATO you could be asked to 60 defend a German's rights or a Belgian's homeland.

So what do you think?

Is the job worth doing?

Next question:

CAN YOU TAKE BOREDOM?

65 We hope you'll answer that boredom is something you hate. And we swear that in the Army we'll do everything we can to allay it.

But the fact is that when major powers 70 are balanced, often all that is needed is a quiet presence.

It would be quite wrong of us to pretend that patrolling the East/West German border is a scintillating 75 experience.

Or that being holed up in a converted school in Ulster is remotely comfortable.

Or that our Army Officers in the UN force who had to take care of thousands 80 of Cypriot refugees recently found their blood tingling with excitement.

Are we putting you off?

If we are laying it on a bit thick it's only because we want you to volunteer out of 85 a mature realisation of what the Army can be like, not out of schoolboy fantasies.

Even so, there is a lot to get out of three years National Service.

90 Perhaps you saw the statement signed last year by leading industrialists about the short service commission?

It said that for them, three years as an Army Officer can equal three years at 95 university.

In their letters the words 'leadership', 'man-management', 'a sense of discipline' cropped up time and again.

Why? What will happen to you to 100 reveal these sterling qualities?

It really boils down to having the awesome responsibility for the lives of thirty men.

It will be your job to train them, care 105 for them and build a trusting relationship with them. So that in a terrifyingly dangerous situation when you give them orders, they will obey you.

It might give you a few sleepless 110 nights but you'll grow into the responsibility until, gradually, leadership will come naturally.

At the same time you'll be making lifelong friends. You'll probably go on 115 exercises abroad. You'll be fit, alert and active.

In addition, you won't be badly off.

As a Second Lieutenant you'll start at £2,675 rising to £3,325 as a Lieutenant. 120 You'll also get a tax-free bonus of £1,395 when you leave.

The first step is to spend three days at the Army Officer Selection Board where you'll confront tasks and stress-situations 125 designed to let you show your worth.

Major C. N. B. Wellwood, Dept. A41, Army Officer Entry, Lansdowne House, Berkeley Square, London W1X 0AA, will send you the details, if you send him 130 yours.

from *The Guardian*, 1976

KEY **6** Which is the writer doing most often:
– giving information
– expressing opinions or feelings
– addressing the reader
Give three examples of each and compare with a partner.

EY

7 Look at the following words as they appear in the text: say whether the writer uses them with a positive, negative or neutral connotation, by writing +, − or N in the first column. Give reasons for your opinion.

	Text	Other		Text	Other
professionals (line 18)			communist (line 57)		
conscripts (line 22)			homeland (line 61)		
deomocracy (line 36)			fantasies (line 87)		
terrorist (line 40)			leadership (line 96)		
dictatorship (line 45)			discipline (line 98)		
exploited (line 51)			responsibility (line 102)		
pacifist (line 57)					

EY

8 Now test the words in other contexts and say whether they could have different connotations by writing 'same' or 'different' in the second column.

EY

9 The words 'boy' and 'man' appear several times in the text. Scan the text and underline these words wherever they occur. Then answer these questions:
   a) What ideas, apart from youth, are associated in this text with 'boy'?
   b) How does the use of 'men' contrast to 'boys'?

What do you think?

10 Do you feel that the advertisement is in any way *not* fair or *not* objective?

11 Do you think the advertisement would achieve its aim?

Section 3 The Art of Persuasion

Part A It's All For Your Own Good

*All advertising aims to influence people. However, public or government advertising is aimed not so much at persuading people to buy things as to **warn** people about dangers, to **inform** them of rights and opportunities, or to **encourage** them to be good citizens.*

1 Does the government in your country issue public notices to try and influence people's behaviour? If so, about what kinds of things?

2   What kind of information do you think governments *should* issue to help the public?

In Britain many government publications of this kind are concerned with health, for example, how to stop smoking.

3   What ways can you suggest to help anyone who wants to give up smoking?

4   Now read the extract:

Plans of Action

   PLAN 1. Cut down your smoking gradually over 2 or 3 weeks. And then stop for good.
   PLAN 2. Many smokers find it easier to give up if they change their day to day habits or routine. Sit in a different chair. Read another newspaper.
   PLAN 3. For some reason eating seems to trigger the craving for a cigarette. There's probably no physical explanation. More likely, smokers just light up out of habit after eating.
   So for the first few days it's worth trying to make a really conscious effort not to smoke after meals.
   Do everything you can to counter temptations.

   1. Give up with a friend.
   2. Travel in 'No Smoking' compartments.
   3. Spend the first few days with people who don't smoke.
   4. Tell everyone you've given up. (It'll be harder to go back on your word.)
   Because smoking is largely psychological, a little gimmickry can often be successful where tried and tested methods have failed. Anything you can find to take your mind off your cigarettes could prove to be useful.

5   How many of the ways mentioned did you think of in 3?

Tooth decay is another health issue on which the government publishes advertisements. British people are often said to have particularly bad teeth! The extract below comes from a leaflet printed in 1978.

6   Look at the headline:

Tooth decay among British children is an urgent serious problem

7   What solutions to the problem would you expect to follow?

8 Now read the text:

a)
> Fluoride occurs naturally in almost all water supplies. In a few lucky districts where the natural concentration is about one part per million, tooth decay among local children is over 50% less than elsewhere. Where the fluoride level in other areas is adjusted to the same concentration, the result is exactly the same. Fluoridation to one part per million halves tooth decay in children.

b)
> Fluoridation plant simply adds a suitable compound to the main water supply. The apparatus, chemicals and operation method are arranged to make it impossible to deliver an excessive concentration. Daily sampling and laboratory checks maintain precise control. Millions of people throughout the world live happily and healthily in areas where the natural fluoride concentration is often much greater. Where fluoridation has taken place, no ill effects from this measure, either of a medical or dental nature, have been detectable at any age.

c)
> Countries where some fluoridation is now carried out include:
> Australia, Belgium, Brazil, Canada, Chile, Columbia, Czechoslovakia, Eire, Finland, Germany (West & East), Hong Kong, Japan, Malaysia, New Zealand, Panama, Paraguay, Peru, Romania, Switzerland, United Kingdom, United States of America, Uruguay, Yugoslavia, U.S.S.R., and Venezuela.

9 Each of the three paragraphs originally had a heading. Write your own heading for each.

Other government advertising gives information about opportunities. The advertisement on the next page is addressed to those approaching retirement age.

Retiring soon?
You could stop work up to a year early.

10 Imagine *you* are approaching retirement age in the UK and are quite attracted by this headline. You might ask yourself the following questions.

a) Will I have to pay tax? □
b) Would I get the same as everyone else? □
c) Do all married people get the same? □
d) Can I retire *more* than one year early? □
e) Must my employer agree to let me go? □
f) Can women make use of the scheme at an earlier age than men? □
g) Will I pay National Insurance? □
h) Does it apply to all kinds of job? □
i) Can I do part-time work? □

KEY **11** As you read the text, mark each of the above questions with either a tick √ (for yes) a cross X (for no) or a question mark ? (for don't know)

If your time was your own today, what would you do? Cook up something special? Spend time with friends, perhaps? Take the grandchildren to the park? Now, through the Government's Job Release Scheme, we're offering you the chance to take all or part of your last year off work, if you've up to another year to go before retiring. It's the opportunity for men of 64, women of 59 years of age, on or before 31st March 1979, to apply for Job Release. You'll get £26.50 a week *tax free*, and many married people will be eligible for £35. Think too of all those many expenses you save, like national insurance or pension fund contributions, meals and fares. Applications must reach us on or before 31st March next year when the scheme closes. Your employer must also agree to release you, and take on someone from the unemployed register. This is something for which you've worked long and hard.

Fill in the coupon and find out more about Job Release, or pick up a leaflet at your local Employment Office, Jobcentre or Unemployment Benefit Office.

Post to:- **Eileen Tingey, Job Release Scheme, P.O. Box 702, London SW20 8SZ.**

Name _____

Address _____

Job Release Scheme
Department of Employment DE

Part B Enjoy a Better Life

Much advertising is for commercial products – to persuade us to buy something. Advertisers use various means of getting us to do this.
The implications of an advertisement could be that if you buy the product, you will, for example, get a bargain or become more attractive.

1 Read the advertisements below and on the next page. Show what appeals are made in each, by putting a tick in the appropriate box in the table.

		SHADERS	CROWN PERSONAL TV	MAKE LIFE CH'EASY
a)	gain the admiration of other people			
b)	be more attractive			
c)	save yourself time and trouble			
d)	achieve immediate enjoyment or gratification			
e)	get a bargain – good value for money			
f)	get a good quality product			

Smokey Silver

Pearl Cloud

Beige Mink

Ash Whisper

Golden Sun

Turn a few heads this Christmas with Shaders

This Christmas you can be a different *blonde* at every party. All you do is shampoo with Shaders, and change your hair in less time than it takes to change your clothes. Shaders are a temporary colour, shampoo and conditioner all in one. They do beautiful things to blondes in five wash-in, wash-out colours. So try them all this Christmas and be a sensation every time.

Shaders temporary colours for blondes– wash in, wash out

SMALL ENOUGH TO CARRY, YET BIG ENOUGH TO SEE. THE CROWN PERSONAL TV. JUST £109.95.

SOMEHOW, portable televisions have never really managed to hit a happy medium.

Either they're only portable if you happen to be built like Charles Atlas, or the screens are so small it's a waste of time watching them anyway.

But at the Scotcade price of £109.95 (+p&p), the Crown Personal TV is one that's actually got it right.

The screen is a respectable 4½", yet the Crown weighs just 7½ lbs, excluding batteries.

And not only does it give you an extremely watchable television, it gives you AM and FM radio as well.

With a sound that's as clear as the picture.

Make life ch'easy.

From a snack to a meal. From a sauce to a soufflé. That's the versatility of Cheese. There's nothing simpler, better, or more natural than choosing Cheese. It's always good value for money. You can use exactly the amount you want when you want it.

Cheese is a great recipe for good ideas. So go ahead – make life Ch'easy.

Cheese. **Don't be without it.**

What do you think?

2 Which advertisement seems to fit in best with what *you*
think is important?

3 Why do you think some advertisements focus on one or two
features only?

EY **4** Imagine you are going to buy a car. What kinds of things
would you look for? Below is a list of features you might
consider important. Tick in the first column the features you
think *are* important, and use two ticks to mark the features
you think are very important.

	Points you feel are important	Points stressed in the advertisements			
		Volvo	MG	Maxi	Peugeot 604
a) it's comfortable to travel in					
b) it's attractively designed					
c) it isn't expensive to buy					
d) it isn't expensive to run					
e) it's safe on the road					
f) it suits your personality and lifestyle					
g) it's technically impressive					

EY **5** Now read the following four adverts for cars. As you read,
tick the points in the table above which are mentioned (✓)
or stressed (✓✓).

YOU'VE LEFT THE LIGHTS ON.

IS YOUR CAR AS CONSIDERATE AS A VOLVO?

When you forget to turn the lights off on most cars, they have a sure way of reminding you.
They don't start the following day.
Now for their latest 200 series Volvo have found a much kinder way.
If you haven't switched off, a buzzer goes as you leave the car.
(It also buzzes if you forget the ignition key.)
At Volvo, we know you're only human. You don't have eyes in the back of your head, so when a bulb goes out where you can't see it, a bulb lights up on the dash where you can.
Your back wasn't designed for 300 miles on a motorway.
So we built a seat that was.
It has an adjustable lumbar control that gives you the support nature didn't provide.
The 1979 big Volvos even have washer/wipers on the headlights, so even in bad weather you're beaming.
The fact is, the people who design Volvos never forget who they're designing them for.
PEOPLE.

Psychologists say a saloon car is a wife and a sports car is a mistress.

Beautiful body. A joy to handle. And rumoured to be rather fast. MG BGT

© Jaguar Rover Triumph Ltd

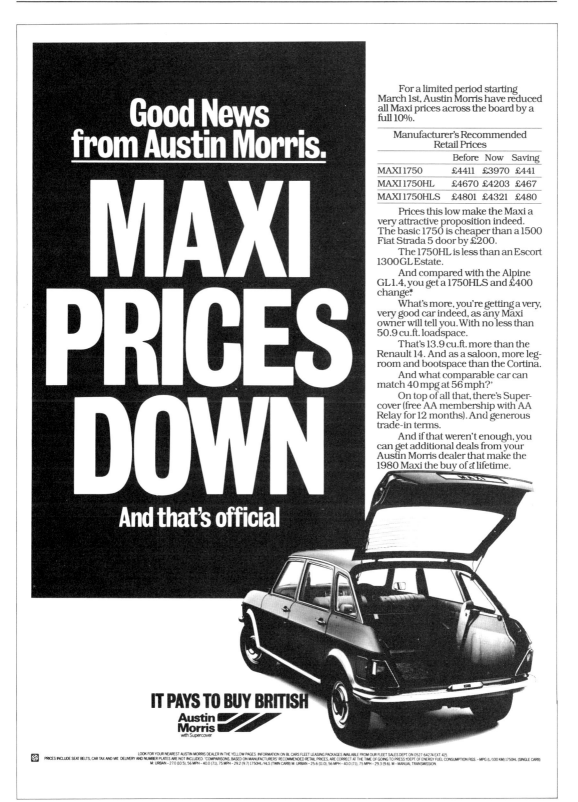

Good News
from Austin Morris.

MAXI PRICES DOWN

And that's official

For a limited period starting March 1st, Austin Morris have reduced all Maxi prices across the board by a full 10%.

Manufacturer's Recommended Retail Prices

	Before	Now	Saving
MAXI 1750	£4411	£3970	£441
MAXI 1750HL	£4670	£4203	£467
MAXI 1750HLS	£4801	£4321	£480

Prices this low make the Maxi a very attractive proposition indeed. The basic 1750 is cheaper than a 1500 Fiat Strada 5 door by £200.

The 1750HL is less than an Escort 1300GL Estate.

And compared with the Alpine GL1.4, you get a 1750HLS and £400 change.*

What's more, you're getting a very, very good car indeed, as any Maxi owner will tell you. With no less than 50.9 cu.ft. loadspace.

That's 13.9 cu.ft. more than the Renault 14. And as a saloon, more leg-room and bootspace than the Cortina.

And what comparable car can match 40 mpg at 56 mph?'

On top of all that, there's Super-cover (free AA membership with AA Relay for 12 months). And generous trade-in terms.

And if that weren't enough, you can get additional deals from your Austin Morris dealer that make the 1980 Maxi the buy of a lifetime.

IT PAYS TO BUY BRITISH

Austin Morris
with Supercover

LOOK FOR YOUR NEAREST AUSTIN MORRIS DEALER IN THE YELLOW PAGES. INFORMATION ON BL CARS FLEET LEASING PACKAGES AVAILABLE FROM OUR FLEET SALES DEPT ON 0527 6424 74 EXT. 415. PRICES INCLUDE SEAT BELTS, CAR TAX AND VAT. DELIVERY AND NUMBER PLATES ARE NOT INCLUDED. *COMPARISONS, BASED ON MANUFACTURERS' RECOMMENDED RETAIL PRICES, ARE CORRECT AT THE TIME OF GOING TO PRESS.† DEPT OF ENERGY FUEL CONSUMPTION FIGS. - MPG (L/100 KM) 1750HL (SINGLE CARB) M. URBAN – 27.0 (10.5), 56 MPH – 40.0 (7.1), 75 MPH – 29.2 (9.7) 1750HL/HLS (TWIN CARB) M. URBAN – 25.6 (11.0), 56 MPH – 40.0 (7.1), 75 MPH – 29.3 (9.6). M – MANUAL TRANSMISSION.

If you are looking for a luxury saloon, the Peugeot 604 range is one not to miss.

The new 604 range combines style, comfort and power with the traditional Peugeot strength and safety.

The 604 is in fact becoming a symbol of a certain measure of success, not pretentious, but a classic blending of elegance and refinement.

The interior of the 604 is perhaps the last word in luxury. The elegant dashboard is the result of carefully engineered styling and houses a bank of well positioned controls and easy to read dials with curved protected glass eliminating the distraction of reflections.

Take a seat, front or rear; you can be forgiven for imagining that you are settled in your favourite arm chair at home, head and leg room are exceptional and there is a large fold down central arm rest at the rear which often doubles as a writing surface.

You have a choice of upholstery, rich velour or on certain models sumptuous leather, and this is complemented with thick pile carpets front and rear.

Technically, the car is a delight. It is powered by an over-square 2.7 litre V6 engine built from lightweight aluminium and has twin cam shafts for maximum flexibility. There are two models to choose from, the SL carburettor, or for those seeking that edge on performance, the TI with Bosch K Jetronic fuel injection system.

The all-round independent suspension system with anti-roll bars front and rear ensures a smooth comfortable ride and excellent road holding.

It has a superb braking system which is servo-assisted with discs all round, ventilated on the front to protect against brake fade.

Automatic transmission is available on both the SL and TI, or alternatively a 4 speed manual gearbox for the SL or 5 speed for the TI.

Equipment is naturally of the highest level, electrically operated sun roof and front windows, halogen headlights, rear fog lights and driver's door mirror adjustable from the inside of the car.

The TI's standard specification is further enhanced with tinted glass all round, electric windows front and rear, superb deep lustre metallic paint finish with a final coat of clear protective lacquer, centralised pneumatic door locking system and electronic ignition.

Leather upholstery, air-conditioning and headlight wipers are available as options on certain models.

Prices for the 604 range start as low as £6715 for the SL and go up to £9227 for the 604 TI with automatic transmission, leather upholstery and air-conditioning.

Main service intervals are once a year or every 10,000 miles and there is a straightforward 12 month unlimited mileage guarantee.

So, if it's luxury motoring you require at a sensible price, why not take a test drive in one of the 604 models from one of our 231 Dealers throughout the country.

Please send details on the 604 SL and TI

Name

Address

Peugeot Automobiles U.K. Limited.
333 Western Avenue London W3 0RS Tel 01 993 2331

Finance and leasing facilities available from Peugeot Finance. Recommended retail prices including VAT, Car Tax and seat belts. Excluding delivery charges and number plates. Prices correct at the time of going to press.

Advertisements can appeal to the senses of sound, touch and smell, to a sense of the exotic or mysterious, or to the idea of health or natural goodness.

KEY

6 Look at the adverts on the opposite page and point out words and phrases which could be grouped under these headings:
a) words which appeal to the five senses
b) words which suggest mystery and excitement
c) words which suggest freedom and adventure
d) words which suggest health or natural goodness

Y
by Yves Saint Laurent

Unafraid to laugh and love, to suffer and cry, she has but one life, and she is going to live it . . . no imitations either . . . this lady demands the real thing. The spirit of freedom itself, she makes her own conventions with a relaxed determination that leaves lesser souls breathless. She's a lover of atmospheres . . . the aroma of fine coffee on sunlit balconies, the lilt of a tune she can only just remember, a smoke filled room just before dawn. She cares more for style than money and dresses with an unconscious chic that makes you think the work was invented for her. To a man she is all things. A woman easy to love, she herself falls in love seldom, but when it happens it's with an intensity that astounds even those who think they know her well. For she lives a life of essences, almost an archetypal existence where each word she speaks comes from her heart. Her perfume: Yves Saint Laurent's Y, hauntingly unforgettable scent whose changing nuances follow her every mood.

UNIT EIGHT

Section 4 Images That Sell

*What other means do advertisers use to sell their products?
There are common tricks or 'gimmicks' used, for example the
use of children or animals. Here is an example, from an
advertisement for butter.*

The next extract is written by a feminist writer.

1 Read the passage below and then answer the questions.

> Every survey ever held has shown that the image of an attractive woman is the most effective advertising gimmick. She may sit astride the mudguard of a new car, or step into it ablaze with jewels; she may lie at a man's feet stroking his new socks; she may hold the petrol pump in a challenging pose, or dance through woodland glades in slow motion in all the glory of a new shampoo; whatever she does her image sells. The gynolatry of our civilization is written large upon its face, upon hoardings, cinema screens, television, newspapers, magazines, tins, packets, cartons, bottles, all consecrated to the reigning deity, the female fetish. Her dominion must not be thought to entail the rule of women, for she is not a woman. Her glossy lips and matt complexion, her unfocused eyes and flawless fingers, her extraordinary hair all floating and shining, curling and gleaming, reveal the inhuman triumph of cosmetics, lighting, focusing and printing, cropping and composition. She sleeps unruffled, her lips red and juicy and closed, her eyes as crisp and black as if new painted, and her false lashes immaculately curled. Even when she washes her face with a new and creamier toilet soap her expression is as tranquil and vacant and her paint as flawless as ever. If ever she should appear tousled and troubled, her features are miraculously smoothed to their proper veneer by a new washing powder or a bouillon cube. For she is a doll: weeping, pouting or smiling, running or reclining, she is a doll.
>
> from *The Female Eunuch* by Germaine Greer, 1971

5

10

15

20

25

KEY **2** What point is the writer trying to make with the use of the following expressions?

a) *She may lie at a man's feet stroking his new socks* (lines 4–5)
    The writer's implication is:
    i) women like being subservient
    ii) women are obsessed with clothes
    iii) this is a typical posture of women in advertising
    iv) women enjoy this kind of intimacy

b) *dance . . . in all the glory of a new shampoo* (lines 6–7)
    The writer's implication is:
    i) women are represented (in advertising) as rejoicing in trivial things
    ii) a new shampoo makes one feel exhilarated
    iii) the launching of a new shampoo is a cause for celebration
    iv) the girl in the advertisement has beautiful hair

c) *She sleeps unruffled, her lips red and juicy and closed*
(lines 17–18)
Which word sums up the writer's attitude here?
  i) amused
  ii) admiring
  iii) envious
  iv) contemptuous

d) *she is not a woman* (lines 12–13)
The writer implies here
  i) women are not really used to promote sales
  ii) the 'woman' is a young girl
  iii) the 'woman' is artificial, unreal
  iv) most women are not so attractive or glamorous

e) In *the inhuman triumph of cosmetics* (lines 15–16)
the *triumph* is described as *inhuman* because, it is
implied:
  i) it is very impressive
  ii) no human could achieve it
  iii) it involves cruelty
  iv) the result is very unnatural

KEY **3** In the left-hand column below ten words from the text are
used in more usual contexts. In the second column, note
whether in the more usual context the words carry positive
(+) negative (−) or neutral (N) meaning.

The third column tells you where to find the word in the
text.

In the fourth column say what connotations you think the
words have in this text – watch out for words which are not
normally used to describe people. In the fifth column, note
the clues in the text which tell the reader how the writer
uses these words.

I was enjoying the *glory* of my success.	(line 7)		
The student produced a *flawless* piece of work – not a mistake in it.	(line 14)		
An *extraordinary* coincidence happened the other day.	(line 14)		
Our front door is *painted* black.	(line 19)		
She is very smart – always *immaculately* dressed.	(line 19)		
It was a perfect *tranquil* summer's day.	(line 21)		
His car was a wreck but *miraculously* he was unhurt.	(line 23)		
The surface of our piano is badly damaged, especially the *veneer*.	(line 24)		
The child was given a *doll* for her birthday.	(lines 25–26)		

Feeling Great

Section 1 You and Your Body

Most people are obviously concerned about their health. Being ill is not something which you can ignore: you usually do something about it.

But perhaps people vary in the extent to which they are concerned about it.

What do you think?

1 Are people in your country over-concerned about their health? If so, how do they show this? Is there something they are always complaining about?

2 Read this passage from a weekly magazine: what do the French, the Germans and the English often complain about?

The imagery that we use for reconstructing our own insides seems to vary from country to country. For example, the French seem to have an obsession with the liver, while in Germany, they explain all their peculiar feelings in terms of an organ which they call 'the circulation' – whatever that is. I remember, when I was producing an opera in Frankfurt about six months ago, that whenever singers arrived late for rehearsal they would always apologise for it by saying they had had 'ze circulation collapse' which had somehow reduced their efficiency.

It is very easy to get the impression that everyone outside the English-speaking world is a hypochondriacal loony, or a visceral fantasist. This is not altogether so, because, although I have not been able to find, so far, an American 'national organ', among the British, the last four feet of the intestine seem to loom larger than they ought to.

The word 'constipation' is used so often that it is very hard to know what is being referred to – regularity of the bowel, headaches or lassitude. A vast laxative industry is based on our national fantasy, and even the medical profession has sometimes fallen victim to the same obsession. In the early 1900s, there was a surgical craze for removing yards and yards of intestine at the slightest excuse.

from *The Listener*, 1978

3 Do you think there is any truth in what the writer says about the French, the Germans and the English?

4 Do people in your country have a favourite explanation for feeling unwell?

 5 People go to the doctor for different reasons. Would you go if you:
– had a bad cold?
– had a headache?
– felt depressed?
– had a sprained ankle?
– felt breathless after physical exercise?
– felt you were putting on too much weight?

The next passage comes from a book on people's attitudes to the body and to illness.

 6 Look at the chart below; as you read the next text, complete the chart with the following information:
a) four ways of assessing symptoms
b) how the symptoms of breathlessness and acute breathlessness might be assessed in each of these ways. Mark the degree of seriousness by using a 1–10 scale as follows:

```
1                              10
|——————————————————————|
```
hardly worth attention   acutely serious

	Ways of assessing symptoms			
	1	2 *alarming implications*	3	4
breathlessness		*5*		
acute breathlessness			*9*	

    There are four independent scales which can be applied to a symptom to decide whether or not it demands attention. First, there is the symptom's intrinsic nastiness. Pain is intrinsically nasty, and most people would agree that nausea is, as well. The straightforward feeling of having either of these symptoms is quite enough to make you wish you hadn't.

    In contrast to these, there are symptoms whose nastiness has to be inferred. The painless appearance of blood in the

urine is not obviously unpleasant as a thing in itself. It is
unsettling not because it causes discomfort, but because it
carries alarming implications. The same principle applies to a
painless, invisible lump in the breast.

Symptoms are also complained about because they
reduce efficiency or restrict freedom of action. A patient who
becomes steadily more breathless when he exerts himself
eventually complains because he is frustrated by the way in
which this cuts down his movements. It is not the feeling of
breathlessness as such, but the results of it which lead him to
complain. This also applies to tremor or muscular weakness
of one kind or another: unless they come on rapidly enough to
cause immediate suffering or alarm, they excite complaint
because of the frustration they cause.

Finally, there is the question of embarrassment or shame.
Patients may complain about a symptom simply because
they regard it as unseemly. A painless blemish on the mouth
can bring a patient to the clinic much sooner than a large,
painful lesion on the shin. This applies to any publicly notice-
able anomaly – a squint, drooping eyelid, hairlip, rash, loud
intestinal noises, hoarseness – which seems to threaten the
patient's self-esteem and which might be regarded as a
stigma.

Obviously, a symptom can appear on more than one scale
– perhaps on all four.

Breathlessness is an interesting example. It is more or less
unpleasant in itself, and if the patient associates the symptom
with his heart or his lungs he may also be alarmed by it. But,
as with angina, the sense of incapacity may weigh most
heavily, and if the patient prides himself on being able-bodied
he may experience an intolerable sense of shame when his
friends or colleagues leave him panting on a short stroll.
However, if it comes on very rapidly or very severely, the
scale changes. Someone who is awakened at night by an
attack of paroxysmal breathlessness finds the feeling almost
insufferable in itself, so that it now hits the very top of the
intrinsic nastiness scale. Since most people would interpret it
as a serious threat to life, it notches up a heavy score in terms
of sheer alarm as well. And when breathlessness is extreme,
the patient is often bed-ridden, so it also appears very high up
on the incapacity scale. However, anyone preoccupied with
drawing his next breath has very little time to feel ashamed of
it, so that it doesn't even appear on the stigma scale, although
a sense of shame and embarrassment can survive even the
most fearful emergency – I can remember patients struggling
for breath, waving a weak apology for what they obviously
regarded as humiliating panic.

from *The Body in Question*, by Jonathan Miller, 1978

UNIT NINE

Check your understanding

7 Guess the meanings of the following words from the way they are used in the text.

    a) *Nausea* (line 4) is likely to be:
- i)   a painless symptom
- ii) an embarrassing symptom
- iii) a symptom unpleasant in itself
- iv) a symptom which is painless but worrying

    b) If you *infer* that a symptom is nasty (line 8)
- i)   you learn from the doctor that it is dangerous
- ii) you feel immediately that it is painful
- iii) you guess that it might be dangerous
- iv) you deny that it is nasty

    c) *Unseemly* here means (line 25)
- i)   painful
- ii) ugly
- iii) dangerous
- iv) invisible

    d) A *blemish* (line 25) is likely to be:
- i)   a mark
- ii) a blow
- iii) a wound
- iv) a taste

    e) A *lesion* (line 27) is likely to be:
- i)   a fracture
- ii) a headache
- iii) a pinprick
- iv) a wound

    f) A *squint, drooping eyelid . . . hoarseness* (lines 28–29) are likely to be:
- i)   symptoms which draw people's attention
- ii) unpleasantly painful symptoms
- iii) invisible symptoms
- iv) visible symptoms people pay no attention to

    g) *Panting* (line 40) is likely to mean:
- i)   sleeping
- ii) feeling fit
- iii) breathing fast
- iv) walking fast

8 Now check the exact meanings of these words in a dictionary.

What do you think?

9 Now look at the following symptoms and fill in the chart according to how you think they would score in each category on the 1–10 scale.

	Ways of assessing symptoms			
	intrinsic nastiness	alarming implications	incapacity	embarrassment
pain in the chest				
severe headache				
alopecia (hair loss)				
sprained ankle				

10 Now compare your chart with your partner. How far do you agree?

Section 2 You Are What You Eat

1 Read these two paragraphs, noticing the differences between them. Which one is more formal? Can you see why?

a)

There are apparently very few areas of agreement amongst doctors and nutritional experts these days, upon what constitutes a safe and healthy diet and what is to be avoided. No sooner is a product declared by one group of scientists to be the key to vigour and longevity, than it is dismissed by another group as being acutely dangerous to health.

b)

People like doctors and such, who should know about these things, don't seem to agree about what food is good for you and what isn't. One day you hear that something will make you healthy and help you live to a ripe old age and the next they are saying it's poisonous.

UNIT NINE

KEY **2** Below is a passage extracted from a book on food technology. Make it as formal as possible by choosing the more formal alternative in each bracket.

A menace to { many / a great number of } foods, particularly raw products, is

{ the food heating up by itself / spontaneous heating } { after mould has grown on the top / following surface growth of mould }

or { after insects have attacked it / the attack of insects } . This risk is { accelerated / speeded up }

{ by humidity conditions in excess of normal / if there is more dampness than usual } . { Another thing which leads / Another prerequisite }

to spontaneous heating } is high storage density, which reduces

{ the amount of air reaching the food / ventilation } . If tightly packed,

{ the heat which is produced / the produced heat } is not readily { dispatched / got rid of } and the

buildup of { high / elevated } temperatures is { enhanced / greater } . { So / Thus }

{ controlling the temperature and also the dampness is / temperature and moisture control are } the basic physical

requirement in storing { farm / agricultural } products. { Cleanliness / Sanitation }

{ is supplemental / also helps } , to { stop / prevent } loss by micro-organisms, insects and

{ rats and mice / rodents } .

from *Slimming Magazine*, 1978

KEY **3** On the following page, there is a letter to a health magazine and a reply to that letter. Make both as informal as possible by choosing the less formal alternative in each bracket.

{ There is / We've heard about } a slimming treatment which consists of being rubbed

with a herbal gel; { you are / one is } then tightly wrapped in bandages for an hour

or so, and { are / is } supposed to lose inches .... Is this a permanent

solution to overweight?

Answer

{ How *can* it be? / This isn't possible } · { Closer analysis of the facts should make this obvious / In your heart, you know this as well as I do, don't you? } ·

The truth is { surplus weight will be lost / you will lose surplus weight } only if { more calories are / you expend more }

{ expended / calories } than { are consumed / you are consuming } { which forces the body to / thus making your body } draw

on its fatty reserves. Bandages { could come to your aid / could be used } { if you tied / by tying }

some together and { used / using } them as a skipping rope.

from *Slimming Magazine*, 1978 (answer by John Yudkin)

4 Make the sentence below more informal by splitting it into 4 or 5 shorter, simpler, sentences.

> In countries such as America and Britain, where vast sums are expended in promoting vitamin preparations, millions of vitamin tablets and tons of special vitamin foods are consumed each year by people who not only have no need of them, but who are more likely to suffer ill-effects from over-consumption than enjoy the benefits promised by the promoters.

Three factors affecting STYLE are:
i) **choice of vocabulary**
   e.g. *accelerated* **or** *speeded up*
ii) **the use of personal or impersonal forms**
   e.g. *more calories are expended* **or** *you expend more calories*
iii) **the complexity of sentences**

KEY **5** Read the following text, which is quite formal, and then use the information from it to complete the second text, which is more informal.

> Today almost everyone is a consumer of caffeine. The drug is contained in many non-alcoholic drinks, including tea. A cup of tea or coffee contains between 100 and 150 mg of caffeine. Even a cup of cocoa, favoured by some as a
> 5   non-stimulating bedtime drink, can contain up to 50 mg and chocolate too can contain a little caffeine. It is also to be found in the popular cola drinks. Perhaps it is because we like caffeine so much that many still believe it might be in some way harmful. Those with a puritan streak may
> 10   even feel that it should not be so widely enjoyed without some penalty!
>
> Is there any justification for this feeling? Caffeine may be regarded as a mildly addictive drug and if it were introduced nowadays as a new product of the
> 15   pharmaceutical industry it might well be available only on a doctor's prescription. Reaction to caffeine certainly has some of the characteristics of a drug of addiction. For instance, withdrawal symptoms in the form of severe headaches can occur. The ability to become addicted to the
> 20   drug is, however, not confined to man. If rats are given a taste for caffeine by making them take it in their drinking water they come to prefer caffeinated water when they are later given a choice between that and plain water.
>
> Many people believe that caffeine counteracts the effects
> 25   of alcohol. Because of this folklore the drug has been used in the treatment of alcoholism and drunkeness. Experiments with rabbits and rats, however, show clearly that a dose of caffeine significantly increases the impairment of performance caused by alcohol. If the
> 30   traditional sobering effect of coffee is real, therefore, it would seem to work despite the caffeine present. Also, though tradition has coffee as the sobering drink, tea contains almost the same amount of caffeine per cup. Caffeine can certainly cause a feeling of wakefulness in
> 35   man and it is used in a few preparations for the treatment of hay-fever and asthma, perhaps to reduce the drowsiness caused by other ingredients.
>
> from *The New Scientist*, 1978

6 Now fill in the gaps in the text below.
(Only one word missing from each gap.)

> Nearly all of . . . drink some caffeine. You can . . . the
>
> drug in many non-alcoholic drinks including tea. A cup of
>
> tea or coffee . . . between 100 and 150 mg of caffeine in it.

You may . . . cocoa at bedtime, because it doesn't keep you . . . . Well even that can have up to 50 mg in it and chocolate . . . some too. You can also . . . it in the popular cola drink. Perhaps it is because we like caffeine so much that a . . . of us still believe it can do us . . . . If you are a . . . of a puritan, you may even feel that you . . . enjoy it without feeling . . . .

(There may be several words missing from the gaps below.)

Is it . . . . .to feel like . . . .?
Caffeine is mildly habit-forming and if it had only just come on the market, ...And, what's more, caffeine does the same kinds of things to you that habit-forming drugs do. For instance, if you stop drinking caffeine, ...But it's not just humans who can get hooked on caffeine. You can give rats . . . . .if . . . . water. Then if you . . . . caffeinated water.

Perhaps, like a lot of people you think caffeine can sober you up. It's certainly been used to . . . . .But tests with rabbits and rats show that if . . . .
So, if a cup of coffee really does . . . ., it's in spite of . . . .
In fact, although people . . . ., a cup of tea has . . . . But it's certainly true that caffeine can . . . . .For instance, some asthma and hay-fever remedies tend to make . . . . .and caffeine is sometimes added to these . . . .

Section 3 In Good Shape

Keeping healthy is not just a question of eating the right things. You also have to keep physically fit. But people differ in their opinions of what is the best way to stay in shape.

What do you think?

1 What is the best way to keep fit through exercise? Five ways of keeping in shape are given here. Which do you agree with? Fill in the first column.
(You may add other ways if you wish)

		Your opinion	Jenny	Sue	Kate	Molly	Ted
a)	Make exercise part of your daily routine						
b)	Just keep generally active and busy						
c)	Only do a form of exercise which you really enjoy						
d)	Discipline yourself – be strong-minded, so you exercise even if you do not feel like it						
e)	Go to a gymnasium						
f)	Other ways						

On the following two pages five people talk about the ways they choose to keep fit.

KEY **2** Read what they say very quickly. Each person makes one major point about exercise. What is it? When you have found it, fill in the chart above.

Yes, Exercise is Good for You—

but how do you start and once you've started how do you stick at it? On the next two pages, five people with very different lives give their views

Jenny is a housewife with 2 small boys

"My stay-slim aids are two little boys, three sheep-dogs and one weight-prone husband. Luckily, I don't put weight on easily; I hate to be bulky and worked very hard at getting back into shape after my babies were born. But after getting really trim, thanks to a strenuous schedule – the odd extra pound can creep on once you let up. Still, I cope without a formal daily dozen, simply because I'm so active. I just make sure that I keep extra active. For example, I do hours of dog-walking. Young Billy and Tom keep me on my toes, too. And I'll keep my husband company if he jogs or plays golf. No crack-of-dawn stuff, though. It would be unrealistic for me to start because I'd never keep it up!"

Sue is a university student who discovered she was not as fit as she had thought

"At 22, I didn't think I needed to worry about fitness. But, heavens, how a bout of strenuous activity can show you up! So I decided I must get really fit. And I did it by building my exercise into my day first thing, then it can't get crowded out later. I set my alarm for just before 7 am, take a cool shower to wake up, then I go and do 15 minutes concentrated jogging. Then I come back for a warmer bath and feel different all day: much more alert, more alive, and I ride over little crises that might have bothered me before. I've also taken up rowing (my bust is better for it) and I try to be more active all day. I've been jogging for five months now: it's part of my life. I think you must slot exercise into your routine as firmly as teeth-cleaning or you won't keep it up."

Kate is a teacher and a keen sportswoman

"I'm a weight-prone person. I can put on those extra pounds very easily indeed. But I tend not to think of exercise as primarily burning up calories: I find its mental effect, the uplift it gives you, far more important for keeping me in shape. If I feel fit, I am definitely in better control of my eating; I'm 'stronger'. If I haven't been able to get my usual exercise, I feel heavier long before any surplus pounds have time to appear. I've had some painful proof lately of how much exercise means to me: I hurt my hand badly and couldn't hold a racquet for months. Apart from the annoyance and the aches, the forced inactivity was definitely a mentally depressing experience: I missed the lovely lift you get after a really energetic work-out and I noticed my weight started to creep up from a previously fit 9 stone. To stick at exercise, I think you must enjoy what you do for its own sake: if it's just like a dose of nasty medicine, you won't keep it up or get much out of it. That's why I don't jog; to me, it's so boring! But it's fun to fix up a good game of tennis or squash with friends and I've spent many a happy Sunday afternoon on the tennis courts. I enjoy swimming, too, and once a week I call in at the local pool and swim a swift twenty lengths. It's always a bit of an effort to take the plunge on a cold winter's evening but it gives me that marvellous tingling-fit feeling – which, once you've experienced it, makes you sure that, yes, it is worth all the hard work."

Molly is mother of 3 grown-up children: she is a freelance journalist living in the country

"I have no easy answers to: 'How do you stay in good shape?' All that has ever worked for me is old-fashioned self-discipline and never letting up. I steer clear of all fatty foods. And sweets. And I couldn't keep slim without my exercise routine. I do a set of exercises first thing every day. I walk our English setter, for two hours whatever

110 the weather. I *make* myself do all this, even when I'd much rather not. Yes, it's often very hard work, but I've never discovered any other way to get as-good results – alas!"

Ted is in the music business, working in a recording studio

"To be quite truthful, getting a daily dose of exercise can on 115 occasion be an awful effort. Still, I really do believe in it – enough to *make* myself take it. And I'm always very glad afterwards! Being tired doesn't stop me. But 120 I wouldn't slog on if I didn't feel too well; that would be daft. I think the best thing is to persevere till whatever kind of exercise you choose is not 125 something special but an automatic habit. My day feels all wrong now if I don't do something active. You tend to get a very closeted sensation 130 from working in a studio; that's why so many showbiz people go in for golf, I think. But I prefer tennis in the fresh air. Otherwise, I'll play table tennis. In fact, my 135 wife and I often amaze hotel reception staff by making 'Where's the table tennis room?' practically our first question; everyone else usually wants to 140 be pointed towards the bar! If tennis is impossible, I do own one of those chest-expander wire things supposed to build your muscles. It does, too: I 145 daren't use mine too often or I'd bulge out of all my shirts."

3 The words and phrases below occur more than once in the previous texts. Find out what they mean by looking back at the texts. Then use each word in a sentence of your own.

a *dose* (lines 77, 114)
to *let up* (lines 11, 100)
weight-prone (lines 3, 49)
jog (lines 19, 35, 80)
strenuous (line 27)
stay in shape (lines 97–98)
get into shape (line 6)
keep it up (lines 22–23)

KEY **4** One feature of informal style is the use of phrasal verbs, e.g. I have taken up rowing (line 41) = I have started to row as a hobby.

Look at the phrasal verbs in the extract below. Replace the informal expressions in italics with more formal alternatives.

'I noticed my weight started *to creep up* from a previously fit 9 stone. *To stick at* exercise I think you must enjoy what you do for its own sake; If it's just like a dose of nasty medicine you won't *keep it up* or *get much out of it*. That's why I don't jog; to me it's so boring! But it's fun to *fix up* a good game of tennis with friends . . . . . . I enjoy swimming too, and once a week I *call in at* the local pool and swim a swift twenty lengths.

KEY **5** Look again at Molly's views on exercise. Summarise the
extract, using a formal style. An outline is provided to help
you. Fill in the gaps with one word only.

Molly . . . . that the only . . . .

of . . . . slim is . . . .

self-discipline and . . . . of fatty

foods. In order to remain slim, daily . . . . is . . . . .

For example, ... of the weather, she exercises

her dog for two hours . . . . despite frequent . . . . . .

to do so. She . . . . that it is . . . . . . but adds

that she has not discovered a satisfactory . . . .

KEY **6** Now attempt a summary of Ted's comments; the
words given below may help you.

Ted admits that . . . . but adds . . . . However,

he thinks . . . . Speaking from his own

experience, he . . . . because . . . . This is the

reason why . . . . However, he himself . . . . Failing

this . . . .

Section 4 Hospital

What do you think?

1 Have you ever been in hospital yourself, or visited a friend
or relative?
What was the experience like? Write notes under these
headings:
– the patients
– the nurses
– the doctors
– the hospital conditions

*In the following extracts Polly Toynbee describes the experience
in hospital of a patient, Meg Harris. Polly, a journalist, spent 5
months observing in a teaching hospital.*

KEY **2** Read the extract below.
Who do you think is talking here? What illness is suspected?

'Mrs Harris is forty-six, married with two children. Two weeks ago she noticed a lump on her right breast. On examination she has a large craggy lump on the breast. It does not appear to be attached to the skin or muscle. I can't find any indication of other swellings.

5 ... Family history – she has a sister who had a breast removed twenty-five years ago and who is alive and well. She breast-fed both her children. Her younger son has cardio-vascular disease and is awaiting surgery.'

Later, Meg's husband Bob talks to Polly about his concern that Meg should get the best possible treatment . . .

'I'd do anything in the whole world for her, you know, Polly,' he said. 'I'd sell everything and get it done private. I wouldn't mind

10 if I spent the rest of my life paying it back. Would it be better to have gone private? I did think I would, except they took her in here so soon. Would she get better doctors?' To have been able to work and pay would have made him feel so much better.

15 The helplessness of sitting and waiting and contributing nothing made him feel bad.

I said that for something serious, there was nowhere better than a big teaching hospital. The only reason for going private was to be in a private room, to get better hotel conditions, but

20 not better medical treatment. Otherwise, for something that was an emergency, where the National Health would admit someone at once, as they had admitted Meg, there was nothing to be gained. She had already jumped the waiting list, so it would just be a waste of money. I explained that the best specialists in

25 Harley Street were the same people who were consultants in the best hospitals, like this one. You paid your money to see the same man, get the same treatment, but in nicer surroundings. He was a little comforted but still not quite believing. 'I thought the rich always got better medical treatment?' I said that for

30 minor ailments, they did. They didn't have to wait three years to have their varicose veins out, or to have a painful arthritic hip or knee replaced. But when it came to the big operations, you could pay out a fortune, and, perhaps, in a small private clinic get worse nursing care, even if you got better food. The rich

35 don't queue, and don't mix with the hoi polloi, but they don't live longer.

---

3 Do you agree with Polly's last point? Comment, from your own experience.

KEY **4** What do we learn about public and private medicine in Britain?

5 Now read on . . .

Meg goes into the ward to prepare for her operation in a few days time . . .

Meg had gone into the ward carrying her neat navy coat over one arm. Her brown mock crocodile shoes with a gold buckle had made a crisp clacking on the floor. Then she had disappeared inside the
40 curtains round her bed. She had been shown her locker, told to unpack and undress. All her possessions had been closeted away in the cupboard. Her shoes went away and instead her slippers were tucked under her bed. All the clothes that belonged to the outside world were hidden away – and when the curtains were pulled back,
45 Meg Harris had turned into the patient in number ten bed.

---

6 Does this remind you of any experience you have had yourself?

KEY **7** What general point is the writer making here about life in hospital?

Later, Meg has the operation for the removal of the lump on her breast. It is expected that the breast too will be removed. The surgeon, examining the lump which he has now removed from Meg's breast, says:

'We won't bother to send it to the laboratory,' he was saying. 'I'm absolutely sure, just from looking at it. We'll send it along later just as a final check, but I'm quite sure.'

I turned quickly to the students, to be certain that I had under-
50 stood what he was saying. 'What's he mean?' I whispered.

'It's all right!' said one of the girls, breaking into an enormous smile. Then everyone in the room, the surgeon too, was smiling and looking pleased. It wasn't cancer, and she was going to be fine!

The pleasure on their faces was a surprise and a delight. They
55 were really, genuinely very pleased and very happy. Most of the people in that room had never seen or heard of Meg Harris until she was wheeled into the theatre, looking like a not-quite human thing that morning, and yet they had cared – not just that a good job

---

should be done, but they cared that her breast should be saved, and
possibly her life. I had misjudged them. The calm and uninvolved
way in which the operation was carried out had led me to believe
that they all regarded her as just number three on the list, just
another probable mastectomy case. It wasn't their own skill that had
made them so pleased, but the fact that they weren't going to have
to use it after all. I would have expected a moment of euphoria at the
end of a difficult heart by-pass operation, a celebration of their own
tremendous surgical prowess, but here was everyone being pleased
because Meg didn't have cancer. Even the students were moved and
pleased, even the student nurses, even the hardened operating
theatre Sister. Did they have time to be pleased or sad at the end of
every operation every day? I think they probably did.

8 Do you think Polly is right? Were the nurses genuinely
pleased?

9 What do we learn here about the procedure of an
operation?

*So Meg is able to leave. Polly observes her last few moments in
the hospital.*

Meg pulled the curtains round the bed while she dressed and put
her last few things into her suitcase. She'd been fiddling around with
her packing since seven o'clock that morning. She poked her head
out of the curtains and handed her two vases of flowers to the deaf
lady. Her chocolates and grapes she gave to her other neighbour.
She finally shut her case and pulled back the curtains. There she
was, transformed from the woman they all knew, in her familiar
dressing-gown, to a strange person from the outside, in clothes they
didn't know, her hair smart, her face made up. It often surprises
people to see patients in their street clothes, as they suddenly seem
like a different sort of person.

Meg managed her good-byes and her exit with great tact. She
looked a little embarrassed, a little regal and very friendly, as she
went round each person wishing them luck. Most of her warmth was
reserved for her two neighbours.

The deaf lady smiled and held her hand firmly. 'I'm so glad for
you, dear, that it all turned out so well. Don't you worry about me. I
like it here. Such a nice place.'

The woman with the mastectomy held her hand too and smiled
affectionately. Meg was a little lost for words. What comfort could

she offer? 'You've been so good to me. If it had been me I couldn't have been brave like you,' she said.

'Oh nonsense,' said her friend. 'It really isn't so bad when it
95 actually happens. You had the worst of it, the waiting, and the going into the operation.'

Meg said a last good-bye to the whole room, and in a moment was gone.

There was a small silence.

100 'Lucky bugger,' said a young woman at the other end of the ward.

'You'll be home soon too,' someone answered.

Two auxiliary nurses came to change Meg's bed, to wash down her locker with disinfectant, to remove every trace of her. I sat for a little while chatting to one or two of the women. Soon there was no
105 sign that Meg had ever been there.

'Wonder if there's someone else coming in today?' someone asked.

'Bound to be. With waiting lists the way they are, they never leave them empty long,' someone else said.
110 'Hardly time to let a bed go cold!' said another woman.

from *Hospital* by Polly Toynbee, 1977

 10 What point does the writer make in this last sentence?

11 Describe in your own words the feelings of
a) Meg
b) Meg's two neighbours
c) the young woman

Check your understanding

 12 Select the best alternative in the questions below:
a) Which sentence best sums up Bob's feelings about Meg's treatment (lines 10–36).
   i) He is sure that the National Health treatment Meg will receive is the best that exists
   ii) He is convinced that private medicine is always better
   iii) He is wondering if he should have paid for private medicine, although he could barely afford the cost
   iv) He is worried about the expense of the operation Meg is about to have

b) Has Meg (line 22)
  i)   been admitted to hospital quickly as her case is considered serious?
  ii) had to wait a long time because she cannot afford to pay?
  iii) been admitted quickly because her husband decided to pay for private treatment?
  iv) been admitted quickly although her case is not an emergency?

c) Do you think that Harley Street (line 25) is
  i)   the street where this particular hospital is?
  ii) a street famous for private specialists?
  iii) a street famous for specialists on the National Health Service?
  iv) a street full of hospitals which operate under the National Health Service?

d) Which statement represents Polly's view best (lines 17–27)
  i)   The rich always get better medical treatment.
  ii) The one advantage of paying for your treatment is that you receive better nursing care.
  iii) The advantage of private medicine is that you do not have to wait so long for relatively minor operations.
  iv) Paying for medical treatment brings no advantages at all.

e) What had Polly 'misjudged'? (line 60)
  i)   the nature of Meg's illness.
  ii) Meg's feelings about the operation.
  iii) the competence of the nurses.
  iv) the feelings of the nurses and doctors about the operation.

KEY **13** What do you think the following words and phrases mean in the context? Substitute another word or phrase.
a) *swellings* (line 4)
b) *consultants* (line 25)
c) *the hoi poloi* (line 35)
d) *locker* (line 40)
e) *the theatre* (line 57)
f) *just number three on the list* (line 62)
g) *mastectomy* (lines 63, 90)
h) *euphoria* (line 65)
i) *prowess* (line 67)
j) *hardened* (69)

It Takes All Sorts . . .

Section 1 'Er-Down-Under and 'Er-Up-Atop

What do you think?

1   Do you know anyone whom you would describe as an
eccentric? What is it that makes you describe this person in
this way?
The following headings might help you:
- how they look or dress
- what their house looks like
- how they behave to others
- habits they have
- opinions or beliefs they hold
- how they like to spend their time

2   Read the passage. The references in the margin will help
you to guess the meanings of the words in italics.

Granny Trill and Granny Wallon were rival ancients
and lived on each other's nerves, and their perpetual
enmity was like mice in the walls and absorbed much of
my early days. With their sickle-bent bodies, pale pink
eyes, and wild wisps of hedgerow hair, they looked to me
the very images of witches and they were also much
alike. In all their time as such close neighbours they
never exchanged a word. They communicated instead by
means of boots and brooms – jumping on floors and
knocking on ceilings. They referred to each other as
''Er-Down-Under' and ''Er-Up-Atop, the Varmint'; for
each to the other was an airy nothing, a local habitation
not fit to be named.
    For as long as I can remember, the lives of the two old
ladies continued to revolve in intimate enmity around
each other. Like cold twin stars, linked but divided, they
survived by a mutual balance. Both of them reached
back similarly in time, shared the same modes and
habits, the same sense of feudal order, the same rampag-
ing terrible God. They were far more alike than unalike,
and could not *abide* each other.

Look at lines 2–3, line 15

5

10

15

20

They arranged things therefore so that they never met. They used separate paths when they climbed the bank, they shopped on different days, they relieved themselves in different areas, and *staggered* their church-going hours. But each one knew always what the other was up to, and passionately disapproved. Granny Wallon worked at her *vats*, boiling and blending her wines; or crawled through her cabbages; or tapped on our windows, gossiped, complained, or sang. Granny Trill continued to rise in the dark, comb her waxen hair, sit out in the wood, chew, sniff, and suck up porridge, and study her almanac. Yet between them they sustained a mutual awareness based solely on ear and nostril. When Granny Wallon's wines boiled, Granny Trill had convulsions; when Granny Trill took snuff, Granny Wallon had strictures – and neither let the other forget it. So all day they listened, sniffed, and pried, rapping on

Look at lines 22-25

look at *boiling and blending her wines*

floors and ceilings, and prowled their rooms with hawk-
ing coughs, *chivvying* each other long-range. It was a
tranquil, bitter-pleasant life, perfected by years of cus-
tom; and to me they both seemed everlasting, deathless
crones of an eternal mythology; they had always been
somewhere there in the wainscot and I could imagine no
world without them.

Then one day, as Granny Trill was clambering out of
her wood, she stumbled and broke her hip. She went to
bed then for ever. She lay patient and yellow in a calico
coat, her combed hair fine as a girl's. She accepted her
doom without complaint, as though some giant authority
– Squire, father, or God – had ordered her there to
receive it.

'I knowed it was coming,' she told our Mother, 'after
that visitation. I saw it last week sitting at the foot of me
bed. Some person in white; I dunno . . .'

There was a sharp early rap on our window next
morning. Granny Wallon was bobbing outside.

'Did you hear him, missus?' she asked knowingly. 'He
been a-screeching around since midnight.' The death-
bird was Granny Wallon's private pet and messenger,
and she gave a skip as she told us about him. 'He called
three-a-four times. Up in them *yews*. Her's going, you
mark my words.'

And that day indeed Granny Trill died, whose bones
were too old to mend. Like a delicate pale bubble, blown
a little higher and further than the other girls of her
generation, she had floated just long enough for us to
catch sight of her, had *hovered* for an instant before our
eyes; and then had *popped* suddenly, and disappeared
for ever, leaving nothing on the air but a faint-drying
image and the tiniest cloud of snuff.

The little church was packed for her funeral, for the
old lady had been a landmark. They carried her coffin
along the edge of the wood and then drew it on a cart
through the village. Granny Wallon, dressed in shower
of jets followed some distance behind; and during the
service she kept to the back of the church and everybody
admired her.

All went well till the lowering of the coffin, when there
was a sudden and distressing commotion. Granny Wallon, ribbons flying, her bonnet awry, fought her way to
the side of the grave.

'It's a lie!' she screeched, pointing down at the coffin.
'That baggage were younger'n me! Ninety-five she says!
– ain't more'n ninety, an' I gone on ninety-two! It's a
crime you letting 'er go to 'er Maker got up in such
brazen lies! Dig up the old devil! Get 'er brass plate off!
It's insulting the living church! . . .'

Look at lines 8–10;
lines 35–37

Look at *without complaint,
authority . . . ordered*

Look at *bird* (line 60) and *up*.

Look at *bubble* (line 65),
floated (line 67)
Look at *suddenly, disappeared
for ever.*

90 They carried her away, struggling and crying, kicking out with her steel-sprung boots. Her cries grew fainter and were soon *obliterated* by the sounds of the grave-diggers' spades. The clump of clay falling on Granny Trill's coffin sealed her with her inscription for ever; for no one knew the truth of her age, there was no one old 95 enough to know.

Granny Wallon had triumphed, she had buried her rival; and now there was no more to do. From then on she faded and diminished daily, kept to her house and would not be seen. Sometimes we heard mysterious 100 knocks in the night, rousing and summoning sounds. But the days were silent, no one walked in the garden, or came skipping to claw at our window. The wine fires sank and died in the kitchen, as did the sweet fires of obsession.

105 About two weeks later, of no special disease, Granny Wallon gave up in her sleep. She was found on her bed, dressed in bonnet and shawl, and her signalling broom in her hand. Her open eyes were fixed on the ceiling in a listening stare of death. There was nothing in fact to 110 keep her alive; no cause, no bite, no fury. 'Er-Down-Under had joined 'Er-Up-Atop, having lived closer than anyone knew.

from *Cider with Rosie* by Laurie Lee, 1959

Look at *cries grew fainter* and *sounds of . . . spades*

3 Now look up the words in italics in a dictionary.

4 Which of the following words would you apply to the old ladies?
Put a tick in the relevant box below. Support your opinion by referring to the passage.

	Granny Wallon	Granny Trill
regular in her habits		
physically active		
sociable		
sad		
mild-tempered		
inquisitive		
religious		
superstitious		
lonely		

5 Look back at question 1. Would you say the old ladies were eccentric in any of these respects?

Section 2 A Prime Minister's Husband

*The passage below from a daily newspaper in October 1979
describes Denis Thatcher, husband of the British Prime Minister,
Margaret Thatcher.*

1   Read the text. If you find any references to unfamiliar things,
people or events, scan the texts on pages 168–9 for the
information you need, or use the clues given in the
margin: ↑ means 'look back in the text'; ↓ means 'look
forward in the text'.

It is Sunday lunchtime in the Home Counties and your host
for the weekend has taken you for a drink at his golf club.
After a while you are joined by a trim, balding man in his early
60s. He is wearing cavalry twill trousers and a chunky knit
5 sweater. His voice has a surprising drawl, as if the vowels
were having trouble escaping from his throat; it is the voice
developed by some middle-class officers during the war as a
medium for addressing the other ranks. However, he seems
amiable and without any pomposity; he suggests that it is
10 'time for a *tincture* or two' and inquires 'what's your *poison*?'

    a) *What* is he offering? ↑

Conversation does not range widely. The game of golf he
has just finished is exhaustively discussed as is a rugby
match he recently watched on television. There is a good deal
of talk about cars, big ends, petrol injection and so forth, and
15 he mentions his Rolls Royce. Other people at the bar begin
some routine banter about wives, who are referred to as 'the
boss' or, in mock cockney, 'the trouble and strife' but he does
not join in. He seems slightly in awe of his own wife.

There are two things which everyone who knows him says
20 about Denis Thatcher. The first is that he is extremely nice, a
view even shared by his first wife who was also called
Margaret. She said he was 'one of the kindest men I have
ever known'. The second is that he is perfectly captured in the
Private Eye column 'Dear Bill,' which is presented as a
25 fortnightly letter from Thatcher to one of his golfing chums and
drinking companions.

The column is so accurate about his language and tastes
that there is some gossip in Westminster that there is a *Mole*
in the Thatcher camp who reports to the author, John Wells.

    b) A 'Mole' here is
      i) A dull person
      ii) a spy
      iii) a dishonest person
      iv) a shortsighted person

30 Recent columns about the trip to Lusaka and a disastrous
holiday on the island of Islay have particularly delighted those
in the know. One associate says that the real summer holiday
was actually worse than the Private Eye description. 'It's
exaggerated, of course, and it doesn't catch his real affection
35 for Margaret, but it really does give a fair description of the
way he talks'.

He accompanies her on most of her set-piece trips, and
during the election could be seen constantly with her, a
respectful few feet behind. As she plunged into crowds he
40 would cry 'get her out of there or there'll be an accident!' On

the embarrassing occasion when sne cradled a new-born calf he said grimly 'If we're not careful, we'll have a dead calf on our hands.'

Only rarely does he let his own views become public. At the Tory conference this year one speaker praised the arrival of the South African mixed rugby team. The delegates burst into loud applause, as did Denis until he noticed that the whole of the Cabinet was silent, when he too suddenly froze.

Like a lot of people with strong political views, he is not terribly interested in politics as such. He has an almost unbounded admiration for his wife, and will excitedly praise a speech or a Commons performance. Then, realising that he is not the most unbiased judge, he will add diffidently 'you have to remember, I'm a *fan*'.

They met in 1949 when he had been invited to *make up the numbers* at a dinner on the night she was adopted Tory candidate for Dartford. He gave her a lift back to London that night, and they began their courting more or less in secret. Their engagement leaked out just before polling day in the 1951 election.

He was 10½ years older than her and was joint general manager of the family firm, the Atlas Preservative Company of Erith. This was the subject of successive takeover and was the reason why he ended his business career on the board of a Burmah Oil subsidiary. His compulsory retirement at the age of 60 was within two months of her election as Tory leader.

Friends say that he was *'staggered'* at her *elevation*, which came as suddenly to him as to everyone else including her. 'You must remember that Denis is the kind of chap who would never imagine that a woman might become leader of the Conservative party,' one associate says. 'He was shattered. For a year he was like a man in a trance: he simply didn't have the faintest idea of what to do.'

He now seems to enjoy the round of trips and has achieved a certain social relaxation. At factories and businesses he will linger behind occasionally to chat with evident genuine interest.

He is, those close to Mrs Thatcher say, highly influential but not in a direct political sense. In other words she doesn't ask for his views on immigration or the unions or monetary policy, though she might consult him on business matters. But he is good at persuading her to delegate.

She also depends on him at times for judgements about people. The Tory party runs to a large extent on the kind of opinions formed in the clubs and smoking rooms. It's a world which she knows nothing about, and her ignorance has led to some woeful choices as personal aides. 'But Denis can spot *a wrong 'un'* one MP says, 'and she seems to trust his advice about people.'

At home he is entirely supportive, buoying her up at her lowest moments. 'When she gets back for those famous little weeps he's always there to console her,' one former aide says. George Gardiner's biography of her quotes him at the time of the 'milk-snatcher' row which caused her intense unhappiness and anguish. He said 'to hell with this, why not pack it up?' though she gritted her teeth and carried on.

c) of whose? ↑
d) This refers to the dinner-party convention of
   i)   having a large number of guests
   ii) having more men than women
   iii) having an equal number of men and women
   iv) having a man to help the hostess
e) What does *'staggered'* mean here? ↓
f) What kind of elevation?

g) What does this mean? ↑

100 Visitors to the various Thatcher homes say that he plays a Johnnie Craddock role, fixing the drinks and the wine while she does the food. He is successful in this task: 'Denis has a sharp eye for the *refill*,' one guest says appreciatively.

One visitor complained tentatively that cooking dinner was perhaps not the best use of the Leader of the Opposition's time 'Oh don't stop her, it's her form of therapy,' he explained.
105 But he is not spared her infuriating habit of *putting people down* in small ways.

Another dinner guest, this time in Kent, says that Denis was pouring the wine at lunch and remarked 'I think you'll rather like this claret.' She replied crisply 'how do you know? You only bought it at the *off-licence* this morning.'
110 'He's had to learn how to be married to the Prime Minister after 28 years of being just married to Margaret Thatcher,' a friend says, 'and there's no doubt he's learning fast. She doesn't like being disagreed with, and so instead of just leaping in with his opinion, he'll start by saying 'you're
115 probably right my dear, you usually are . . . . .'

'It has been a very happy marriage,' one close associate says, 'and he deserves great credit for keeping the family together and united. Sometimes I think she might have preferred someone a bit more dashing, a bit more politically
120 sophisticated – . But really she couldn't have done any better than she has.'

from *The Guardian*, 1979

h) of what? ↑

i) What does this mean? An example follows ↓

j) a shop selling what? ↑

A writer has a specific audience in mind. If he writes for an audience in the UK, for example, he may presume that they share the same background of cultural, historical and political information as he does, and he will make references to this background which he does not need to explain.

Readers who do not share this background may find these references obscure. This is especially true of political commentary, political satire and literature.

Sometimes it is possible to make a guess at the significance of the reference by studying the context. Otherwise the only solution is simply to find out more about the background from other sources.

Conservative Leaders of the last 20 years

After the Suez fiasco of 1956 it was Harold Macmillan who led Britain through the relatively prosperous fifties, and who remained, after his resignation in 1963, a respected elder statesman of the Conservative Party. Sir Alec Douglas-Home succeeded briefly but it was Edward Heath who, in 1965 on Douglas-Home's resignation became Conservative leader, who signalled a radical change in style. For Heath, unlike his predecessors, was not an aristocrat. Until then the Tory leadership had been inevitably associated with privilege, with the world of exclusive gentlemens' clubs, large country houses and grouse shooting in Scotland every August.

Edward Heath came from a working class background – unheard of for the party of Winston Churchill and other members of the great aristocratic families. Heath is likely to be remembered primarily for taking Britain into the Common Market in 1973 a move consolidated by the British Public in the 1975 referendum under a Labour government. Margaret Thatcher emerged as a rival to Heath's leadership of the party, following his humiliating defeat, after less than 4 years of government, in the General Election in January 1974.

Springboks Arrive

South Africa's first mixed rugby team arrived in Britain today surrounded by controversy. The question that is being asked is how far the team is genuinely racially mixed, consisting as it does of exactly equal numbers of whites, coloureds and blacks. The team manager . . .

THATCHER MILK-SNATCHER!

Secretary of State for education Margaret Thatcher yesterday announced that school milk provision for the over-sevens will be cut. When questioned further, Mrs Thatcher said

Golf originated in Scotland where it has for centuries borne the title of the Royal and Ancient Game, the headquarters of the Royal and Ancient Golf Club being situated at St. Andrews on the east coast. The sport is played throughout Britain and there are golf courses in the vicinity of most towns, some of which are owned by local authorities. The main event of the golfing year is the Open Golf Championship; other important events include the Walker Cup match for amateurs and the Ryder Cup match for professionals, both of which are played between Britain and the United States.

ELECTION 1979

MAGGIE DOES IT!

Fletcher's Book of Rhyming Slang

Glossary

Tea leaf Thief
Teapot lid, or God forbid Kid (child)
Tea, two, and a bloater Motor
Thomas Tilling Shilling
Tin tack Sack
Tin tank Bank
Tit for tat Hat
Tit willow Pillow
Tod Sloan, or Jack Jones, or Pat Malone Own (alone)
Tom and Dick Sick
Tommy Tucker Supper
Touch me on the knob Bob (shilling)
Trouble and strife Wife
Tumble down the sink Drink
Turtle doves Gloves
Two-thirty Dirty
Typewriter Fighter

I asked Mrs Thatcher whether she didn't sometimes find the burdens of her job too difficult to bear. "Well, I must admit," she said, "when things get particularly hard I just have to have a little cry to myself when I get home. It helps, you know."

A sermon in slang

(Given by the Rev McVitie Price, vicar of the church of St Cain and Abel, Hampstead Heath)

How many of you here tonight will know that Cain and Abel, and Hampstead Heath, are cockney rhyming slang. *Cain and Abel* means table, and *Hampstead Heath* means teeth. We are glad to welcome tonight a large group of cockney worshippers to Evensong: and it is to them that I wish to address my sermon. I want to tell you a story. A long time ago, in the days of the Israelites, there lived a poor man. He had no *trouble and strife* – she had run off with a *tea leaf* some years before

Although it is possible to practise golf shots on an indoor driving range, the game is essentially an outdoor one, played on a golf course or links.

Modern golf courses vary in length from 6,000 to 7,000 yards and have 18 holes each of about 100 to 600 yards. The first shot on each hole is made from a level teeing ground or 'tee' and in playing this shot the ball may be placed on a small plastic or wooden peg, also called a 'tee'. The holes are designed so that a good player should hole out in either three, four, or five shots, according to the length of the hole. Most holes are fours, that is, the player should drive his ball more than 200 yards along the fairway, strike his second shot on to the putting green and hole out with two putts.

Television Programmes

BBC 1

6.05 pm Fanny and Johnnie Craddock: Home Entertaining

6.35 Nationwide

UNIT TEN

The following text is an extract from the satirical magazine 'Private Eye' referred to in the article above. 'Dear Bill' is an imaginary letter from Denis Thatcher to an imaginary friend 'Bill'. This particular letter describes the Summer holiday on the Isle of Islay mentioned in the preceding article (though the island is referred to here as the 'Isle of Muck'). Denis Thatcher is describing his first experience of grouse-shooting.

2 Read the text. Use the questions in the margin to help you. If you need other information, scan the texts on pages 168–9. Don't expect to understand everything in the text; in a satirical passage like this even native-speakers would have difficulties. Some words are explained in footnotes.

10 **Downing Street**
Whitehall

Dear Bill, 22/8/79

We got back from Scotland at seven o'clock this morning, and I'm still feeling pretty groggy. However much I hate *this place*, a week on the Isle of Muck or whatever it's called makes it seem like a positive
5 Shangri-La.[1]

a) What place is meant? ↑

I'm very confused about the whole thing, but it seems all to have been Macmillan's fault. He told the Boss that the done thing was a week in Scotland every August going after the grouse. Damn silly idea if you
10 ask me, especially when all good men and true are out on the links at the Royal and Ancient.

I never caught the name of our host, but he had a handle[2] to his name and used to be something very big in M's lot. He lives in the most ghastly
15 God-forsaken castle on this frightful island covered with boulders and fir trees and not so much as a putting green in sight, somewhere out in the *Celtic* twilight you get to in a little aeroplane from Glasgow.

b) Why is the word *Celtic* chosen? ↑

You know me, Bill. I can't tell a grouse from a bloody
20 emu and I haven't fired a shot in anger since we went on that *TA*[3] *booze-up*. However, when I asked to be let off games, M. got unbelievably shirty. Down to the

c) Do you think this refers to
   i) an all-male drinking session
   ii) a game of golf
   iii) a dinner-party
   iv) a wedding

---

1 paradise   2 title   3 Territorial Army (voluntary)

gun-room by the ear, kitted out in His Lordship's
spare waterproofs and a damn silly hat with a lot of
25 flies stuck in it, all several sizes too big. I ask you,
Bill.

Everything they say *about the Scots* is *absolutely true*.
Lord Whatsisname's idea of a *snort* looks as though a
gnat's[4] pissed in the bottom of the glass. Luckily prior
30 to the Shooting Expedition I struck up a great friendship
with the Factotum, and he loaned me an awfully
ingenious flask that fitted down the gumboot, filled
with his own favourite *tipple*, made at a secret still up
in the hills somewhere.

35 Anyway, picture the scene. Rain bucketing down, His
Lordship's reachmedowns leaking like the proverbial
colander. M. got up in her best tweeds with a macintosh
hat, deep in conversation with *His Nibs*.

After an eternity of waiting, barbaric cries from the
40 undergrowth, a few bedraggled *boiler fowl* came
winging in, barely visible in the mist. Ben the ghillie[5]
strikes me heavily between the shoulder blades and
grunts something in *Gaelic* which I fail to catch, fowling-
piece[6] discharges, into the butts[7] Thoughts of D.T. at
45 this juncture need not be described.

Scene Two. Another part of the forest. Same set-up:
wind up to Force Nine, rain now horizontal, specs
entirely steamed up, Wellingtons filling up nicely. A
few sheep cropping the rocks. Lord Thingummybob
50 plainly in his element, talking to M. about the old days
with Winston. At that point, Bill, something snapped.
No one was watching, so I gave Ben five quid and the
gun, and buggered off back to the castle.

Hot bath, dry togs, large noggin of firewater, and
55 settled down in Back Nursery to watch International
Golf. Much to my relief my absence did not appear
to have registered with the *Big White Chief*, or indeed
mine host. Ghastly dinner of boiled birds, all bones
and *buckshot,* no *fizz* in sight. Meanwhile Lord
60 Whatsisname is telling M. how much he approves of
axeing the students, far too many long-haired clever
dicks about the place as it is. High time students'

d) What do they say? — Example ↓
e) Slang for what? ↓

f) *Tipple* is
    i)   something to eat
    ii) something alcoholic
    iii) a gun
    iv) reading material

g) *Who* is *His Nibs?* ↑

h) Refers to what? ↑

i) A language spoken
    where? ↑

j) Refers to whom? ↑
k) Why were they filled with
    buckshot? ↑
l) What does he expect
    besides food?

---

4 a very small insect   5 servant
6 gun   7 shooting range

grants were cut out altogether, and they were all turned over to potato picking.

65   What else is new, you ask? Well, everybody's getting very steamed up about the Common Market, as is only right and proper.

M. knows my views on the subject, i.e. that we should never have got mixed up with the bally thing

70   in the first place. It was obvious from the start that *the Frog* in the street wasn't going to jump at our stuff, give or take the odd woolly[8] from Marks and Sparks, and they can always come over on the boat train if they want one of those. So what's the point?

75   Personally I blame that damn fool Heath.

Reggie says there's a rather nice little indoor driving range near London Airport. Would that be a possible venue to *bob back a few scoops*?

Yours, through a glass darkly,

Denis

from *Private Eye*, 1979

m)   *The Frog* is English slang for
    i)   the Germans
    ii)   the Australians
    iii) the French
    iv)   the Japanese

n)   What might he do besides practise golf?

8 pullover

Section 3 'I Was an Ordinary Housewife Until . . .'

The following is a true story called 'My Life on Sealand' from a woman's magazine.

1   As you read note the words and phrases in italics. They suggest certain things to a British reader, which are not directly revealed in the text. What do they suggest to you?

MY LIFE ON SEALAND

PRINCESS JOAN BATES

This rusting lump of metal 140 feet by 40 feet out in the grey North Sea is the place Joan Bates considers her home and country.

What do you think Mrs Bates is doing in the North Sea?

Calling herself Princess of Sealand the former Southend housewife lives there under the protection of armed guards, and uninvited visitors are repelled or imprisoned. It's the year's most bizarre story. What is Mrs Bates' life like, and what is she up to? With a protective invitation—and her passport—Ruth Brotherhood flew to Sealand to find out.

The helicopter hovered in a great blue sky. "There she is," said the pilot, "that's Sealand." Below, in the vast grey waters of the North Sea, a few boats bobbed. Then, small at first but getting larger, a tiny tin island rose into view.

Princess Joan of Sealand turned in her seat and smiled at me. "Nearly there," she said, and beamed down onto what she considers her beloved homeland—a lump of iron 140 by 40 feet.

She had the *gracious air of an English lady about to show you round her stately home.* Then I saw the guns, all pointed at our bubble in the sky, and the day-trip atmosphere vanished.

Why were there guns on the island do you think?

173

Below lurched armed guards, black against the sun, ready to snipe at anything foreign – including, possibly, us. The self-styled Princess waved regally.
40 "They know this helicopter – we always use it. But I sit in the front just to make sure they recognise us," she said.

If the gunman slipped, pulled his trigger and shot me dead, there would
45 be nothing anyone could do about it –

Why would there be nothing anyone could do?

– because
Sealand is literally a law unto itself. This rusting World War Two fortress that Joan Bates and her husband Roy call home sits safely out of British ter-
50 ritorial waters, seven miles off the coast of Harwich.

They're not there
for the sea view

In 1967 the couple declared it a princi-
55 pality and have "ruled" there as the Prince and Princess of Sealand ever since. Are they mad? Harmless eccentrics – or what? I took the helicopter trip to this curiosity to find out. The
60 ominous iron platform loomed nearer, standing firm on two enormous cylindrical legs that plummeted to the depths.

The wind lashed at our hair, making
65 us reel when we at last stepped out. There was no shelter, no protective rail around the heli-pad. It was bleak, bare and unwelcoming.

The Bates didn't choose this white
70 elephant because they liked the sea view,

Why *did* they choose it?

but because
it was the biggest and most brilliant financial investment they could think of.
75 Being outside British law also means being away from the taxman and financial controls. If their plans work out, in a few years' time they will have trans-
80 formed their iron hulk into a hotel and leisure complex complete with casinos, shops, and even factories.

Incredible, yes. Impossible, no. At least, not according to the Princess, a slick, fast-talking lady who doesn't
85 expect raised eyebrows as she gives her rundown of Sealand's future.

"Millions of pounds have been invested in this venture, by busi-nessmen from all over the world," she
90 explained in her neat, clipped voice. "We ourselves have put a vast fortune into the project from businesses we owned and have now sold.

"We intend to build three gigantic
95 hexagonal modules in Germany containing everything we need from hotels to factories, and then float them over here. The idea is they will slot on to Sealand. The first section should be
100 completed by the spring.

"When it's finished, we will reclaim land from the sea.

Why are they able to do this?

We have territorial
waters just like anyone else and plan to reclaim 3,000 acres in 18 months."
105 The Bates go to extraordinary lengths to protect their investment – they won't let anyone near it without express permission from a member of
110 the family. I'd been half expecting a merry crowd of rosy eccentrics. Now the Sealanders were beginning to look like a *bunch of 007-type individuals* who really meant business.

115 It wasn't a game – the frisking was for real. The photographer and I had been searched at Southend airport. Now – apparently in case we'd slipped any
120 hand grenades or sub-machine guns into our bags in transit – we were searched again. The atmosphere was menacing –

What was it about the atmosphere that was *menacing*?

Molotov cocktails in ketchup bottles lined the deck walls.
125 "We have to be careful," the Princess explained. "Other people now see the potential of the island and would like to take it over.

130 "It has all been done properly – we had our coins made in a Mexican mint, and our stamps by genuine stamp makers in Italy. We haven't actually used either yet, but we have sold samples for people to keep.

135 **A 24-hour armed guard**

"We have guards on watch 24 hours a day. Even so, there have been several attempts to take over the island."
140 To underline the point, the gunmen paraded a "prisoner" in front of us –

What sort of *prisoner* was he, do you think?

– a German lawyer called Gernot Putz. Princess Joan caught my wave of sympathy and
145 snarled: "I don't feel anything for him except disgust. He tried to take over my island, my home."

The anxious-looking Putz stood sheepishly in the wind. He had been
150 taken prisoner after a dramatic attempt

to take over the island with a band of other men, and was being punished for it.

"It was greed that made them do it,"
155 said Mrs Bates. "They realised the value of the island. But they only held it for one day before my husband and son took it back again."

Putz has since been released, but not
160 before completing an eight-week sentence at *their majesties' pleasure*. My visit grew more bizarre by the minute. "This way for passport control," the Princess announced, tapping elegantly
165 across the bleak iron in her *Gucci shoes*. She looked chic in a silk shirt and well-cut trousers. "You have got your passports with you, haven't you?"

Was she joking or not?

Do you think she was joking?

I de-
170 cided Princess Joan appeared to take the sovereignty business very seriously. I quickly found my passport. Looking up, I saw her disappearing down a ver-
175 tical ladder that led to the living area. Gingerly I followed her down wooden rungs and along a cold metal corridor to the radio room, one of several rooms tucked under the top platform. It was
180 suddenly a lot more welcoming.

What made a woman who so obviously loved the luxuries of life choose to live on so barren an island – and for so long? "I love it here," she insisted.
185 "I'm at peace. There's so much to do developing the island all the time – finding out about the legal side, company registration and banking – it's a massive project."
190 When Mrs Bates set off for the island 13 years ago in a smelly old fishing boat, she didn't anticipate staying so long.

In those days, the wasting fortress was called Rough's Tower and had been left to the mercy of the wind and sea since the war because the British Government didn't know what to do with it.

Then Roy Bates had a brainwave. An extremely successful businessman who owned several factories as well as Britain's biggest inshore fishing fleet he'd had his eye on the tower for some time.

Every day as he looked at the rusting hulk that once housed 200 marines, he formulated more of his plan.

He employed lawyers, offering to double their money if they could give him one reason why he could not take over the tower. They weren't able to think of one. So on the dark and wintry Christmas Eve of 1965, Mr Bates arrived home windswept and chapped-cheeked to tell his wife he'd put men and tools on the island. "I wasn't surprised," said Mrs Bates. "I've learned not to be surprised at anything my husband does."

In October she left her comfortable house on the Southend seafront and headed for Rough's Tower. "I was an ordinary housewife until that day," she told me. "I didn't work – I have two children who are now grown up – but at that time I was a great believer in the old-fashioned idea of mother being at home.

"When we first came here we had very little. Now you can ask for *bay leaves or champagne* and we have it. The best thing to arrive I think was my electric blanket. I'm perfectly happy now. We have our own small boat, which is very fast, but we often hire boats to come out with provisions when one of us is in England."

Beneath Mrs Bates's room stood six more like it getting rustier and rustier. They were all used to accommodate marines – 20 to 30 in each. I climbed to the very bottom, about 50 feet down to the sea bed, accompanied by an armed guard.

It was cold, echoey, dry – still piled with the original shell cases. It seemed indestructible. Putz, the German, had been thrown down there in the early days of his imprisonment.

Upstairs, Mrs Bates was cooking spaghetti bolognaise in the tatty, depressing kitchen. There were two electric cookers and a row of shabby, rusty pots. It didn't look Mrs Bates's style. Perhaps she wasn't actually there all the time? She *insisted rather loudly* that she was: "I live here, this is my home. I have no other. I do go abroad a lot on business and also for pleasure, but my home is here.

"When the complex is built I shall have my own accommodation with a lovely bath. It will be a wonderful place. The people who work in the factories will live in flats we provide. There will be taxes to pay – to us, of course – but nowhere near as high as in England.

"If someone wants to build a factory, we will give them permission. The Prince is the law here, he can say what goes."

from *Woman*, 1978

2 Make notes to summarise what is said here about the island.
   – the past history of the island
   – protecting the island
   – the Bates' plans for the future of the island

KEY **3** Some phrases in the text are printed in italics. The following statements express the meaning of these phrases in another way. Match the statements with the phrases. For example:

Mrs Bates has aspirations to grandeur –
She had the gracious air of an English lady about to show you round her stately home

a) The writer does not believe all of Mrs Bates' claims . . . . .

b) Mr and Mrs Bates are ruthless in their dealings with people
   i) . . . . .
   ii) . . . . .

c) Mr and Mrs Bates are arrogant in their claims to absolute power over the island . . . .

d) Mrs Bates' appearance suggests that she may not spend all her time on the island . . . .

e) Mrs Bates tries to give the impression of having a comfortable life on the island . . . .

Section 4 Two Portraits

The following extracts are from articles published in a Sunday newspaper magazine. In each, a journalist interviews a famous person to find out how they spend a day.

The first article is about Ronald Biggs, still wanted by the British police for his part in the Great Train Robbery in 1963 in which several million pounds was stolen. After serving 2 years of a 30-year jail sentence in Britain, he escaped and went to Australia where he secretly rejoined his wife and three children. Later, he went alone to Brazil, where he now lives, in a small fishing village.

KEY **1** As you read, note down words or phrases in the passage which are connected with
   a) money (e.g. income)
   b) alcoholic drink
   c) criminals, or criminal activity

With no regular income, many people think Biggs still has a suitcase with the odd 1963-style fiver in it to draw on. Not so. Life on a beach in Brazil is still very cheap. He pays £80 a month rent: windfalls from Australian television, English punk rockers and French publishers cover most of this and he taps his visitors for funds, hand on heart, face straight and eyes-a-giggle.

I rise at 7 a.m. I sleep naked. I have a pot of tea – Lipton's best Indian – and two fried eggs with a rasher of bacon. I like my eggs sunnyside up and my bacon crisp. When I can, I have toast and marmalade.

I lunch soon after noon on freijoada, a bean stew I prepare myself which looks like something the dog threw up on a raw morning but tastes fine. I take my freijoada with hot peppers on my verandah: my son usually settles for ketchup indoors.

I had to give up the maid three years ago – simply couldn't afford her, old chap, you know how it is – so I spend a lot of the day pottering round the villa and the garden. I do all the cleaning and washing for the two of us. Any free time I spend in the sea – it's only 300 yards away – or the local bar on the beach.

I dine at 7 p.m. on eggs and toast. If in funds, I'll have a few nightcaps of imported Scotch, but it's £28 a bottle so that's not often. I'm more likely to write poetry or read. Right now I'm reading John Fowles's *Daniel Martin*. My favourite author is Marcel Proust. At 11 o'clock I get out of my swimming trunks and go to bed. If the mosquitoes are bad I spray Autun body mist on the sheets.

The craziest thing is that I'm not allowed to work. As a young crook in England they were always telling me to work. Now I want to, they won't let me. So I spend a lot of time lounging about and looking after Mike. His mother came over in January to see him. I've taken him to meet his grandparents in Maranhão. But now I'm divorced from Charmian, I hope to be able to give him my name.

It's awkward, though. I don't officially exist in Brazil. They still know me as Mike Haynes, the name I came off the boat with. I do the whole one-parent family bit. Washing up, tidying, shopping.

We seem to be on the tourist circuit. Just before you arrived, two landladies from Blackpool came here to pay their respects. They said that coming to Brazil and not seeing Biggsie was like going to Egypt and not seeing the Pyramids. An Englishman who had done nine months for corrupting a police officer was here between Christmas and Carnival. He runs a restaurant in Cornwall and he was discussing a winter holiday with his wife when he said, 'I know, let's go to Brazil and see Ronnie Biggs.'

There are lots of Germans, very keen on autographs. And New Zealanders, and stacks of Australians. I've just done a TV film for Australia, and an introduction for a cook-book. And of course Slipper of the Yard came four years ago in January 1974 to arrest me. He was so confident of success that he had booked me a first-class one-way ticket on British Caledonian.

I'd been at my lowest. I was missing Charmian and the kids, missing Australia, even missing England. I was tired of running. The money was long gone. I was living in a crummy flat doing house conversions and painting jobs. I thought if I gave myself up, went back and said 'OK, it's me folks,' they'd take it into account with the sentence.

So I got a friend who was going back to London to fix a deal with the *Express*. He said 'Ronnie, you're mad, but I'll see what the *Express* will come up with for the story.' Thirty-five grand. To send to Charmian in Australia. Not bad – but then it was a bloody good story. I was all fixed up and ready to go – and who turns up on Copacabana beach? Slipper of the Yard.

Now that wasn't what Biggsie had in mind at all. I wanted to go back sure, but as the guy who'd gone straight and done the decent. Not hauled back in cuffs like a screaming felon.

The morning they came for me, my bird, Raimunda, told me she was pregnant. Now, on the normal sort of day, that would have made an impression. But not with Slipper and the whole of Fleet Street after me.

I found myself in a cell, feeling very sour, with a couple of Rio taxi drivers who shared the bedclothes with me – gave me the sports pages to sleep under.

There I am, all upset, and one of these blokes says to me, 'If you could pretend to have got a Brazilian girl pregnant, they can't extradite you. Only deport you.' I said, 'Look fellas, you're not going to believe this, but . . .'

Superintendent Slipper duly departed Rio minus Biggs. Biggs's next run-in was with the Royal Navy. He met some ratings from the frigate Danae, in Rio on a courtesy visit in April last year.

They insisted I go aboard for a few pots. I had to cross the cruiser Tiger to get to the Danae. Lots of Nelsonian blind eyes. We're having a quiet jar when a fuss starts up and Biggsie exits pronto.

I get on well with the neighbours round here, but one day I came back from the beach to find that my record player had gone. I was bloody mad. And then I thought, well, that's justice. They have an expression here – *ladrão que rouber ladrão tem cen anos de perdão*. A thief who steals from a thief has 100 years of pardon.

In fact, the silly bastard who nicked it tried to sell it in a bar where I drink and the barman recognised it and I had it back in a day.

I don't see myself getting back to Britain. If you offered me Britain or Brazil now, I'd choose Brazil. But I do not believe that I shall ever go to prison again. I am quite satisfied in my own mind that I am rehabilitated. Why put me back in prison in a criminal environment when I've been straight for so long?

What do they want to do – make a criminal out of me?

from *The Sunday Times*, 1978

Check your understanding

2 Choose the best answer.
   a) Where does Biggs get money to live on?
      i) He still has some of the money he stole in 1963.
      ii) He has an income from a regular job.
      iii) He writes poetry, plays for television, songs for pop musicians and articles for French publishers.
      iv) He gets it from various sources, including asking visitors for money.

   b) Why doesn't Biggs officially exist in Brazil?
      i) The police don't know he's there.
      ii) He's in hiding from the authorities.
      iii) He's supposed to be in an English jail.
      iv) He entered the country under a different name.

   c) How did Biggs see himself returning to England in 1974?
      i) Secretly.
      ii) Of his own free will.
      iii) With a lot of publicity.
      iv) Under arrest.

   d) Why did Slipper of the Yard go back without Biggs?
      i) He couldn't find him.
      ii) Biggs decided not to give himself up.
      iii) Brazilian police arrested him first.
      iv) The father of a Brazilian child cannot be extradited under Brazilian law.

   e) Why was Biggs invited aboard the *Danae* when it was docked in Rio?
      i) The sailors were just being friendly, offering a fellow-countryman a few drinks.

ii)   The ship had been sent specially to take him back
      to England under protection.

iii) The sailors were trying to trick him into being
      captured by them.

iv)   Biggs persuaded the sailors to do it
      so he could avoid the Brazilian authorities.

3   Now read the next extract about a famous actor

Tom Baker was born in Liverpool. His mother was a chamber-maid in an hotel and his father was a punter. He spent six years as a monk in a very strict order in France and left when he decided it was time "for the pubs and women". He first caught the eye of the public when the played Rasputin on television. He is now known and acknowledged as being the best of the actors who have played 'Doctor Who' in the legendary series. Tom Baker is a great believer in always travelling light. Note the toothbrush which he carries in his top pocket.

You could say that yesterday was fairly typical of a day in my life when we're not recording *Dr Who*. I woke up at 5.15 a.m. in a brown cork-lined room in Soho and then got into bed. But where am I? I dreamt about a tall, thin woman, but who is she? I suffer recurring images of tall skinny ladies. They look so good and really release all those fantasies. I woke up again and it was 6.10 a.m. I got up and began the daily process of dragging my feet to their final destination at night: I was hit by terrible waves of anxiety. The feeling of loneliness that smacks of self-pity. I drank a glass of water and felt for a toothbrush wondering where on earth I was. If I'd had a radio I would have put it on but it's too early, of course, for Radio 3. The anxiety persisted and I thought suicide is the answer. I got out of bed and looked at some eletrical flex. The ceiling was too low. How could I have hanged myself in a room only 5ft 10in. high? I gave up the idea, found a radio and switched it on. I heard some news and my anxieties instantly increased. Then I took a sly bath and checked my pockets. I found £114 and a pair of clean underpants and began to walk confidently.

All you really need for confidence is always to have a toothbrush and a hundred or two in your pocket. Usually when I wake in a strange house I like to get out before *they* wake up without leaving a single clue that I've been there. I went out and bought *The Times* and read the obituaries. There was no pleasure in them for me. Then I went of Valerie's in Old Compton Street for some coffee and tried to do the crossword puzzle. At 9.30 a.m. it was 'voice-over' time at a Soho recording studios. I performed for Norsca Foam Baths and they seemed pleased by my enthusiasm. I find it quite interesting to try and give credibility to a blatant sell. After the voiceover I signed an autograph for a child called Donal-bain and a few mintues later I signed one for a child called Wee Peng. There is a constant stream of hallos, nods and autographs. All very good medicine for anxiety. At midday, I went to the Yorkminster for a drink in the hope of seeing Eva Johansen and also hoping for the miracle that I might see someone I'd never seen before. I bought 10 pence worth of money from Gaston. [Gaston Berlemont the guvnor, charges 10p to cash a cheque.] It's the cheapest cash in town. After lunch in the Paparazzi – I usually eat the calf's liver and bacon – I went to a rehearsal for the BBC at North Acton. It's Kafkaville. I worked for a bit as a paid fantasist and it went quite well. On the train back to town I tried to learn some lines but there was a girl sitting opposite with a transistor. It was playing *I Am Your Automatic Lover.* Curiously I felt embarrassed. I wonder why? Another wave of anxiety swept over me. At teatime I arrived at The Colony Room Club and Francis Bacon bought me a large gin and tonic. The anxieties went away and the conviction grew that I had something to say on any subject. At 5.30 p.m., after a vaguely lunatic afternoon, I went back to the Yorkminster in the hope of finding some conversation before bedlam set in. Then I met the beautiful Moe Jenns and invited her to Madisons in Camden Lock. Dinner and cabaret at 9.00 p.m. costs £9. But before that I went to Gerry's Club and played some pool and lost. Dee Lynch, the manageress, embraced me and that was nice. Then I talked about cancer for a while with a man who had a bad cough. After that I was introduced by an actor acquaintance to a Welsh school teacher who said he was delighted to meet me. We shook hands and he promptly had a heart attack. Astonishingly enough there were two doctors in the house – well, three if you included me – and the poor man was carried out and put into an ambulance. And then we embarked on a conversation about having heart attacks.

After that we went on to Madisons. The cabaret that was appearing there was called Gotham and they were very merry. But they declined into barber shop trios which was disappointing.

I tottered off back to Gerry's Club and had several nightcaps and felt relieved that another day had passed. As usual there was someone there with whom to discuss crumpet and the meaning of life.

I then popped into Ronnie Scott's club and sat there at the bar self-consciously affecting a knowledge of jazz that I haven't got. The recurring image of tall, skinny ladies came back and they still looked good.

from The Sunday Times, 1978

Check your understanding

KEY

4 Choose the best alternative

a) Tom Baker carries a toothbrush with him
   i) because he hates heavy suitcases.
   ii) because he has no home.
   iii) because he visits friends a lot.
   iv) because he's never sure where he's going to sleep.

b) He didn't commit suicide
   i) because he wanted to listen to the radio.
   ii) because he couldn't work out how to do it.
   iii) because he was too tall to hang himself.
   iv) because he wasn't serious about it in the first place.

c) On the train back to town he tried to
   i) practise a selling technique.
   ii) learn his part for an acting job.
   iii) learn nice things to say to people.
   iv) remember something from a textbook.

d) He gets rid of anxieties
   i) by thinking of other things instead.
   ii) by socialising.
   iii) by drinking.
   iv) by dreaming of women.

e) During his second visit to Gerry's club, Tom Baker discusses 'crumpet', which here, means:
   i) sexually desirable women.
   ii) political matters.
   iii) sports results.
   iv) food.

KEY TO THE EXERCISES

UNIT ONE

Section 1

9 a) very little space, smelly, washing hanging inside, lonely

b) sharing facilities can cause rows, sharing bills can cause rows, lack of privacy

c) landlady is like a mother

d) person who is not naturally sociable

e) person who values privacy

10 iv)

Section 2

1 The most suitable advertisements are:

●**WILLESDEN GREEN,** 5th person, own room in large mixed house with garden. Non-smoker. £31 pcm.
●**MALE 24**+ share house, E7. Own room. £8 p.w. Pref non-smoker.
OWN LARGE ROOM in shared house with lounge, colour TV, kitchen, garden etc. Near countryside, near Orpington. £39 pm.

3, 5 ABBREVIATIONS

b	bathroom
CH or ch	central heating
cmfts	comforts
CTV	colour television
dec	decorated
Dep	deposit
ea.	each
excl.	excluding, exclusive
F	female
fac	facilities
furn	furnished
g/f	ground floor
K	kitchen
lux	luxury
M	male
mxd	mixed, i.e. men and women
O/R	own room
p.w.	per week
p.c.m.	per calendar month
prof.	professional
recep.	reception room, i.e. living room
Refs	references

rm.	room
s/c	self-contained
Sh	share
stn.	station
unfurn.	unfurnished

4 **NW9.** 2 share rm mxd hse. £11 pw. Ring ⟨...⟩
N13 2 girls to share rm, mxd flat. £48.50 inc pcm. ⟨...⟩ ⟨...⟩ at 10 am.
CHISWICK
W4 s/c flats. 2 twin bedrms lnge, dining rm. k & b, for 4 sharers. £12.50 pw each. Tel ⟨...⟩
N21 2sh hse. £14 pw. ⟨...⟩ Fri 6–8.

6 **HAMPSTEAD.** Luxury furnished flat. 2 dble bedrms, colour TV. Phone serviced etc. £85 pw. ⟨...⟩
KENS. SW10. Nicely furnished 2 dble bedrms., living/dining room, kitchen, bathroom. Colour TV. Telephone, etc. £80 pw. Telephone ⟨...⟩

Section 3

4 e) something a building can stand high on
something between two streams

f) people in a team
people employed on a job
people doing restoration work in the castle

g) something situated by the entrance gate of the castle
something which was once flooded and has now been re-flooded, i.e. something which contains water

h) something which sums up high cost, heat loss, breakdown in the hot water system etc; i.e. problems

i) part of the entrance hall
something which makes the entrance hall look like a church
something to do with the ceiling, like Gothic drapery

j) something which is baked
something which is eaten for tea
something Jane makes 'mountains', i.e. a lot of
a word which has a plural

5 The actual words in the text were:
a) portcullis
b) ramparts

c) battlements
d) stronghold
e) promontory
f) mason
g) moat
h) hassles
i) barrel-vaulting
j) scones

6 a) i)
b) iii)
c) ii)
d) iv)
e) iii)
f) i)
g) iv)
h) i)
i) iii)

The Text	Living in a Castle	Living in a Tent
The people: Age	middle-aged	20s/30s
Social background	middle-class	mixed
Job	husband is MP	self-sufficient; some odd jobs
The facilities: Cooking		open fire
Heating	central heating	open fire
Sleeping	14 bedrooms	mats
Cost	'unspeakable'	very little
Advantages	beauty, romance, peace	low cost independence
Disadvantages	cost work involved	physically hard life
Other points of interest (suggestions)	open to public on Sundays	some draw social security

Section 4

3 a) iv)
b) i)
c) i)
d) iii)
e) i)
f) iii)
g) iii)
h) iii)

UNIT TWO

Section 2

2 MOODY GRAN

*My <u>gran's moods</u> are very
<u>changeable</u>. Sometimes she can
be very domineering and
difficult, at other times she'll be
pleasant and quite happy. But
whichever it is, the good is
never quite as good as it might
be and the bad is always worse
– whenever my mother or I are
involved. Frankly she seems
<u>happier</u> to <u>hear about</u> our
<u>problems than</u> our successes.
<u>I haven't seen very much of her</u>
<u>since I married</u>, although my
mother still sees her about every
three or four weeks.
Occasionally she <u>has outbursts</u>
<u>about me</u> and tells mum <u>I'm no</u>
<u>good</u>. Other relatives have had
this treatment and have moved
away or lost contact. My mother
tells me about her visits and I
feel weighed down just by
listening. But I <u>feel guilty</u>. She's
my grandmother, not getting
any younger and I'm taking the
easy way out by <u>not</u> going to
<u>visit</u> her.*

4 iii)

☐ **6** She feels as though she has no friends and no identity of
her own and wants to escape her mother's overwhelming influence.

☐ **9** She and her husband have accepted very good jobs in
the USA, but her mother's life is in the balance after an
accident. If her mother comes out of her coma, she
would need her daughter's help. The job arrangement
cannot be postponed and she doesn't know who to put
first, her husband or her mother.

☐ **10** MY OPINION: It would be harsh to tell you that this is
your life, and you must go with your husband, but in
some ways this would be right. On the other hand, I
quite see that if your mother returns to consciousness
and asks for you, and finds you have left England, it
would be grim for her. Only *you* can make the final
decision, and the only glimmer of light I can shed on it
is that if your mother did live and you were there, then
she heard how much you had sacrificed for her she
would probably be the first to say you should have
gone. However, if you do decide to go, you could come
home during your first break from college and see her.
Perhaps you could find one of her friends to keep in

touch with the hospital, and be there if she comes out of the coma — when surely, in such an emergency, you could fly over to be by her side for a day or two, and explain.

Section 3 Part A

8 *Boredom*
strain of . . . cohabitation.
relapse into . . . silence when guests have gone

Gender Roles
women — chore obligations
men — home is dull
wife — overdependent
man regards woman as prey
woman regards man as source of loot and flattery

Parenthood
children command all time and attention

10 a) ii)
b) iv)
c) ii)
d) iii)

Section 3 Part B

2 a) c) and d)

6 a) no
b) no
c) yes, if long enough
d) no

9 defects of one partner
e.g. insanity
alcoholism
crime
relations between husband and wife
e.g. work in different places
incompatibility
overwhelming passion for another person
mutual consent

Section 4

2 a) iv)
b) iii)
c) i)
d) iii)

UNIT THREE

Section 1

3 a) hostile
b) contemptuous
c) sympathetic

5 a) rather brutal, with one exception
b) unused to other boys, frightened, but brave

Section 2

5 The sentences in the right hand column come from paragraphs:
a) a) b) c) a) d) a) c) d) a) b) c) d) a) b) b) c) d) a) b)

6 Original topic sentences:
a) The main argument against the co-education is that boys and girls differ.
b) The main argument in favour of co-education is that it is 'natural'.

Section 3 Part A

2 a) all too often fully justified./fulfill her potential/reach a decision./as poor as reputed./headmaster/how intelligent children are catered for./move to a new school which offers a more stimulating curriculum.

b) a better education for an intelligent child./of payment of fees./to win a scholarship/from the education received at the prep school./the children who had stayed with the state education system,/having had a superior education./send Penelope to the private prep school for as long as you can afford it.

Section 3 Part B

2 a) ii)
b) i)
c) iv)
d) iii)
e) iv)

10 destroys creativity — learning too rigid — discourages initiative — exams cause fear of failure and lack purpose

Section 4

3 a) ii)
b) i)
c) iii)
d) i)

4 a) ii)
b) iii)
c) ii)
d) i)

UNIT FOUR

Section 1

1 a) i) expenses/work
b) ii) work late, iii) c) in order to work late
c) i) this is the word you use to refer to fellow trade-unionists
c) iii) in order to make sure you are in the office in the morning
d) ii) at the fact that the boss has a new Rolls-Royce

e) ii) in order to shut out the noise
e) iii) about the noise
f) i) your friend
f) ii) 'out of the job', i.e. be dismissed
f) iii) the sacking
g) i) making the tea
g) iii) tea
h) iii) the match

4 a) i)
b) ii)
c) i)
d) i)
e) ii)
f) iv)
g) iii)
h) i)

Section 2

1 a) 'period of social change' (line 1)
b) 'period of social change' (line 1)
c) 'the deadly acts of the terrorist, serious crimes that go undetected, violent protest' (line 4)
d) as c)
e) the police (line 7)

2 a) conflicts (line 1)
b) 'the deadly acts . . .' etc are dramatic; 'to see that ordinary life goes on . . .' etc is less dramatic.

3 a) 'forces between four and five times your body weight, operating on the hip joint'
'when you take a step' and when you run (line 1)
b) 'The Bionic man' (a TV programme) (line 6)
c) the hip-joint
d) the previous statements about the joint: 'It is after all . . ., it has . . ., it needs . . ., it must . . .'. (lines 8–11)
features, aspects
e) the idea illustrated in the first paragraph
f) the way in which engineers . . .' (line 16)
g) Mechanical engineers, farmers, horticulturalists, biologists working together (line 19)
h) the production of waist-high crops (line 24)
i) than previously

6 a) puts a small lump of 'rag' onto a scale/If the weight is correct/it is incorrect/empties its contents/puts another lump on the scale
b) conveyor belt/labelling/four/too many slipping out/conveyor belt/ the unwrapped/stacks extras at the side
c) eight/hand/labelled packets/slotting/a new box/ flattened card/lot of packets comes along the conveyor-belt

Section 3

1 a) Clerk who can type required for busy office. Experience is essential. £3000 per year plus lun-cheon vouchers (tickets of a certain value, acceptable at restaurants, given by employers as a means of subsidising the cost of an employee's meal). Flexible working hours. 3 weeks' holidays.
b) Carpet salesperson required by large company. Basic wage plus 10% commission. Dynamic person essential.
c) Import/export clerk required in busy shipping office. Quick with figures (good at arithmetic). Should be able to do some typing and be a willing worker.
d) Friendly boss needs a person able to do all kinds of work (remember Defoe's 'Robinson Crusoe' who had a manservant called 'Man Friday' who did any job his master demanded). Must have good telephone manner and secretarial skills. Generous conditions of work.

2 a) possible ads are:

LOVELY SPOT near the river in SW1 for an energetic young Clerk/Typist looking for more variety & interest. Pleasant working conditions; open plan office with two others. Plenty of perks, discounts, travel scheme, etc. Good salary too! Miss Baines CHALLONERS (Employment Agency) 870 ....

MEET THE STARS at big TV co. Some typing & phone work. £2600 m/f. ... BROOK STREET BUREAU

MUSIC CO. req. bright young clerk typist £2400. Phone ... 323 DT Selections Agency.

PERSON FRIDAY. m/f. with typing for friendly publishers £2000 neg. ....

RECEP/TYPIST. m/f. £2300 neg. Great new job at city co. Good prospects. ....

RECEPTIONIST. £3000 + Greeting clients & arranging appointments for this specialised co. Slow typing. 5 pm finish. Phone Chris Manley on ....

SCHOOL/COLLEGE LEAVER with audio typing ability required for friendly West End solicitors office. Salary up to £2300 and subsidised lunch. Please phone Personnel ....

THEATRICAL PRODUCERS W1 need young, bright Sec/Sh. Plenty of involvement. To £3000 aae. Phone .... Hard Graftino Staff Agency.

b)   possible ads are:

EXPERIENCED retail carpet sales person wanted. SW11 area. Good basic wage plus comm. Phone Mr Mack. 22~ ~~~~.

SALES ASSISTANT required for exclusive children's shop in Kensington. Phone ~~~ ~~~~.

SALESPERSONS required for modern jewellery in London stores. Good salary. Phone ~~~ ~~~~.

Section 4

3 young people (line 2)/a rise of 163,901 ... (line 8)/100,000 (line 10)/problem (line 16)/the fact that the young unemployment problem used to be seen as a seasonal one etc. (line 16)/school leavers (line 23)

5 163,901/over 1.6 million/the war/60/ unemployed/ chronic/seasonal/Great Britain/3rd/Belgium/West Germany

7 a) NAME: Tessa
AGE: 17
QUALIFICATIONS: 5 O-levels; 2 A-levels
JOB INTERESTS: nursing; has applied for Assistant Scientific Officer Civil Service
REMARKS: well qualified; no definite interests
SUITABLE JOB: needs a series of temporary jobs to help her decide what she wants to do

b) NAME: Ian
AGE: 16
QUALIFICATIONS: has taken 3 CSEs (passed 1?)
JOB INTERESTS: craft apprenticeship at Parsons or Vickers
REMARKS: keen; but has been out of work for 9 weeks; needs a job soon before he becomes unemployable
SUITABLE JOB: unskilled factory job?

c) NAME: John
AGE: 16
QUALIFICATIONS: ??
JOB INTERESTS: garage mechanic
REMARKS: shabby in appearance; off-putting attitude; probably involved in crime; needs a job before this gets more serious
SUITABLE JOB: unskilled job (in a garage?)

UNIT FIVE

Section 1

4 a) a better education and career prospects; a 'gentleman's manners; courage; honours and higher rank in his previous military career

b) relatively poor education; poor career prospects; somewhat shabby appearance

6 He feels he doesn't have the money, influence or the clothes that the members of the club have.

7 a) the centre of power and influence
b) a person from a working-class background without power or status
c) a middle-class person with power and status

Section 2

1 a) but
b) However
c) rather than
d) In fact
e) However
f) For
g) Thus
h) but
i) so
j) Firstly
k) lastly
l) therefore
m) but

2 (possible sentences)
consequently characterised by an ignorance of the way most working people live
but . . . there are so many other ways of telling what a person's social background is
for example . . . whether he speaks standard ('Oxford' or 'BBC') English or whether he speaks a dialect
however, this piece of information will immediately reveal a great deal about the person socially
for example, are filled by people who have been educated at one of these universities
moreover . . . tend in the end to appoint Oxbridge students in much higher numbers than would be justified by the small proportion of British students who actually study at these universities

Section 3

2 a) III (M)
b) I
c) III (N)
d) I

3 No. The figures in the third line are not the average of the figures in the other two lines.

4

	Non-manual	Manual	All
Male	35	65	100
Female	56	44	100
Both	43	57	100

5 a) The ballot in the UK is secret
b) Conservative
c) Labour
d) Yes, Class I

8 a) two-thirds; less than
b) 1 in 80
c) 1 in 20

9

	The typical British male worker	The typical British female worker
belongs to social class number:	III (M)	III (N)
votes:	Labour	Conservative
is by religion:	Church of England	Church of England
has an average working week of:	over 36 hours a week perhaps over 48 hours a week	36–40 hours

Section 4

3

The family	The Cutters	The Tranters
Where they live: – the area	professional middle-class suburb of Manchester	coal-mining estate in Yorkshire
– the house	elaborate detached house	council house
The husband: – job	small business man	installs freezers – foreman works: joinery
– spare-time occupation	?	
The wife: – job	housewife	housewife; works part-time in textile mill goes dancing at a working-men's club
– spare-time occupation	golf, amateur dramatic and operatic societies A-level class in sociology	

Earnings	not well off but comfortable	enough for 'a nice standard' of living
Political inclinations	Conservative	Maureen has voted Labour twice
Other points of interest (suggestions)	Nick is against Comprehensive schools	not concerned about education Parents strong Labour voters

(in relation to the UK standard of living)

4 a) ii)
b) iv)
c) i)'
d) iv)
e) ii)

UNIT SIX

Section 1

5 a) Aims: planting trees; Activities: organising campaigns, conferences, tree-plantings
b) Aims: preservation of places of historical interest and natural beauty; Activities: purchasing and preserving buildings and land for the public
c) Aims: making people aware of the environment, campaigning for its preservation and changing life-styles; Activities: exerting political influence, direct action, raising money
d) Aims: avoidance of cruelty to animals in the preparation of cosmetics; Activities: making available non-animal cosmetics

Section 2

2 a) ii)
b) i)
c) iii)
d) The elm regularly produces flowers
The flowers rarely ripen into seed
The seed very rarely germinates
e) iii)

4 a) i)
b) i)
c) ii)

5 a) roots; bark; timber; root suckers; hedge; flowers; seed; clones; pollen; wood; bole; trunks; grain
b) coppiced; pollarded; bored out; turned; harvest
c) keels; pipes; (parts of) water mills; wheel hubs; chair seats; furniture; bowls; tableware

KEY TO THE EXERCISES

Section 3 Part A

2   a)   change
      b)   (the danger from) the atom bomb
      c)   the decision described (lines 13–18)
      d)   the insurance companies
      e)   that of nuclear power
      f)   an active menace (line 39); satanic mills (line 42); nuclear power stations (lines 45–46); unsightly monuments (line 46)
      g)   the field of nuclear energy development
      h)   the real development of nuclear power
      i)   the rise in radiation levels; the increase in harmful mutations
      j)   damage caused by radiation
      k)   the level of a small dose

3   a)   3
      b)   3
      c)   1
      d)   1
      e)   3
      f)   2
      g)   3
      h)   1
      i)   2
      j)   3

Section 3 Part B

2   a)   F
      b)   T
      c)   D
      d)   T
      e)   D
      f)   F
      g)   T
      h)   F

Section 4

3   Lethal, long-term/pesticides/electronic equipment/ fisheries.

increase/decrease/cotton./migration/increasing the dosage/sales./exploited./equipment/be wiped out.

it is making money out of it./underdeveloped countries./ grows/decreases/famine, for example./are being born/ are dying/plague/nuclear war/famine./

pessimist/horrible./be welcome./maturity./latter./ cruelty and suffering/greatness and splendour./poverty/ illness/loneliness/fear/expectation of happiness/ genius./conquest/achievement.

UNIT SEVEN

Section 2

3   a)

regulated	–	N
correct	–	N
dolls	–	N
stubborn	–	–
mist	–	N
imperialism	–	–
socialists	+	N
snobbery	–	–
subservience	–	–
authoritarian	–	–
equality	–	N
commitment	+	+
tribal	+	N
political	+	N
ordinary	+	N
unity	+	N
magnetism	+	N
instincts	+	N
longing	+	+
convenience	–	N

4   a)   *trundles* –; *moves* N, possible; *glides* +, would sound odd.
      b)   *scheming* –; *clever* +, possible; *cunning* –, possible; *quick-witted* +, possible.
      c)   *gawping* –, *gazing* N, possible; *staring* –, possible; *observing* N, possible
      d)   *complacent* –; *happy* +, would sound odd; *self-satisfied* –, possible; *satisfied* +, would sound odd.
      e)   *subservience* –; *obedience* +, would sound odd; *loyalty* + would sound odd.

7   86%
       8
       over 9 out of 10
       8
       three-quarters
       over 9 out of 10

8   The text but not the table gives information about the numbers *very strongly* in favour of the monarchy.

Section 3

1   a)   pro
      b)   pro
      c)   anti
      d)   anti
      e)   pro
      f)   anti
      g)   anti
      h)   anti
      i)   pro
      j)   anti
      k)   anti
      l)   pro

2 b) just outsiders

c) machine . . . nothing like as democratic as our own

d) regain this self-government . . . free of interference

e) weight and influence . . . vigorously in defence . . . help to shape

f) crazy . . . destroy

'g) alien . . . artificial . . . throw away

h) swallowed . . . ruled . . . bureaucracy . . . rigid regulations . . . wrangling . . . crises

i) British . . . not . . . dull uniformity . . . nor . . . damage . . . British

j) scare stories . . . ruined . . . good sense to say 'No' . . . prospered . . . revalued upwards . . . plummetted

k) reduced . . . mere

l) Sovereign

3 a)-c)-d)-b)-e)

4 d)-b)-a)-e)-c)

6 in favour of Britain staying in: h)-e)-c)-f) or h)-c)-f)-e)
in favour of Britain leaving: a)-g)-d)-b)

Section 4

3 a) strong action . . . . . urging them on in defiance . . . . . quite unsuitable . . . . superior accommodation . . . . neighbours complaining . . . . . councils do not need to consult.

b) is factually correct

c) well-stocked larder . . . . . . new homes very close to present home Weatherhill thinks this is reasonable . . . . children would benefit from move.

UNIT EIGHT

Section 2

4 a) ii)

b) i)

c) iii)

d) ii) iii)

e) ii) iii)

f) i) iii)

6 ii) occurs most frequently

7, 8

	Text	Other
professionals	+	DIFF
conscripts	−	DIFF
democracy	+	SAME
terrorist	−	SAME
dictatorship	−	SAME
exploited*	−	DIFF
pacifist	−	DIFF
communist	−	DIFF
homeland	+	SAME
fantasies		DIFF

leadership	+	DIFF
discipline	+	DIFF
responsibility	+	DIFF

*Negative when applied to people

9 a) laziness, fantasising

b) men are responsible, mature

Section 3 Part A

9 Original headings:

a) Fluoridation fights tooth decay

b) Fluoridation is simple, safe, inexpensive

c) Fluoridation has been adopted in countries throughout the world

11 a) x

b) x

c) x

d) x

e) ✓

f) ✓

g) x

h) ?

i) ?

Section 3 Part B

1

	SHADERS	CROWN PERSONAL TV	MAKE LIFE CH'EASY
a)	✓		
b)	✓		
c)	✓		✓
d)			✓
e)		✓	✓
f)		✓	

4,5

	VOLVO	MGB	MAXI	PEUGEOT 604
a)	✓		✓	✓✓
b)		✓	✓	
c)			✓✓	
d)			✓	✓
e)	✓			
f)		✓✓		✓
g)	✓✓	✓✓		✓✓

6 **Badedas**

a) stimulating
caress
invigorating
delicious

b) mystery
daring

c) abandon yourself
discover
extravagant

d) extract of horse chestnuts
    freshness
    herbal essence

Chamomile+Mullen Leaves Shampoo

a) velvety
    fragrant
    fair, white and yellow, brightens
    soft, silky and shiny
    mild, gentle

b) —

c) —

d) leaves, Mullen, Elderflower
    the natural colour
    Charmomile

Y

a) the aroma of fine coffee on sunlit balconies
    the lilt of a tune
    smoke-filled room

b) going to live it
    breathless
    only just remember
    just before dawn
    an intensity that astounds
    hauntingly
    changing nuances

c) unafraid to
    demands the real thing
    spirit of freedom itself

d) —

Section 4

2   a) iii)
    b) i)
    c) iv)
    d) iii)
    e) iv)

3   *glory* +, −, gimmick . . . . . shampoo
    flawless +, −, unfocused eyes . . . . vacant . . . . paint
    extraordinary N, −, inhuman
    *painted** N, −, . . . sleeps unruffled (hence unnatural)
    immaculately N, −, false
    tranquil +, −, vacant
    miraculously +, −, washing powder . . . bouillon cube
    *veneer** N, −, miraculously smoothed . . . . washing powder
    doll * N, − weeping, pouting, smiling, running, reclining

    * These words are often negative when applied to humans

UNIT NINE

Section 1

6   a) intrinsic nastiness; alarming implications; reduction of efficiency; embarrassment

b)

	1	2	3	4
	5	5	8	7
	10	8	9	0

7   a) iii)
    b) iii)
    c) ii)
    d) i)
    e) iv)
    f) i)
    g) iii)

Section 2

2   a great number of/spontaneous heating/following surface growth of mould/after the attack of insects/accelerated/by humidity conditions in excess of normal/Another prerequisite/ventilation/the produced heat/dispatched/elevated/ enhanced/Thus/temperature and moisture control are/agricultural/sanitation/is supplemental/prevent/rodents

3   We've heard about/you are/are/How *can* it be?/In your heart you know this as well as I do, don't you?/you will lose surplus weight/you expend more calories/you are consuming/which forces the body to/could come to your aid/if you tied/used/

4   Vast sums are expended in promoting vitamin preparations in countries such as America and Britain. In these countries people consume millions of vitamin tablets and tons of special vitamin foods. In fact they have no need of them. On the contrary they are more likely to suffer ill effects from overconsumption than to enjoy the benefits promised by the promoters

5   us/find/has/prefer/awake/has/find/a lot/harm/a bit/can't/guilty

    right/this/you might well need a doctor's prescription for it/you can get headaches/a taste for caffeine/you put it in their drinking/give them a choice between caffeinated water — and plain water —, they prefer

    treat alcoholism and drunkenness/they are given caffeine on top of alcohol, their performance is even worse/sober you up/the caffeine in it/have always thought of coffee as a sobering drink/got almost as much caffeine in it/keep you awake/you drowsy/to lessen this effect

Section 3

2   Jenny b) Sue a) Kate c) Molly d) Ted a)

4   rise gradually/persevere with/continue doing it/gain much benefit from it/arrange/visit

5   maintains/means/remaining/constant/ avoidance exercise/essential regardless/daily/reluctance admits/arduous/alternative

6 daily exercise can involve considerable effort/that he makes himself do it, even when tired

it is stupid to carry on until one is unwell

finds his day feels wrong if he is inactive/he feels closeted working in a studio

so many people in show business take up golf

prefers tennis or table tennis

he uses a chest expander to develop muscles

Section 4

2 One of the medical staff

Cancer of the breast

4 *Private medicine*: it is expensive; you can have private rooms; you get better hotel conditions; treatment is not better than in public hospitals; you get quicker treatment for minor ailments

Public medicine: it is free; you get good treatment especially in big teaching hospitals; the best private specialists also work in public hospitals

7 It is rather impersonal.

10 The hospital is very busy; every bed is needed all of the time.

12 a) iii)

b) i)

c) ii)

d) iii)

e) iv)

13 a) lumps protruberances

b) specialist doctor in a hospital

c) ordinary people

d) a small cupboard for personal possessions

e) place where operations are carried out

f) the third person to be operated on that day

g) the removal of a breast

h) a feeling of elation

i) skill

j) used to facing unpleasant things

UNIT TEN

Section 1

4

	Granny Wallon	Granny Trill
regular in her habits	√	√
physically active	√	√
sociable		
sad		
mild-tempered		
inquisitive	√	√
religious	√	√
superstitious	√	
lonely		

Section 2

1 a) a drink (line 2)

b) ii)

c) Mrs Thatcher's (line 51)

d) iii)

e) shattered (line 71)

f) election as Tory leader (line 66)

g) a person unsuitable for the job (line 87)

h) of his guests' glasses (line 98)

i) making people feel small or embarrassed (line 108)

j) alcoholic drinks (line 108)

2 a) Downing St. (letter-head)

b) it refers to Scotland (line 1)

c) i)

d) they are mean (line 29)

e) a drink (of spirits) (line 29)

f) ii)

g) his host 'Lord Whatsisname' (line 28)

h) game birds

i) Scotland (line 1)

j) Mrs Thatcher

k) they had been shot as game

l) alcoholic drink

m) iii)

n) have a few drinks

Section 3

3 a) insisted rather loudly (line 256)

b) i) bunch of 007-type individuals (line 113)

ii) Molotov cocktails in ketchup bottles (line 123)

c) at their majesty's pleasure (line 161)

d) Gucci shoes (line 165)

e) bay leaves or champagne (line 230)

Section 4

1 a) income, 1963-style fiver, rent, cheap windfalls, taps (his visitors) for funds, afford, £28, thirty-five grand.

b) bar nightcaps, Scotch, pots, a jar, barman.

c) a crook, done (nine months) for corrupting a police officer, running, Slipper of the Yard, arrest, gave myself up, sentence, gone straight, cuffs, felon, cell, extradite, deport, thief, steals, 100 years of pardon, nicked, prison, rehabilitated criminal.

2 a) iv)

b) iv)

c) ii)

d) iv)

e) i)

4 a) iv)

b) iv)

c) ii)

d) iii)

e) i)